Retrospections on Social Psychology

Edited by
LEON FESTINGER

OXFORD UNIVERSITY PRESS
New York   1980   Oxford

Library of Congress Cataloging in Publication Data
Main entry under title:
Retrospections on social psychology.
Includes bibliographical references and index.
1. Social psychology—United States—History—
Addresses, essays, lectures.
I. Festinger, Leon, 1919– II. Title.
HM251.R474   302   80–10919   ISBN 0-19-502751-5

Printed in the United States of America

Dedicated by all of us

to the memory of Alfred Marrow

Preface

The reader of this book, even the most thoughtful and careful reader, may not realize that there are characters in it—and that it has a plot. Therefore I want to describe the characters, elaborate the plot, and explain why the story is so well hidden in the following chapters.

In 1934, a young graduate student of psychology at New York University wrote a letter to Kurt Lewin, recently arrived in temporary sanctuary at Cornell University—a refugee, escaping, and very much aware of the magnitude of the growing horror in his land, Germany. The letter asked for permission to visit Lewin to get advice about his Ph.D. dissertation.

Kurt Lewin answered the letter and the student, Alfred Marrow, made the trip. They talked for two days—sometimes about the dissertation, mostly about the world, the Jews, the coming storm, a State of Israel, and how the scientific study of humans could address such problems without deserting science. The lives of the forty-four-year-old famous man and the graduate student became and remained closely connected for thirteen years —until the death of Kurt Lewin.

In 1969 Alfred Marrow wrote a biography of Lewin, *The Practical Theorist,* and he dedicated it to the Research Center for Group Dynamics —a curious dedication. The meaning of that dedication lies in the personal and intellectual history of the relationship between these two men.

Kurt Lewin left Cornell University in 1935 for the University of Iowa, where he began to direct his talents into a new area—the functioning of social groups and their impact on the person. Soon there emerged a series of studies on the effects of autocratic and democratic group atmospheres, studies that reflected his desire to build a science that would relate to the social problems that concerned him. These studies were unique in their time for, in addition to the substantive findings, they showed the way to use controlled experimental methods for the investigation of complex social phenomena. It is for this that many regard Lewin as the founder of modern experimental social psychology.

Alfred Marrow received his Ph.D. from New York University in 1937 and was diverted from a scientific career, but not from his interest in Kurt Lewin and their joint dedication to solving social problems. Alex Bavelas and John R. P. French, Jr., who had worked with Kurt Lewin, were invited to come and explore the application of their research findings in the factory that Alfred managed. The Harwood Manufacturing Company became, in part, a laboratory for bringing together science and the complex social world.

Exciting as these developments were to both Alfred and Kurt, they were not enough, and they were all still too far removed from the issues that neither could ignore. By 1942 some people knew what was really happening in Germany and in the areas of Europe occupied by the Germans, facts that the world at large would not be convinced of until 1945. Kurt and Alfred both knew that whatever remnant of European Jewry might survive, a homeland for them was needed. They further knew that the Jewish problem was only symptomatic of deep social ills that needed cure, not just alleviation. And they believed that through the pursuit of new knowledge could come the basics for cure. Action without knowledge is akin to wandering in the dark—ineffective no matter how determined and moral the wandering is. To them science, the pursuit of new knowledge, had to be supported in close proximity to action.

Kurt Lewin wanted to found an institute dedicated to this purpose. Alfred Marrow helped, and the Research Center for Group Dynamics came into being in 1944 at the Massachusetts Institute of Technology. That Research Center for Group Dynamics still exists, although now, and since 1948, relocated at the University of Michigan. Through its work over the last thirty-five years, it has exerted a profound influence on social psychology—an effective monument to Kurt Lewin. Alfred Marrow dedicated his biography of Kurt Lewin to an ideal, to a goal, and to his relationship with a man.

Then what is this book about? Let me first tell you who planned and wrote it. It was written by representatives of three "generations" of the

Research Center for Group Dynamics. Dorwin Cartwright and I were among those fortunate enough to have joined the faculty of the Research Center close to its inception. Alvin Zander was reluctant to come at that time, but the Center came to him at Michigan and he could then no longer stay apart. Kurt Back, Morton Deutsch, Harold Kelley, and Stanley Schachter were part of that talented group who were students at the Research Center at M.I.T. I call them "second generation," but the distinction between them and the "first generation" blurs. And then we have the "third generation"—the later students and even students of the students: Elliot Aronson, Richard Nisbett, Jerome Singer, and Robert Zajonc. These names represent a good proportion of those who built modern social psychology.

This book, then, is dedicated in the same manner and with the same spirit as the dedication of Alfred Marrow's biography of Kurt Lewin—but in the reverse direction. And it seems a fitting time to look back over the last forty years of social psychology and to ask ourselves: What has been accomplished? What do we know and understand today that was unknown forty years ago? Are there examples of the cumulative effect of forty years of searching for new knowledge about humans?

That endeavor, the search for new knowledge, is a precarious thing—and forty years is a very short time. Each of us was willing to try and each of us selected his own topic, one on which he thought a good, exciting story of progress could be told. So the book will not represent an examination of all of social psychology but, rather, a selection of what certain individuals think would show the field in its best light.

I do not know how the story ends. I am writing this Preface before anyone has even begun to work on his chapter.

New York
May 26, 1978

Leon Festinger, representing the
Research Center for Group Dynamics

Addition to the Preface

In February 1979, we met together to discuss the plans for the book. We hoped, by discussing what each of us had in mind, to avoid undue duplication—while not interfering with the personal, idiosyncratic character of the book. It was a good meeting.

Unforeseen events and demands sometimes interfere, and ours were not even "the best laid plans." We have fared rather well but, unfortunately, some unanticipated events made it impossible for Doc Cartwright to complete the chapter he wanted to write. We do, however, thank him for his very constructive help at our February meeting.

New York   L. F.
April 1980

Contributors

ELLIOT ARONSON
Professor of Psychology, University of California at Santa Cruz

KURT W. BACK
James B. Duke Professor and Chairman of Sociology, Duke University

MORTON DEUTSCH
Professor of Psychology and Education and Director of Social Psychology
Program and Laboratory at Teachers College-Columbia University

HAROLD H. KELLEY
Professor of Psychology, University of California at Los Angeles

RICHARD E. NISBETT
Professor of Psychology and Faculty Associate at
the Institute for Social Research, University of Michigan

STANLEY SCHACHTER
Robert Niven Professor of Social Psychology, Columbia University

JEROME E. SINGER
Professor and Chairman of Department of Medical Psychology,
Uniformed Services University of Health Sciences

ROBERT B. ZAJONC
Professor of Psychology and Faculty Associate at
the Institute for Social Research, University of Michigan

ALVIN ZANDER
Professor of Psychology and Program Director in the Research Center
for Group Dynamics, University of Michigan

LEON FESTINGER
Else and Hans Staudinger Professor of Psychology,
New School for Social Research

Contents

Retrospections on Social Psychology

1

Persuasion via Self-justification: Large Commitments for Small Rewards

ELLIOT ARONSON

Historical background

In the 1950s and early 1960s, there was a great deal of excitement among social psychological researchers in this country. Partly this was the result of Kurt Lewin's legacy of enthusiasm and optimism about the potential benefits which a new scientific social psychology could bring to society. Partly it flowed from the more general zeitgeist of those decades, the development of computers and spaceships, the seemingly limitless possibilities of technology, and the unprecedented linkage of humanitarian and scientific concerns exemplified by scientists like Lewin. A generation of social psychologists grew up with the conviction that through laboratory experiments it would be possible to discover scientific principles of human behavior which, in turn, would lead to social change. It was in this era that Leon Festinger invented and developed his theory of cognitive dissonance, and in my opinion, social psychology has not been the same since. The first dissonance experiments introduced ideas and approaches which had a strong effect on the mainstream of the field. They served as a pivotal point, allowing the integration of a cognitively oriented approach to behavior into an experimental framework.

It is too early to write a historical or retrospective account of dissonance theory. For one thing, the theory itself is still expanding and growing and is not ready for either a eulogy or an obituary. In addition, I

This article was written while I was on a grant from NIMH. My research assistant, Erica Goode, provided a great deal of hard work, much encouragement, and even some ideas. I am grateful.

think that it is one of the occupational hazards of being an experimental social psychologist to be oriented toward the present and future and to become impatient, after a time, with soul searching and backward looks. Yet the early dissonance experiments provided certain hopes and expectations— hopes and expectations which are sometimes forgotten and at times need to be recalled. And undeniably there are occasions when it is useful to take stock of what we have learned over a period of years. This, in fact, is the general purpose of the present volume. Thus, rather than write still *another* descriptive analysis of the theory of cognitive dissonance—something which I have done in the recent and not so recent past (Aronson, 1968, 1969, 1978) and which others have done far more completely than I (Wicklund and Brehm, 1976)—I would like, in this chapter, to discuss the role dissonance theory has played in the field and the directions in which it has expanded in the last several years. As with most things I write, it is both personal and idiosyncratic.

When I first became interested in social psychology as an undergraduate in the early 1950s, there was already a sizeable experimental literature on persuasion. If, at that time, I had been able to assemble a panel of expert social psychologists and asked them what we know for sure about how to persuade people, my guess is that they would have included the following techniques:

1. Offer tangible rewards for compliance and clear punishments for espousal of opposing views.
2. Present an audience with a reasonable communication attributing it to a highly credible communicator (e.g., Hovland and Weiss, 1951).
3. Present the individual with the illusion that everyone else in sight agrees with one another and disagrees with him (e.g., Asch, 1951).

In the early 1950s the overwhelming trend in American psychology was, "Let's find the external reward." If a person does something, there must be a reason, and that reason had to be the gaining of an identifiable reward such as food, money, or praise, or the removing of a noxious state of affairs such as pain, fear, or anxiety. If food will induce a hungry rat to press the lever of a Skinner box or turn left in a Y-maze, surely similar rewards can induce a person to hold a given opinion (see Miller and Dollard, 1941). Let us look at Solomon Asch's well-known experiment in which a unanimous majority apparently disagrees with the individual subject on a simple, unambiguous perceptual judgment. Why do so many people conform to this kind of group pressure? Perhaps it makes them anxious to be alone against a unanimous majority; they fear being considered crazy, being held in low esteem, and so on. It's comforting to be in agreement with others. Why do people tend to believe a credible source? Perhaps it increases the probability of being right—and being right reduces anxiety and makes them feel good, smart, and esteemed.[1]

While the research on which these general propositions were based was reasonably clear and replicable, the effects do not seem very powerful or long-lasting. For example, in the classic experiment by Hovland and Weiss (1951) it was found that, while students tended to believe the distinguished physicist J. Robert Oppenheimer when he allegedly wrote that atomic submarines were feasible, the effects of his credibility faded rather rapidly. That is, one month after the communication was presented, the high credibility communicator showed a marked decrease in effectiveness. Indeed, the slippage was such that there was virtually no difference left between the effectiveness of the highly credible source and a source having low credibility. Hovland himself (1959) clearly recognized the weakness and flimsiness of the existing methods of persuasion. The brief duration of the effectiveness of the "persuasion" is probably even more pronounced in the Asch experiment. Asch, of course, realized that most of the effects produced in his procedure were the result of temporary conformity rather than an actual change in belief. That is, the typical yielding subject did not become convinced that the majority was right; rather, he went along with the majority in order to avoid unpleasantness. This process was subsequently confirmed in a more elaborate experiment by Deutsch and Gerard (1955). In one condition of this experiment, subjects were separated by partitions so that they might respond anonymously and in privacy. In this condition, there was far less conformity than in the condition that replicated the more public situation that existed in Asch's study.

Enter dissonance

Most experimental social psychologists seemed sanguine about their inability to produce important and long-lasting changes in opinions or attitudes and apparently were content with reward reinforcement theory

---

1. There were, of course, some notable exceptions to this general zeitgeist—most notably, the work of Kurt Lewin and his colleagues. But this work was not in the mainstream. More will be said on this later on in this chapter.

as an explanation for conformity and persuasion phenomena. Then, in 1959, an experiment was performed which presented a strikingly different approach to persuasion. Picture the following scene:

A young man is instructed to perform a monotonous, boring task as part of an experiment. After completing the task, he is informed by the experimenter that his formal participation as a subject is over. The experimenter then appeals to him for help. He states that his research assistant was unable to be there and asks the subject if he would help him run the experiment. Specifically, the experimenter explains that what he is investigating is the effect of people's preconceptions on their performance of a task. He goes on to explain that he wants to see if a person's performance is influenced by whether he's told either good things about the task (in advance), bad things about the task (in advance), or nothing at all about the task. There is another participant about to arrive; that person is designated to be in the "favorable information condition." The experimenter asks the subject if he would tell the incoming participant that he had just completed the task (which is true) and that he found it to be an exceedingly enjoyable one (which is not true, according to the subject's own experience). The subject is offered either $1 or $20 for telling this lie and for remaining on call in case the regular assistant cannot show up in the future.

This is the scenario of the classic experiment by Festinger and Carlsmith (1959). The results of this experiment are now old hat to students of social psychology. The subjects who said that they found the task enjoyable in order to earn $1 came to believe that it actually *was* enjoyable to a far greater extent than those who said so for $20.

The experiment was, of course, derived from Festinger's (1957) theory of cognitive dissonance. Basically, the theory states that if an individual simultaneously holds two cognitions that are *psychologically* inconsistent, he will experience discomfort. Consequently, he will strive to reduce the inconsistency (dissonance) by changing one or both cognitions to make them more consonant or by adding a third cognition which will render the original cognitions less inconsistent with one another. Thus, if I were a subject in the Festinger-Carlsmith experiment, my cognition that the task I performed was boring is dissonant with the fact that I informed another person that it was enjoyable. If I were paid $20 for making that statement, this cognition provides external justification for my action. However, if I were paid only $1, I lack much external justification for having made the statement. This produces cognitive dissonance. One way to reduce dissonance is for me to convince myself that the task was somewhat more interesting than it seemed at first. In effect, I convince myself that my statement to the other student was not a great lie, in the process persuading myself that the task actually was interesting. This change in opinion through *self-justification* is not limited to trivial judgments (like the dullness of a boring task). It has been extended to much more important opinions, such as a reassessment of the dangers of smoking marijuana among students at the University of Texas (Nel, Helmreich, and Aronson, 1969) and the softening of Yale students' attitudes toward the alleged anti-student brutality of the New Haven police (Cohen, 1962). And theoretically, because the attitudes dealt with are important ones and are not directly linkable to an obvious source of persuasion, one would expect the effects to last longer than those resulting from the persuasion techniques in earlier experiments.

This point deserves some elaboration. The major reason for the power of dissonance effects is that the arousal of dissonance always contains *personal involvement,* and therefore the reduction of dissonance always involves some form of *self-justification.* This self-justification is necessary because the individual has usually done something that makes him feel either stupid or immoral (see Aronson, Chase, Helmreich, and Ruhnke [1974] for an elaboration of this point). Moreover, the greater the commitment or self-involvement implied by the action and the smaller the *external* justification for the action, the greater the dissonance and, therefore, the more powerful the attitude change. Thus, in the Festinger-Carlsmith experiment, to deceive another human being would make an individual feel immoral or guilty. So, he convinces himself that he didn't really deceive anyone—that it *was* a rather interesting task. This justifies his previous action. A similar process occurs in Aronson and Mills' (1959) experiment on the initiation effect. In this experiment, college women chose to undergo an initiation in order to be admitted to a discussion group that turned out to be a boring waste of time. As predicted, those who underwent a severe initiation convinced themselves that the group was *more* worthwhile than those who underwent either a mild initiation or no initiation at all. To go through a difficult or embarrassing initiation in order to become a member of a silly and uninteresting discussion group would make the individual feel stupid; therefore, she convinces herself that the group was *not* silly and was *not* uninteresting. This justifies her decision to work hard in order to become a member of the group.

Compare this with a typical communication-persuasion study (e.g.,

Hovland and Weiss, 1951). Here the reason I'm changing my opinion is that someone smart and trustworthy thinks that something is true. Very little of me is invested. Accordingly, it's easy for me to forget the source, forget my opinion, etc. Moreover, if my new opinion is challenged, I can always change back. I have nothing invested in it. In the dissonance studies, the individual's self-esteem is involved. Therefore, it is expected that an individual's opinions on important matters can be changed, that these changes can be large and truly significant (not just *statistically* significant!), and that they will be permanent.

Some evidence for large and truly significant changes about important opinions comes from an experiment by Nel, Helmreich, and Aronson (1969) in which college students who believed that marijuana should not be legalized were induced to make a counterattitudinal videotape extolling the use of marijuana. In the no dissonance condition, there was little or no change in opinion. In the maximum dissonance condition (small external justification *and* being informed in advance that the tape would be shown to malleable high school students), there were huge and dramatic changes in opinion. Subjects in this condition came to believe that marijuana should be legalized. The change in opinion was enormous—73 percent of what was possible.

In that experiment, we would predict that those large changes in opinion would last a considerable amount of time, partly because in the late 1960s college students would not lightly change their opinions about an important (to them) issue such as the legalization of marijuana. Moreover, it is unlikely that opinion change based on the need for self-justification would shift sporadically. Any regression in the subjects' opinions on the legalization of marijuana would be certain to reinstate their feelings of dissonance and guilt about having misled some innocent and malleable high school students. Unfortunately, we have no direct data on the permanence of the change of opinion about marijuana. Why not? On the surface, it would seem easy to come back thirty or forty days later and reassess the subjects' opinions. But, of course, it would have been highly unethical for us *not* to have debriefed our subjects immediately after assessing their initial change in opinion—in view of the fact that we *were* dealing with an important and highly salient issue. To leave people running around for thirty days believing that atomic submarines are feasible (as Hovland and Weiss did) is relatively harmless. To leave them running around for 30 days with a laboratory-induced belief that marijuana is a good deal less harmful than they had previously thought would have been unthinkable. Thus, ethically, as the importance of the issue increases, so too does the need for immediate debriefing and reinstatement of the initial opinion. This makes it impossible to assess the permanence of the effect under these conditions.

Fortunately, there are some solid data on the permanence of dissonance-induced opinion change. These come from an experiment by Jonathan Freedman (1965) and confirm our speculations. Freedman performed a conceptual replication of Aronson and Carlsmith's "toy" study (1963) in which children were threatened with either severe or mild punishment if they played with an attractive toy. In the original experiment, Aronson and Carlsmith predicted and found that the children complying in the face of mild threats subsequently convinced themselves that the forbidden toy was *less* attractive than did those children who were confronted with severe threats. The derivation should be clear to the reader. If I am a child eager to play with a specific attractive toy and you (an adult authority figure) tell me that you will break my arm if I play with it, I will not play with the toy and I will experience no dissonance. The cognition that you will break my arm is more than ample justification for my abstinence. But suppose you issued a mild threat which was just barely sufficient to induce short-term compliance but was not a superabundant justification. Here, my not playing with the toy will be dissonant with the attractiveness of the toy. I will seek additional justification for my abstinence—by convincing myself, for example, that the toy isn't all that attractive anyway.

Freedman conceptually replicated these results. The experimenter admonished children (either with mild or severe threats) not to play with an extraordinarily attractive toy (a battery-powered robot). As in the Aronson and Carlsmith experiment, all of the children resisted the temptation to play with it. Several weeks later, a different person visited the school and, in a totally unrelated activity, happened to be administering a test to the students in the same room where the toy study had been conducted. The toys were casually scattered about the room. The visitor administered a paper and pencil test to each child. She then asked him to stick around while she graded it—and suggested very casually that, while he was waiting, he might want to amuse himself by playing with those toys that "someone must have left here." The results were striking. Those children who had been admonished previously with a severe threat tended to play with the forbidden toy. After all, the person who had threatened them was no longer around; why *not* play with an attractive toy? On the other hand, the children who had previously refrained from playing with the robot in the face of a mild threat had had little external justification for this restraint. Accordingly, at the time of the initial threat, they had a much stronger need for *self*-justification. In other words, they needed to convince themselves that they weren't playing with the toy because they didn't want to—and that they didn't want to because they didn't like the toy. As predicted, this cognitive activity had a relatively permanent impact. As much as nine weeks after the mild threat, the overwhelming majority of the children in the mild threat condition refrained from playing with the toy that virtually all children (who were not subjected to dissonance arousal) would certainly consider to be by far the most attractive and exciting toy in the room. The power of self-justification *does* produce important and long-lasting changes in attitude.

While the results of these early experiments on cognitive dissonance (especially Festinger and Carlsmith [1959] and Aronson and Mills [1959]) may seem boring and obvious to the reader in the 1980s, they startled the social psychological community at the time of their publication. For many working social psychologists, these results generated a great deal of enthusiasm and excitement; for others, skepticism and anger. As a community, we have yet to recover from the impact of this research—fortunately! The reasons for the *skepticism* and *anger* are complex and will dribble out from time to time throughout this essay. One reason will be mentioned here. The findings departed from the general orientation accepted either tacitly or explicitly by most social psychologists in the 1950s: High reward (not *low* reward, and certainly not high punishment) has *always* been accompanied by greater learning, greater conformity, greater performance, greater satisfaction, greater persuasion, and so on.

The reason for the *enthusiasm* was that for some social psychologists, these results represented a striking and convincing act of liberation from the dominance of a general reward-reinforcement theory. The results of these early experiments demonstrated dramatically that, at least under certain conditions, reward theory is inadequate. Moreover, the early dissonance experiments sounded a clarion call to cognitively oriented social psychologists, proclaiming in the most striking manner that *human beings think;* they do not always behave in a mechanistic manner. When in situations which allow them to think, human beings engage in all kinds of cognitive gymnastics aimed at justifying their own behavior. Perhaps most important, this theory inspired an enormous number and variety of hypotheses which were specific to the theory and could be tested in the laboratory.

In the past twenty-five years, the wide array of research that dissonance theory has inspired has been truly astonishing. As Sears and Abeles pointed out in 1969, in the early years of the theory "no behavioral phenomenon was safe from the ravages of the imperialistic dissonance hordes." Dissonance research runs the gamut from decision making to the socialization of children; from interpersonal attraction to the antecedents of hunger and thirst; from color preference to selective informational exposure; from the proselytizing behavior of religious zealots to the behavior of gamblers at a race track—and much, much more. And because it led into domains that had never before been tested in the laboratory, the theory inspired a range and depth of methodological ingenuity unparalleled in the history of social psychology. This proved to be a curse as well as a blessing—providing still another reason for the annoyance and skepticism of its critics, as Jones observed in his perceptive Foreword to Wicklund and Brehm's (1976) *Perspectives on Cognitive Dissonance:*

> The methodological style of the dissonance proponents also fed the flames of controversy. Those who fashioned the dissonance literature were, by and large, uncommonly bright and inventive. But their inventiveness was usually coupled with the use of deceptive scenarios and a procedural complexity that made precise replication difficult. Those bred in the tradition of cumulative research in experimental psychology thought they saw serious vulnerability in this complexity and in the apparent disregard of standardized dependent variable measurement.
>
> Instead, and this was difficult to realize at any given moment, there was developing a body of literature that was conceptually cumulative and therefore more impressive than permutations on a measuring device or a statistical inference rule. No one can read this book without appreciating the development of a solid research consensus on a number of important and once controversial issues. No one can any more claim that dissonance effects are artifacts or that dissonance is at most a contrived laboratory experience. Undoubtedly many readers of this volume will have reservations about specific interpretations and prefer their own alternatives. Nonetheless, the cumulative reach of dissonance research is remarkable. We may now have reached a less flamboyant stage of tidying of loose ends and charting out the relations between dissonance theory and other psychological conceptions, but whatever the future holds, the dissonance research "movement" has

been the most important development in social psychology to date.
(p. x)

Precursors to dissonance theory

Obviously, Leon Festinger was not the first psychologist to notice that human beings try to justify their actions in complex cognitive ways. Nor was he the first to theorize about this fact. In the 1930s, for example, both Kurt Lewin and Prescott Lecky were interested in the new physics of Einstein and Planck. Both were familiar with European psychological schools, and both were developing theories which emphasized the cognitive, active nature of the human organism. Lecky, who had studied with the psychoanalyst Alfred Adler, working at Columbia University within an experimental framework, took issue with the idea of reinforcement as the sole mechanism through which humans learn. Reinforcement was unable to account for a great deal of human behavior that Lecky considered to be important. He developed a theory of self-consistency, which portrayed human beings as active, organized, unified organisms seeking to predict and having the tendency to create (1945). "Prediction and control," Lecky maintained, "is the problem of the subject as well as the experimenter." Human learning, according to Lecky's view, involves conflict between the organization of the individual's expectations or values and new information or stimuli. In resolving this conflict, the person tries to maintain consistency. In some cases, the conflicting or inconsistent stimulus may be distorted or ignored, particularly if it is threatening to the self-concept. In other cases, the individual actively tries to integrate the new information.

> The point is that all of an individual's values are organized into a single system the preservation of whose integrity is essential. The nucleus of the system, around which the rest of the system revolves, is the individual's valuation of himself. The individual sees the world from his own viewpoint, with himself as the center. Any value entering the system which is inconsistent with the individual's valuation of himself cannot be assimilated; it meets with resistance and is likely . . . to be rejected. (pp. 152–153)

Lecky's thinking is close to Festinger's. In Lecky's formulation there is a willingness, and even a need, to view humans as active, organizing beings.

Kurt Lewin, too, particularly in the group decision studies carried out as part of his channel theory, foreshadowed dissonance theory. Lewin astutely observed that the process by which group members' attitudes are changed in a more or less permanent way could be described in three steps: 1. in which the old attitude is "unfrozen"; 2. in which the person is "moved" to the new attitude level; and 3. in which the new attitude is "frozen." This "unfreezing"—"moving"—"refreezing" conception became central in the development of dissonance theory. Festinger used similar terminology to describe the process of postdecision dissonance reduction. In fact, Lewin's explanation of why a group's voluntary decision is more effective in changing attitudes than a lecture or command to the group is carried all but intact to the later dissonance formulation and has been borne out by subsequent research. The group decision, Lewin maintained, provided a link between motivation and action. The relatively small behavioral commitment of the group decision served to "freeze" the decision and link it to later, more concrete behavioral changes. The individual who has committed himself as a member of the group will show a tendency to "stick to his decision."

The link between behavioral commitment and change is, of course, a very important aspect of Festinger's work, as we have already seen. The specific carryover of Lewin's studies may be seen clearly in Freedman and Fraser's (1966) experiment on the "foot-in-the-door-technique," in which it was demonstrated that once a person has made a small behavioral commitment, he becomes more willing to make larger commitments in the future. The results of the "foot-in-the-door" experiment are clearly and easily derivable from the theory of cognitive dissonance: Commitment produces a need for self-justification, which increases the probability of future action. The astute reader will be able to make the same prediction from Lewin's more general theoretical approach.

Trained in the Gestalt tradition, Lewin was dissatisfied with a purely mechanistic view of causality and convinced that to adopt a Newtonian approach to the psychology of human behavior was inadequate. The causes of behavior could not be traced solely to sources internal or external to the person. Rather, human behavior was the result of a complex interaction of the person and his environment: the life space. Humans, according to Lewin, were not completely passive, driven organisms but took an active role in constructing and deciding. In short, they were able to think, and this ability had enormous consequences for persuasion and social action. Tolman (1948), in a tribute to Lewin, saw Lewin's ideas of systematic rather than historical causation as intimately bound up with his commitment to social action, to the notion that human behavior could be changed. Festinger himself, in his contribution to Marrow's biography of Lewin, saw change as central to Lewin's work:

> This theme, that in order to gain insight into a process one must create a change and then observe its variable effects and new dynamics runs through all Lewin's work. To Lewin life was not static; it was changing, dynamic, fluid. Lewin's unfreezing-stabilizing-refreezing concept of change continues to be highly relevant today. His understanding of the importance of change was part of his philosophical approach to science and a basic ingredient of his "metatheory." As such, it helped change much of social psychology from art into science. (Marrow, 1969, p. 235)

Fritz Heider's extension of Lewin's work also shares a similar cognitively oriented approach to behavior. Heider's conception of causal attribution, of course, provided the basis for what was later developed by Kelley (1973) and Jones and Davis (1965) into attribution theory. In addition, Heider's balance theory works on a common premise with dissonance theory and other consistency theories. Consistency of relationship is, in many cases, of itself desirable for the individual; and lack of consistency or its loss, an unbalanced relationship, causes the individual to seek it, restoring balance.

What's the hullabaloo about?

If dissonance theory is firmly rooted in earlier conceptualizations, why do I credit dissonance theory with a larger direct impact on social psychology than the earlier theories of Lewin or Lecky? Why did dissonance theory provide such enthusiasm and anger? Some of the answers to these questions are implicit in the statement by Jones (presented earlier). While Lecky's ideas were clearly consistent with dissonance theory, there was little or no original research generated. On the other hand, Lewin's general theory was not only rich with complex cognitive and dynamic subtleties, Lewin and his students produced a good deal of interesting research. Yet, this research did not have the impact on the field that dissonance research did, partly because as research it did not directly engage or challenge existing mainstream theories. That is, while Lewin's theory was both cognitive and dynamic, for the most part the data themselves could (at least superficially) be fit under the rubric of reward theory. For example, if one looks at the classic study of leadership (Lewin, Lippitt, and White, 1939), the results are not troublesome to a reinforcement theorist. After all, if you expose youngsters to a stiff, dogmatic, punitive, autocratic leader, this would be less rewarding than a more casual, attractive leader who allows them to make their own decisions. It falls easily within the general reward zeitgeist to assume that the latter would produce more satisfaction and greater productivity among the children. Similarly, while the theorizing underlying the group decision research (Lewin, 1947) is complex and cognitive, the actual data are not so far removed from the data of the Asch experiment that the conformity cannot be explained in terms of anxiety reduction.

What Festinger and his band of irreverent students brought to bear on the scene was not a brand new conceptualization. Rather, it was a theory stated in terms that opened the door wide for a diverse set of hypotheses and, more important, stated those hypotheses in a way that existing theories *had* to pay attention to: Either reward theory made no prediction at all or the opposite prediction.

I recall vividly the atmosphere in which Judson Mills and I, as graduate students at Stanford University in 1957, presented the hypothesis and procedure of the initiation experiment to a group of our peers: "Undergoing an embarrassing initiation in order to become a member of a group will increase the attractiveness of that group." The dominant response was that our hypothesis was silly—that it went against common sense. Clearly a stimulus (the group discussion) associated with unpleasantness (the embarrassing initiation) would be liked less through association. "Common sense" is, of course, defined as the climate created by the global acceptance of existing theories. When the results supported our "nonsensical" hypothesis, the first response of serious critics (e.g., Chapanis and Chapanis, 1964) was to conclude with great confidence that our data were an artifact—that what we called an embarrassing initiation was actually a pleasant, even an exciting, event. As the reader knows, the experiment has been successfully replicated several times, using such clearly unpleasant initiation procedures as severe electric shock (e.g., Gerard and Mathewson, 1966).

Of course, a prediction that is nonsensical in one decade can become "common sense" several years later—and even old hat and boring in a third decade. In one sense, it is the duty of a theory to become boring, and fortunately, this fate seems to have befallen dissonance theory. But in the early days of the theory, a great deal was made of the "nonobvious" predictions which were generated. The battle over who can be most nonobvious was part of the growing pains of dissonance theory in the 1950s and 1960s. The claim of nonobviousness was uttered both as a criticism of the theory and as a source of pride and pleasure among the people working most closely with the theory. Kiesler, Collins, and Miller (1969) have pointed out that "nonobvious" is a misnomer in the sense that a new theory *should* be able to handle predictions which other theories cannot, and that dissonance predictions are no more nonobvious than predictions in other experiments where competing hypotheses have been ruled out. But "nonobvious" is a misnomer in another sense, as I have mentioned elsewhere (1968). Dissonance predictions are nonobvious only when seen against the background of a reward-reinforcement framework. They are quite consistent, however, when taken in the context of other theoretical traditions such as Lewin's and Lecky's.

While dissonance theory was in its brash infancy, Sears and Abeles (1969) were not unfair in characterizing us as "the imperialistic dissonance hordes." However, it eventually became clear that we were not opposed to peaceful coexistence. Most specifically, we spelled out both theoretically and empirically under which conditions reward-incentive theory would make its clearest predictions and under which conditions dissonance theory would make its predictions. Most generally, people will strive for rewards and may even change their opinions in the face of a reward under conditions where they are not *personally involved* (Aronson, 1969; Carlsmith, Collins, and Helmreich, 1966; Linder, Cooper, and Jones, 1967). This state of affairs prompted Sears and Abeles (1969) to exult over the fact that the "youthful brashness of dissonance theory is [being] replaced by well-fed middle-aged generosity."

Increasingly, in recent years, dissonance experiments have been aimed less at breaking new ground and certainly have not attempted to outrage the establishment by violating either traditional notions of common sense or traditional notions of the conduct of scientific inquiry. As the theory has continued to amble through middle age, it has moved more and more in the direction of defining the parameters of a variety of social psychological situations, clarifying the conditions under which dissonance phenomena do or do not exist. Here I refer to the admirable research on forced compliance by Collins and Hoyt (1972); on the necessity of arousal for attitude change (by Cooper, Zanna, and Taves, 1977); on the conditions under which dissonance theory and self-perception theory apply (Fazio, Zanna, and Cooper, 1977); on personality differences in selective exposure to information (Olson and Zanna, 1977); and on dissonance and attribution (Zanna and Cooper, 1974). I have recently reviewed this research (1978) and see no good reason to repeat that review here. Rather, I would prefer to spend my last few pages on a longish summary of what we now know for sure about persuasion that we didn't know some three decades ago.

A longish summary

The difficulties which researchers were having in achieving long-lasting effects for persuasion techniques, based on a reward-reinforcement incentive theory, were part of what made the first dissonance experiments appealing. Dissonance theory provided a theory and a method for affecting deep-seated, rather than superficial, attitudes. "Who says what to whom with what effect," while seemingly effective in inducing short-term opinion change, did not change important attitudes—and didn't change even unimportant ones for very long. Although a credible communicator under the best of circumstances (the appropriate technique and audience) could probably sell you one brand of toothpaste or breakfast cereal over another, it was not clear that he could convince you to be less prejudiced against blacks, induce you to support the development of solar energy, or modify your opinion about the legalization of marijuana.

Dissonance theory was different in this respect. In linking the cognitive and motivational components of attitudes to behavior, it offered the possibility of advancing the field in two directions: 1. providing insight into the mechanisms behind deeper set attitudes and 2. pointing the way toward methods of effecting long-term changes in attitudes of a non-superficial nature. Festinger achieved this by suggesting that, at least in regard to important issues, people would not simply respond to the communication package with the greatest incentive value. Rather, people are involved in justifying their attitudes and behavior and in maintaining consistency. And again, this insistence on the link between motivation and behavior was carried over from the Lewinian tradition. The implications of this approach were completely different from those of a strict reinforcement theory, suggesting that the best way to change attitudes was to get people to persuade themselves. And as Lewin implied, techniques which made use of behavioral commitment had the possibility of leading to attitude changes of a more permanent nature. The potential of such an approach added to the excitement and enthusiasm surrounding the beginnings of dissonance theory.

Research concerned with clarifying and defining the parameters of the theory has expanded and continues to expand in many directions. And because of the research generated by the early controversies, this later research stands on a solid foundation—one made up of basics which we really do understand now and did not understand thirty years ago. Before we go on to discuss some of this research, it may be useful to list some of these by now well-known basics:

1. Choice, or volition, plays an important role in the operation of dissonance. In situations where an individual has voluntarily agreed to perform a discrepant behavior, dissonance is most likely to be aroused.
2. If a person's commitment to perform a discrepant behavior, such as arguing against his own beliefs or lying to another person, is high, he is more likely to experience dissonance and engage in subsequent dissonance reduction.
3. In situations in which a person feels responsible for the consequences of a discrepant behavior and is able to foresee its negative consequences, dissonance is aroused.
4. In some cases, even when the negative outcome is *not* foreseen, people will assign responsibility irrationally to themselves and will experience dissonance. This is particularly likely in situations where the behavior has had negative consequences for others besides the individual.
5. What all of these situations have in common is that the self or the self-concept is engaged.

The fact that dissonance predicts most clearly in situations in which the self is engaged and the person feels responsible for the consequences of his action may help to clarify the ability of the theory to address important rather than trivial attitudes. Dissonance predicts more clearly the firmer the expectancies are involved and the less they are subject to individual, idiosyncratic views of what are consonant and what are dissonant cognitions. Almost by definition, our expectancies about our own behavior are firmer than our expectancies about another person's behavior. The fact that most people share some elements of a self-concept (that they are moral and intelligent people, for example) means that predictions which involve the disconfirmation of these elements will be less equivocal and more generally valid than predictions involving other types of expectations.

This line of reasoning may be taken a step further. Our expectations about ourselves are not only firmer, they are more important to us than our expectations about general subjects. Intuitively, the fact that I have misled someone when I consider myself to be a moral person will be more important to me (providing for individual differences) than the fact that you (whom I thought was honest) have misled someone. When cognitions about ourselves are threatened or contradicted, we are likely to devote more energy to restoring consonance than if the inconsistency involves things about which we care little.

As we have seen, the research on dissonance and responsibility confirms this view. In order for dissonance to be aroused in most situations, the person must feel a connection between his own behavior and its consequences. Thus, as mentioned previously, in the experiment by Nel, Helmreich, and Aronson (1969), subjects who knew in advance that their pro-marijuana videotape would be used to change the attitudes of a highly persuasible audience—a group of young people who had no previous opinion on the issue—experienced more dissonance and exhibited more attitude change than those who believed the tape would be played to an audience confirmed in its beliefs. Moreover, subsequent work (Aronson, Chase, Helmreich, and Ruhnke, 1974) indicates that this connection between action and consequences need not necessarily be a rational one. If the results of a behavior are severe, particularly when they are harmful to others, people tend to take responsibility for the consequences *even when they could not reasonably have been expected to foresee them*. In the case of positive consequences, responsibility seems to be assumed only when those consequences had been foreseen (Brehm and Jones, 1970; Lepper, Zanna, and Abelson, 1970).

Let us return for a moment to the self-concept. The notion of responsibility is tied to the self-concept in a number of ways. Wicklund and Brehm (1976) point to the dual components of choice and foreseeability in the concept of responsibility. Both of these describe the connection between the self and the consequences of action. For the consequences of a behavior to arouse dissonance, we must not only see them as connected to us but as connected to us in a way which contradicts an element of our self-concept. The fact that we have harmed others arouses dissonance because most of us carry the expectancy that we are not harmdoers, even unintentionally.

The self-concept, for our purposes, may be seen as composed of a number of statements—such as "I am an honest person," "I am an intelligent person," and so on. Each of these statements, by necessity, must be further defined for the individual, and the subdefinitions must consist of the attitudes, values, and expectancies with which the statement is associated. Thus, for the subjects in the Nel, Helmreich, and Aronson experiment, the general heading "I am not a harmdoer" was further defined by the fact that they regarded marijuana as a harmful substance and therefore their advocacy of smoking it as a harmful thing to do. This further definition, of course, is implicit in the experimental procedure, being determined by the initial attitude measurement.

The suggestion here is that it may be possible to define "deep-seated" attitudes as attitudes which are associated with the self-concept as extended definitions. A peripheral opinion, on the other hand (and it may be peripheral because it was recently acquired, because it falls in a region in which the person claims no expertise, or for numerous other reasons), may be seen as one which has no such association. Whether I buy one brand of soap or another may be reasonably seen as having little association with issues of my intelligence, honesty, and so on.

If this argument holds, it is more easily seen why behavioral commitment in a dissonance-arousing situation may lead to more permanent attitude change. Self-justification, the process of dissonance reduction, involves the reorganization either of the headings themselves or of the sub-definitions. Thus, again in the Nel, Helmreich, and Aronson study, "harmful" is redefined to exclude the advocacy of smoking marijuana. It is likely that in a situation of behavioral commitment where the attitude must be changed to achieve consonance since the behavior cannot, such reorganization will result in relatively long-lasting change. The change of a peripheral opinion, since it requires no substantial reorganization, carries no guarantee of lasting over time.

Although the above is purely speculative, I believe that research along these lines—responsibility, foreseeability, and the self-concept—sustain dissonance as a vital theory. When combined with the other directions of dissonance research, there is indication that continued excitement and enthusiasm are justified.

Twenty-five years of dissonance research have not only illuminated our understanding of social influence and persuasion but, in addition, the cumulated findings have changed our thinking about how people get persuaded on the deepest possible level. Accordingly, researchers of social psychology have shifted their primary focus from an interest in variations in either the nature of a communication or in attributes of the communicator and have placed it on variables involving the person's own behavior—which, in turn, affect his active perception of himself in the situation. Dissonance studies have directed attention to the link between a person's cognition, his affect, and his behavior, to the process by which the subject actively attempts to bring these elements in line with one another. Choice, foreseeability, commitment—all are forces which actively engage the subject, linking him to the situation of which he is a part and inducing him to reconstruct his cognitive environment. What we now know for sure that we didn't know when I was an undergraduate is that when an individual is personally involved in a situation wherein he might consider himself to be stupid or immoral, he engages in self-justifying behavior which involves some form of self-persuasion. That self-persuasion can affect important attitudes and opinions (e.g., as in the experiments by Nel, Helmreich and Aronson [1969] and Cohen [1962]); cause enormous shifts in those opinions (up to 73 percent of the possible range, as in the Nel, Helmreich, and Aronson study); and persist over relatively long periods of time (e.g., in the Freedman [1965] toy study).

Moreover, this process occurs in a wide variety of situations which, before they were linked by dissonance theory, would have appeared to be disparate and unrelated. In addition, what the work on dissonance theory brought into focus more clearly than any other body of work is the fact that the social psychological laboratory, with all of its contrivances and complex scenarios, can produce clear, powerful effects which are conceptually replicable in both the laboratory and the real world.

Having begun this chapter with a rather dramatic description of social psychology in the 1950s and 1960s, I feel some obligation to end it on an equally dramatic note. It seems reassuring to me that over twenty-five years of research one is able to see both continuity and progress. It seems that this should be reassuring to others as well. That both of these qualities have been tied to careful experimental and theoretical work indicates that there is validity in a method which at times feels unproductive or disorganized. In short, there is no reason to think that the work of this decade will be any less productive than that of past decades—or any less exciting.

2

The Role of Social Psychology in Population Control

KURT W. BACK

Introduction

Experimental social psychology has become a consistent field of study; is it, however, also self-contained? Laboratory experiments as well as controlled field studies and experiments have given theoretical insights, but they may have led away from the applicability to social problems which gave an early impetus to the field. Do these elegant systems apply to anything beyond the research situation?

Population control is a good test case for the claims of social psychology. The basic theory of demography relates large-scale social changes to vital rates (such as birth and death rates of large populations). When overpopulation became an important problem, intensive research on fertility change began. Soon it became evident that the macro view had to be reconsidered and that the skills of psychologists, especially social psychologists, were required. The involvement of social psychology in population research coincides with the historical period of the field treated in this volume. The ongoing cooperation of these two fields can give insights into the achievements and difficulties of social psychology when dealing with social problems.

Within the framework of the social sciences we see social psychology as intermediate between the individual and society, dealing with dynamic processes. The impact of these processes is hampered by relatively stable, powerful structures: on the one side, the biological and psychophysiological makeup of the individual organism; on the other, the structures of society. In general, organisms and society provide the parameters of social psychological processes. Changes in these parameters will have powerful effects on any conclusions of social psychological studies.

Again, population control is a good example. It is influenced by the physiological makeup of individuals and by strong social norms. The work of social psychologists in fertility control shows the effects of these limiting conditions. This history can make us sensitive to the limits of social psychology as applied to social problems.

The demographic tradition

For most of human history, overpopulation has not been considered a serious social problem. The rigors of life kept population low, and in the few exceptional cases, war or migration readily settled the balance between territory, resources, and population. This does not mean that population pressure never led to innovations or social change. It does mean, however, that population growth was rarely seen as a concrete problem; nor was birth control considered an important aim, at least for one's own society.

Malthus

Concern about population is associated with the name of Thomas Robert Malthus. During the early Industrial Revolution, when changes in industry, technology, and agriculture, and thus in productivity, raised hopes for a wealthy, almost utopian future, many writers, especially the English reformer William Godwin, predicted an ideal world if only the restraints of social institutions could be eliminated and society protected for the good of all. Malthus objected to such optimism, proposing that material progress was limited by overpopulation. Human populations, he stated, tend to outgrow their food resources. Using available figures, he deduced that population increases in geometric proportion and food supply in only arithmetic proportion. In fact, balance is obtained by "positive" checks on population—that is, increased death rates—through misery, war, and famine. In a later edition of his work, he added the "negative" restraint—a decrease in the birth rate. This was subsumed under the title of "moral restraint," by which Malthus meant delayed marriage without premarital sexual relations (Malthus, 1798, 1803; Peterson, 1979).

Malthus' theory was attacked from all sides. To the reformers, his pessimism was unendurable. Among the economists, for instance, he was singled out by Marx as an opponent of progress. To the conservatives, he was seen as undermining the family and encouraging possible sexual perversion through moral restraint. He was also made responsible for existing birth control measures, positive or negative—which he actually viewed with disgust.

Finally, the industrializing nations of the nineteenth century did not develop as Malthus had predicted, and his theory fell into disrepute. However, he had a great influence on the development of economics—which, thanks to him, became known as the "gloomy science." Malthus' emphasis on competition for dwindling food resources strongly influenced Darwin's theories of the struggle for existence and natural selection; so, his theories remained vital even in periods when his strong beliefs and gloomy conclusions could be denied. The population explosion of the twentieth century again brought his ideas to the forefront—although the solutions proposed would be to him abhorrent.

As we look back, Malthus' thinking was weakened by his taking of both birth rate and mortality as globally given. He made little use of differentiation by age, family condition, or place of residence, all of which influence the conditions of fertility, nor of the sequence of social behavior and fertility throughout the life cycle. This legacy, left by Malthus for demographic theory, has only recently been reconsidered. In today's terminology, Malthus considered only macro events; we must also include micro events, which form the basis of sweeping social trends. The importance of these micro events led social psychologists to undertake population research.

In the first decades after Malthus' writing, the demographic experience was almost a reversal of his prediction. Resources in the industrial societies increased in the nineteenth century, and although population also grew, the food supply, with a few exceptions of local starvation, kept pace. In the early twentieth century, in fact, fertility declined so much that low fertility or race suicide was considered by many to be a social problem. Only the events after the Second World War seemed to vindicate Malthus. While a rise in fertility—the "baby boom"—in the Western countries was easily absorbed and proved temporary, the less developed countries experienced a population increase which threatened to negate all the social gains they had been able to achieve. Even the danger of famine, more widespread than at any previous time, appeared to agree with Malthus' predictions.

Demographic transition

The comparative study of different countries gave rise to the theory of relationships between economic development and population control. This has been called the "theory of demographic transition" (Coale and Hoover, 1958; Robinson, 1964; Thompson, 1929). Essentially, this theory says that given economic, social, and especially medical development, the death rate will drop before the birth rate does. Therefore, we can distinguish three stages of demographic change. The original condition prevailed in pre-industrial societies, where an unrestricted high birth rate prevailed which came close to the physiological capacity of individual women; population was held in check by a very high death rate. With the improvement of medicine, sanitation, and agriculture, mortality declined. As the birth rate was still unchecked, this led to an abrupt increase in population which could be absorbed by the growth of cities and industry. Several factors, then, led to the decrease in the birth rate. Among them were extended education, which led to postponement of marriage; the decrease in infant mortality, which guaranteed surviving children even under conditions of low fertility; the decreasing value of children as a labor force in agriculture or for security in old age (because of social regulation); and finally, birth control through new contraceptives or more efficient means of traditional contraception. This led to the third stage of demographic development, low mortality and low fertility, which stabilized the industrialized nations. Ideally this pattern leads from one level of a stable population to another, with minimum disruption.

The theory of demographic transition fitted roughly the experience of the Western nations. It was also used to predict the development of those areas which used the Western model in guiding their own modernization. The rapid importation of industry and the development of medical techniques led to a decrease in mortality faster than would have been possible in Europe. The population of the developing countries increased rapidly, in many cases negating the gains provided by the new industrial techniques. Demographic transition theory predicted that now, almost as a fact of nature, the birth rate would decrease as well and the population would stabilize, with minimum disruption. This was not happening for several reasons. First, the time span of the European experience would be excruciatingly long for the developing countries. One would have to assume that as these countries copied Europe's industrialization, making the population increases much faster and more extreme, stabilization would occur more quickly too. Also, contraceptives already existed, the social mechanisms were available, the lessening economic value of children was easily demonstrable, and social changes such as compulsory education could be readily introduced. Thus the theory of economic transition promised rapid stabilization of the world population.

Although the theory of demographic transition seems persuasive in its simplicity, it is open to grave objections. It is less a theory than a description of what happened in the Western industrializing nations between the seventeenth and twentieth centuries. And even there, it is not fully accurate. If we look more closely at some of the actual population increases in these societies, we find regional differences which are unexplained by the theory. In addition, the birth rate dropped consistently even during the period of population increase, and the actual growth curves show many variations which belie the smoothness of the theoretical curve.

As the demographic transition theory weakened, it became even more questionable as a guide for future policies. The programs modeled after the European experience did not lead quickly to stability or even to a decline in the growth rate. The question, Does this so-called theory actually describe a unique event, and is it a useful generalizable tool? was no longer academic, but one of social and political import.

Micro-demography: The Indianapolis study

One way to test and improve the theory and to provide additional guidance in its application was to go to a more detailed level. Fertility rates are made up of the actions of individuals. Studying individuals in this social context seemed to provide a good opportunity to view the demographic transition in more detail, to predict the conditions under which it could occur and be speeded up. Some work in this direction had been done, making contraception one of the most important topics in applied social psychological research.

The first major detailed study of population control began in the mid-1930s. It examined birth control at a micro level in a population at the third stage. The practical reason was a fear of a stable or declining population. The study therefore focused on that part of the population whose decline was felt to be especially detrimental to the country and whose dominance demographic measures, such as immigration laws, were designed to protect. Specifically, the study considered the white Protestant population of Indianapolis. Methodologically it was based on a sample survey with individuals, using close-ended interviews. This technique had just become popular and was known to be feasible in political and market surveys. The Indianapolis survey was revolutionary; it assumed that behavior as intimate as birth control could be measured the same way. Its variables were those of social structure, with class position, income, occupation, and age as independent variables; and desire for children, fertility, and contraceptive behavior as dependent variables. Variables between these poles, such as personal or family motivation and other social contexts, were included. Some, which could be used later, were included almost inadvertently as social conditions, such as membership in voluntary organizations.

Because of some delay in the administration and with the interruption of World War II, the Indianapolis study was analyzed almost a decade after it was conducted. At this point, the whole motivation of the study changed. First, instead of the threat of underpopulation, the analysts were working in an atmosphere of the baby boom and growing concern about a population explosion. Second, methods of analysis had changed greatly. Scaling techniques and other ways of summarizing data had been found. Apart from wartime research, the completed study became one of the earliest to which the new techniques could be applied. Finally, the intervening years brought advances in social psychological theory. Some of the new analysts and the authors of the final reports, the younger scientists who had been trained during and after the war, and some older analysts who had started the study also became receptive to these new ideas. Unfortunately, the social and psychological variables had to be derived from broader demographic conditions. These inferred variables included alternative occupations open to a woman, such as paid or voluntary work, questions of career orientation, and liking for children. Attempts at interpretation sometimes went far beyond the data and led the way for a new theoretical approach.

The Indianapolis study was published in the late 1940s and early 1950s as a collection of individual research papers (Whelpton and Kiser, 1946–1958). The results showed very moderate relationships between the demographic variables and fertility desires but suggested intriguing new possibilities for those factors not really measured in the study—namely, general orientation of the woman and the couple. The principal strength of the final results was the proposing of future research.

The rise of population research

The study had been a bold innovation when it started, but the ideas it generated took hold quicker than could be expected. This was not only because of general advances in the social sciences but also because of specific interest in population planning. While questions of depopulation and race suicide had worried only an elite minority, overpopulation came to be seen generally as an urgent problem. The impact of overpopulation on postwar reconstruction, especially in East and South Asia and the Caribbean, attracted the attention of many influential people. This interest led John D. Rockefeller III to establish the Population Council, which was concerned mainly with this problem. Eventually it would lead to the acceptance of population control by government agencies, even in the United States, as well as in international organizations. This new urgency encouraged new research in aid of population control. The biological-technical role of birth control was aided by the development of contraceptives which were safer, easier to use, and more reliable than the ones in use when the Indianapolis study was done. The fact that new techniques existed and were being developed also highlighted the social factors. Contraception could be used. An important condition for its success would be psychological: getting people to use it.

Further social research was also encouraged by the fact that contraception and sexual behavior could be studied closely by social scientists. The Indianapolis study did not go into detail on these questions. Meanwhile, however, Kinsey had shown that sexual behavior could be investigated using standard interviews. Although his techniques were specific and did not represent a sample survey, his success opened the way for others, who were willing to conduct interviews on a random population, using some sexual questions. This improvement in methodology, plus the increased sophistication of survey research, made it possible to enlist more social scientists in studying population control.

Entry of social psychological theories

The results of the Indianapolis study and the need for population control in overpopulated developing countries showed certain paradoxes, if only the demographic factors were considered. Certain social factors which supposedly would cause people to oppose contraception were no longer operating in most countries. Religious prohibition was no longer effective;

children were neither economic assets nor an economic necessity in old age; the ideal family size was two to three children; and most people had at least some knowledge of effective birth control practices. In spite of this, the predicted population decline failed to occur. Sociological factors were not translated easily into a lower birth rate, as could be expected if those two levels had a direct causal connection.

Looking more closely, however, one could find intermediate reasons why the social conditions did not affect fertility in the predicted direction. For example, the influence of organized religion decreased, but religious leaders had sufficient interest and power over political organizations to prevent an effective birth control program. The economic value of children had declined, but people were not used to the new economic system; nor were they sure that their partners or other relevant people would feel the same way. True, the ideal number of children was two to three, but this ideal was not strongly felt and people did not worry too much if they exceeded it. In addition, ideals of balance between boys and girls, or at least of having a minimum number of boys, contradicted the ideal of total family size. Also, although people did know some standard methods of birth control, they did not use them effectively or consistently. All these qualifications point to the following conclusion: These and other social conditions, such as education and work, did not affect fertility directly in some magical way, but only through intermediate conditions—personal decision making within a social context. Fertility is to be understood as personal behavior. It can be seen as a social-psychological problem: a question of attitude change, group decision making, communication within groups, and information transfer. These are all topics which are studied within social psychology. The job of social psychologists, therefore, was to apply their knowledge to a new situation. Researchers needed to combine a variety of theories, concepts, and relationships to address one problem, instead of applying one technique or staying with one conceptual approach and seeing how far they could take it.

Social psychologists were drawn into this work. I had done laboratory experiments and had some experience in survey research before starting to work with J. Mayone Stycos and Reuben Hill on Caribbean fertility studies. I was challenged to combine surveys and educational experiments on one social problem instead of working on controlled "contrived" situations. I concentrated, however, on analyzing fertility behavior, and the studies previously conducted, into their component social psychological terms and then imposed an experimental design, studying these variables.

This was not to be an evaluation of an educational program but a study of how theoretically derived variables worked. In the analysis we grouped the individual variables under three "blocks," or general factors. One was motivation, the values and attitudes which would lead to family limitation. The second was a mechanism by which the family or couple could decide to implement birth control. The third was the means of obtaining information about contraception and the assessment of this information (Hill, Back, and Stycos, 1955; Hill, Stycos, and Back, 1959).

Birth control could therefore be translated from a social or biological problem to a social psychological question. The different aspects of the model were similar to those questions which had been studied extensively in experimental social psychology. Experiments in group dynamics had shown different techniques of attitude change and of combining attitude change with group support. Thus, the social psychologist could turn to the conventional methods of studying mass media and interpersonal influence. The techniques would show the desire for limitation of family size in a social context. The second set of factors, summarized as action possibilities, were also familiar in the group dynamic context. The understanding and cooperation required for effective contraception involve the mechanisms for group functioning, such as communication, empathy, and decision-making ability. Again, research techniques which were used for diagnosing group functioning and for increasing group effectiveness seemed to be directly applicable. In fact, group dynamics had always been concerned with similar problems. Finally, information transfer had also been widely studied in social psychology. Analysis of interpersonal communication as well as the study of large-scale information campaigns had been intense.

Our social psychological analysis led to an additional conclusion beyond that of separating the different aspects of fertility. The effective functioning of a group—in this case, the efficient use of contraceptives—depended on the interplay of all the aspects of group functioning; the interaction between factors became important. In theory, this was a great advance over previous work in demography. It showed how the different aspects were interrelated and why seemingly simple solutions, such as the lessening economic dependence on children, would not lead automatically to a decrease in fertility. We had to study the whole complex of factors at the same time. In constructing a model, we found that there is a plausible sequence of conditions. Only if one is ready to act to limit one's family does the efficiency of the method of contraception become important. The sequence is, of course, not as simple as it appears, and there are feedback mechanisms. For instance, knowledge of certain birth control techniques may make group functioning more simple. Some of the techniques require more of the parties and more cooperation than others. The extreme case of sterilization, for instance, needs no further motivation or family functioning to be efficient once it is performed. This might then explain its popularity in societies where family functioning and cooperation are difficult. Paradoxically, it is also linked to religious prohibition of contraception. It is a resolution of a marked conflict between strong religious feelings and strong motivation for contraception. This interpretation has been popularized as the "one sin" theory (Senior, 1952).

The models were important from a diagnostic as well as a problematic point of view. The models guided the design of the surveys on contraceptive behavior; they also shaped the experiments that attempted to change it. The role of social psychology for these two purposes was different. Under the diagnostic model, the main interest was in identifying the relationships within and between blocks of relevant factors. Within each block, variables could be listed which were indicators of furthering or opposing birth control use. We then conducted a factor analysis within each block to obtain scores and related these "superfactors" to each other and to the dependent variables. (This was done before the modern development of path analysis and linear models.)

In the experiments designed to change contraceptive behavior, the theoretical factors could enter more directly. We intended to change values, family relations, or information and to measure the effect of these changes on initiation and improvement of contraception. The strongest factors in each block could be used as stimuli in the experiment. In this way, the standard methods of experimental design could be adapted to the needs of demographic research. It was obvious to the social psychologist, but not to practitioners in the field, that no particular experimental condition would have an overwhelming effect for practical use. The knowledge gained from the whole study, however, could be used to design more effective programs.

Puerto Rican and Jamaican studies

For several reasons, Puerto Rico became the first country for widespread social psychological research on contraception. The political situation of the island—which benefited by New Deal welfare programs without being restricted by American laws and court decisions on contraception—helped to make it a good laboratory. Puerto Rico had established birth control clinics in the early 1940s and was also the first country where male sterilization was recognized and widely practiced. When in 1948 Puerto Ricans were able to elect their own governor, the victorious party, which was identified with birth control clinics, was opposed by the Catholic Church. Hence, after his victory, the governor was less subject to pressure from the Church than other governments might have been. A series of studies of Puerto Rico saw it as a model of development in what was later to be called the Third World, including the question of population. These studies led to others which concentrated on fertility and birth control.

The first study, by Stycos (1955), was based on a set of lengthy open-ended interviews. It put the sexual-fertility experience, the use of contraceptives, into an individual developmental framework. The strong distinction between sex roles, the protection of women from sexual knowledge, and the stress on male sexual powers all made it difficult to introduce the notion of birth control. Children were proof of male strength. This meaning becomes more pronounced the more a man is anxious about his role. This was called the machismo pattern. Women may exaggerate the man's motives in this matter, even more so because it is impossible for them to discuss sex with their husbands. On the other hand, men will feel threatened if a woman acts independently, such as going on her own to a birth control clinic or using female methods of contraception. Men also feel that, because of the use of male contraceptives with prostitutes, they would degrade their wives by using these contraceptives with them. The detailed interviews provided vivid descriptions of the way men and women developed into their roles, how conditions forced them to repeat the pattern of the older generation even if rationally they would have preferred small families. At some points, the data could be tabulated to confirm the individual description, but generally the first survey gave a set of hypotheses to be tested.

These hypotheses were tested in a large study in which we devised ways to measure the main conditions identified. Here Reuben Hill, a family sociologist, and I extended the study (Hill, Stycos, and Back, 1959). At this point, a social psychological model of the factors could be constructed to test the hypotheses. This study concentrated on the family situation, family relationships, and the conditions for effective influence of contraception information. Data were obtained from husbands and wives or partners and the amount of information and of common information, indicating communication, could be tested by comparing the partners' answers. It was found, for instance, that women systematically overestimated their partners' desire for children. An exaggerated male role did not lead directly to a man's desire for children, but gave the impression that men had this desire and led to a lack of communication between the sexes, a misconception that could not be corrected. This was similar to a model which had been proposed by Newcomb (Newcomb, 1947). In addition, the same impression, based on insufficient information, influenced policy makers and officials of international agencies, who also claimed that Latin macho attitudes made any birth control program impossible. Thus, investigation of individual interactions was shown to be important in correcting the general impression derived from global analysis.

Based on these data, the theoretical analysis in terms of attitudes, family relations, and knowledge seemed justified. Later history would show that researchers fell into two types: those who were interested in attitude analysis and those who were interested in family relationships. In fact, the interest in family relationships probably surfaced only later, with the general interest in women's roles and power within the family. The study of knowledge and attitudes, however, became completely routinized, and the term "KAP (knowledge, attitude, practice) studies" entered the research language. These studies became so frequent that they could be collected; they form one of the largest bodies of data available in comparative analysis.

We extended the Puerto Rican surveys by doing a pilot study in neighboring Jamaica and then by conducting experiments in which we could test, through change, our ideas about the relations between variables. In Jamaica, the pilot study involved a long-range detailed interview with a small sample of pairs. This led us to a somewhat different picture, showing the contrast between a Caribbean English culture and a Spanish one (Blake, 1961). In Jamaica the ideal of sheltering girls clashed with the economic impossibility of protecting them. The importance for research was the prevalence of three distinct sexual arrangements: visiting, cohabitation, and marriage. This was contrary to the situation in Puerto Rico, where there was no difference between common law and church-sanctioned marriage. Another fact of life in Jamaica which was less pronounced in Puerto Rico was the major effort to achieve legal marriage, through sexual favors and pregnancy. On the other hand, promiscuity was a way of controlling family size; the woman could achieve, through abstinence, long periods of infertility. This interaction between marital status and contraception became one of the most important features of the Jamaican scene. In the ensuing study, family status was added to the variables of attitudes, family relations, and information. Comparisons between Puerto Rico and Jamaica show that the general theory of family decision-making was also applicable in dissimilar cultures. The differences between the cultures were dealt with by additional control variables, such as marital status, which had a different impact in each place (Stycos and Back, 1965).

In both places, the survey was followed by an experiment which tried to translate these findings into methods of producing change. These experiments represent the most direct application of social psychological and group dynamic technique to population problems. Therefore, they will be described here in greater detail (Back, Hill, and Stycos, 1957).

A number of neighborhoods were selected, sufficiently separated so that different experimental treatments could be employed. In Puerto Rico a three-by-two design was used. The treatments were distinguished by three kinds of content and two kinds of media. The contents were selected according to the theoretical factors. One treatment was attitude toward family size; another was improvement of family communication and information about birth control; and the third treatment combined both. The message was transmitted in two different ways: by distributing pamphlets giving relevant content, or in discussion groups led by a community worker. An additional group with just pre- and post-interviews acted as a control group. On the preinterview, measures were obtained on amount of information, effectiveness of family relationships, and favorableness of attitude toward birth control. Within each community, women (with their partners) were selected for the experiment who were high on all three measures, low on only one of the three, or low on all of them. This yielded five population groupings.

As dependent variables (measured on interviews two months later), we used changes in the three initial variables and in the use of contraception. The results of the study, in general, validated the model. Changes in values led people to begin contraception, while changes in family interaction led to improved use of contraception. Changes in information were important only for those people who were high on the two other factors and low on information. However, the correlation between program content and change in the theoretical variables was quite low. The ostensive content of the experimental program was the weakest variable. On the other hand, the method of transmission was important. Surprisingly for a group dynamicist, the pamphlet method—the less personal one—was much stronger in its effect than were the meetings. Considering, in addition, the attrition of people who did not attend the meetings (while everyone who was selected was given a pamphlet) and the higher cost of conducting the meetings, communication by pamphlet seemed far superior for practical purposes. The separation of theoretical variables for different experimental conditions, which seemed very sensible as a possible experimental procedure, looked less realistic in a field context. It is somewhat unrealistic first to swamp a village with interviews about contraception and then, a few weeks later, to arrange a meeting which discusses only attitudes toward family size.

The Jamaican experiment was constructed differently (Stycos and Back, 1965). The survey and experiment were planned together, and thus the survey respondents could be classified for the experiment. The experiment itself did not distinguish the two types of content, as this variation had not proved important. The whole program treated values and information together, while family relations were played down. This was done partly because of different social and marital conditions in Jamaica. Also, because of the low level of contraception in general, changes in family interaction—the topic which was designed to maintain an existing contraceptive program—would not have led to any measurable effect. Thus the program dealt only incidentally with marital relationships and primarily with communication and information. Major attention was given, however, to the amount of influence in the program and the manner of communication. We used three methods of giving the message: individual case workers, group meetings, and pamphlets; in a further condition, the three were combined for maximum effect. An attempt was made to follow Solomon's (1946) model of change experiments as far as possible.

In general, the results showed that the programs were effective. The increased use of contraception, as well as the decrease in birth rate, was measurable even after a year. The kind of communication was not particularly important, but the amount of communication was. That is, the more intensive the program, the more effective it was. The combined program, which of necessity took longer, was the most effective. Also, the preinterview could be considered a kind of communication as well, even though it did not try to change opinions or behavior. The additional contact and saliency produced by the interview acted almost as effectively as any intentional educational program. The result fitted a psychological conceptualization, which treats abstract forces and does not describe them by kind of contact. In group dynamic terms, the stronger the force applied to a person, the more likely he is to conform to the influence.

In a summary of the two studies, four conclusions linked psychological insight with the need of educational planning (Back, 1962):

1. It was possible to conduct a program and educational research even on this sensitive topic and in a variety of cultures. The theories and research practices of social psychologists were applicable to people in different societies. The same theoretical terms and relationships apply to human beings in different cultures. Culture defines the possible range of existing variables and their interpretation in concrete measures.

2. The specific program was less important. This again conforms to the abstract statements of social psychology—namely, that the strength of the force is important, but not the particular characteristics. In practical terms, this means that it is more efficient to repeat a stimulus and reach a wider population or the same population more times than to spend time, money, and effort to make features more attractive, such as producing movies or training people in conducting group meetings.

3. The type of recipient was important. Again, one can construct a continuum of strength of reception on which persons can be classified into three groups. One group had little resistance and would comply if only they were reminded of contraception. The second group was amenable enough so that a definite program, the induction of force, would at least lead them to start contraception. The third group had strong resistance, and a novel program would not affect them. Probably the most that can be accomplished with this last group is to provide some information in case they change their view later.

4. As the strength of the force was important, the need for continuing staff and continuing full operations became vital. When a program is initiated, all the skills of a resident community worker are needed. However, keeping up the program is more dependent on such mundane things as availability of supplies, distance from the distribution center, and continuous reminders through follow-up.

These studies were very intricate, difficult to do, and in retrospect, modeled too closely on standard laboratory experiments. They were not duplicated later in all their intricacies. In fact, they are now used in texts of multivariate methods as examples of multivariate design (Namboodiri et al., 1975). They had, however, a salutary effect on further work in family planning by proving that these programs could be initiated and tested with something like experimental precision. Family limitation programs were started under different circumstances and in different countries. The researchers could be confident of identifying crucial variables in the situation, initiating simple programs, and conducting evaluation studies. The experiments familiarized people with the effects of variables such as attitudes, family interactions, and information, which are in essence constant through all cultures. Investigators learned how to start family planning programs in new cultures and to accept the fact that the problem is equivalent everywhere.

Other early studies

Social psychologists were also active in other research which continued the tradition of the Indianapolis study. Elliot Mishler, a social psychologist, joined Charles Westoff, a demographer, in constructing a model for a new study in the United States. The model incorporated some of the ideas which had been used in the Caribbean. The particular conditions were, of course, different (Mishler and Westoff, 1955). Contraceptive knowledge in the United States was widespread, and the norm of the small family was at least verbally accepted. The model therefore concentrated on the family life pattern and on career mobility, which, forcing people to make frequent moves, makes a large family a definite debit. The eventual study was designed to measure the conditions under which a small family decides to become a large one. Mishler and Westoff defined the line between two and three children as the boundary of a large family and decided to concentrate on the decision to have a third child. They took a sample of second children born in nine metropolitan areas and then interviewed the mothers within a month of birth of the child. The interview considered a variety of demographic and social psychological variables, including the intention to have a third child. A reinterview after a few years determined whether the intention was carried through or not. Results of the study were disappointing in finding relevant psychological variables. Career mobility seemed to be less important than the overwhelming importance of religious background. The three religious groups, Protestant, Catholic, and Jewish, had very different patterns which determined fertility, while having different levels of fertility in themselves. The study showed that at least in developed countries, social conditions such as religion were more important than family patterns or careers in determining fertility (Westoff et al., 1961, 1963). A similar study of a national sample of users of contraception and fertility by Ronald Freedman and his associates came to a similar conclusion. Fecundity, the biological condition, and general demographic conditions are important. However, these studies also found that several personality traits, such as confidence in one's own effectiveness, were important predictors in success of family planning. Conversely, studies showed that early unwanted fertility can predict a cycle of low birth control, high fertility, and lack of efficacy in managing one's own life (Freedman et al., 1959).

Freedman, in addition to justifying social psychological conditions in domestic population studies, showed the efficacy of widespread population education programs. Using saturation techniques of mass communication with a controlled sample of different religions in Taiwan, he showed definitely that a mass-media program could significantly decrease the birth rate (Freedman and Takeshita, 1969).

The lack of tradition

The early studies based (even roughly) on psychological theory in the Caribbean, the United States, and Taiwan showed great promise. However, the development did not follow the same cumulative mode as the theoretical approaches in experimental and social psychology. Some variations of these studies were undertaken in different countries to obtain more data on population topics, but the social psychological base hardly expanded.

One of the reasons for this lack of follow-up resulted, paradoxically, from the rapid success of the population control movement. Population control became a widely discussed problem which needed an immediate solution. Funds for intensive programs became available. With this, the focus of psychological research changed. The parameters of the situation were shifted in a way that made questions of intra-personal conflict and personal choice minor problems. As an example, consider the issue of abortion in the United States. In the last six years, it has shifted from the conflict over whether it should be prohibited by law to whether abortion is every woman's right, including the right for government subsidies to pay for it. At the same time, it has shifted from a topic discussed in whispers and circumlocution, to a topic of public debate by both right-to-life groups and freedom-of-choice groups, to an issue fought out in a public arena. Rapid social changes of this kind make social psychological research models, which depend on individual cognitions and emotions, look like unimportant frills.

The change was even greater in developing countries. Government actions, private foundations, and international organizations helped to start population control programs and to make contraception respectable. Two of our study conclusions were vindicated. First, large-scale programs on contraception are possible, and the stereotyped image of the preindustrial society adamantly opposed to family planning is false. Thus, detailed models of the conditions within each country are not necessary for practical purposes. Second, the main finding—that the strength of the forces, and not particular niceties of programs, are decisive—also means that with massive funds, sufficient for reaching large numbers of people with continuous follow-up, effects can be achieved. These efforts will have such an initial success, reaching the appropriate population, that there seems little need for detailed social psychological research and theorizing.

Social psychology and comparative social structure

The rapidly changing conditions of family planning indicate a need to pinpoint the situations in which social psychological research is most effective. Looking at technical and normative circumstances, examining the findings on information and attitude in our contraceptive work, we can find situations where knowledge is either certain or nonexistent, or where norms prescribe or prohibit certain actions. If any of these conditions obtain, action will depend only on knowledge or norms. When neither of them happen, when actions are permitted and knowledge exists, then individual decisions and group interaction become important. Thus, where there are permissive attitudes toward contraception and some knowledge about birth control methods, we find that the social psychological approach is most effective (Back, Hill, and Stycos, 1960).

We may find these situations in special populations within a country, such as teen-age pregnancy in the generally knowledgeable and permissive contemporary United States. We can also classify countries according to their state of knowledge and attitude and predict the appropriateness of social psychological research.

In cooperation with H. Winsborough, I was able to classify governments as if they were individual respondents (Back and Winsborough, 1968). This was possible because the United Nations conducted an inquiry of its members on possible population programs. Enough information was available to pinpoint relevant characteristics. We could identify, for each nation, motivation factors, interest in family planning and information available, and the organizational ability of the country to carry out a birth control program. Based on this and subsequent research, we could propose a classification of countries similar to that of individuals which shows the appropriateness of social psychological research.

At one extreme are the societies in which realization of the population problem, as well as the organization to carry out a program, is nonexistent. Here, as with individuals totally opposed to the idea, we can only begin to make the idea of contraception accepted, at least with an elite part of the population.

The next category would include the nations with some interest in contraception and some clinical or medical planning. The societies which show conflict between the desire for birth control and the level of its achievement are those which best fit into social psychological research. The governmental interest in limiting fertility may be juxtaposed to the traditional value of large families. Sometimes special conditions for delivery systems make organization easier. One of these conditions is spatial limitation; this may be the reason why island nations, such as those of the Caribbean, Taiwan, Mauritius, or Singapore, have been the ones most interested in social psychological studies. These countries also show the limitation of the approach. The first studies are usually extremely successful, showing the ways in which people could change to want small families and to act accordingly. However, this first stage is followed by a massive program or by legislation which is little affected by the subtlety of individual relationships. The strength of the social psychological approach is that it opens the country to the possibility of a birth control program, upon which base government programs can build. A secondary effect, after the government program has been instituted, is to direct attention to groups and conditions which need special approaches. In general, the countries in this condition—the island nations as well as the overpopulated countries of South and East Asia and Latin America—have welcomed research programs of all kinds (Back, 1973).

In industrialized societies, the change from a negative to a positive evaluation of contraception has been amazing. Both knowledge and organization have become available and almost normative. We may recall that up to the late 1950s, U.S. federal agencies could not subsidize any contraception, and until 1973 abortion was prohibited by law. The short-term change saw a massive program of government help for contraception, the contraceptive devices becoming easily available, and abortion being considered practically a human right. Within this social framework of rapid change, let us consider the current social psychological contributions in our society. Here we can find application, not in the general population program but in the problems of special populations.

Current doubts

In social psychology, practice has frequently outpaced theory and research. In the last ten years, social psychologists have been very active in the field of population planning, but more as practitioners than as pathbreakers. This became official when the American Psychological Association created a Division for Population and Environment. On the other hand, the Population Association of America, which is essentially a demographic organization, sponsors a three-day Social Psychological Workshop on Fertility. Publications on psychology and population have been sponsored by the Population Council, by the Society for the Psychological Study of Social Issues, and by the Center for Population Research of NIH to show the range of actual and possible research (Back and Fawcett, 1974; Fawcett, 1970, 1974; Newman and Thompson, 1976).

The past contribution of social psychology to population research is unchallenged. The precise nature of this contribution, however, is not easy to determine. Even more, the practical values of current social psychological research are hard to predict, and skepticism abounds. I shall conclude the chapter by assessing this situation and giving examples of current work.

In preparation for writing this chapter, I talked to many psychologists active in the organizations mentioned above. I asked them what the current contribution of social psychology to demography would be and how they would assess the whole field at the present time. Almost all the answers were quite pessimistic. At present, they said, no precise social psychological approach to the work in population could be pinpointed; nor was there any particularly exciting research which combines the two fields. This is corroborated by declining research support as well as fewer social psychological proposals in population submitted to government agencies. In fact, some people even warned me not to stress this field too much, as there were other aspects of psychology, particularly in measurement techniques, which are quite active. Exposing a generally negative record of social psychology might endanger support for the whole psychological enterprise.

I doubt that such a gloomy view is necessary. It is true that one cannot point to a strong tradition that parallels the precise research models of experimental social psychology in population control or to a current enterprise built solidly on the accumulation of social psychological theory and knowledge. The conditions of experimental research almost preclude successes of this kind. In experimental studies, one is satisfied with changing questionnaire responses and with analyzing these responses as if every change which occurs carries over into socially relevant behavior. With an event as complicated as birth control, which includes a long-term commitment to activities which are connected with intimate and intensely emotional aspects of life, changing answers about the number of children desired could have little relevance for demographic change. Injecting population-relevant content into standard experiments instead of other questions does little either to help us understand population control or to guide policy. On the other hand, population control policy and programs exist; policy makers have specific needs which are not met by the input from current academic research. Those who deal with pregnant adolescents, for example, may be vitally concerned with conducting discussion groups which keep the clients coming back; this makes it possible for agencies at least to distribute the contraceptives. In practice, the work is almost intuitive, without guidance by a theory which explains why clients return and stay interested.

There is a tradition in social psychology which can get beyond this dichotomy between theory and application. Current theory can be used in family counseling or by organizations for massive information campaigns. Large-scale experiments, however, are too expensive and time-consuming for many scientists. They will be undertaken only if the theorist trusts that the theory will be effective in a given situation and is able to convince others that these studies will have a practical payoff. At present, there are almost no studies of this kind. Either theorists do not want to invest their time and believability in such studies or population experts see little to gain by investing in the abstract concerns of social psychology.

Current advances

However, one still finds social psychologists searching for ways to apply social psychological knowledge to practical issues. Let us consider examples from the three fields noted above: values, family relations, and information.

The first example concerns the difficulties of putting a desire for children into a motivational framework. The obvious question to ask of respondents is, of course, "How many children do you want?" Respondents' answers are usually not very realistic, nor do they guarantee relevant behavior. So stereotyped are they, in fact, that they reflect a social norm rather than personal desire. Lois and Martin Hoffman have analyzed the question in greater detail and isolated ten motives which make people want to have children, such as social acceptance, power, or substitute achievements or goals (Hoffman and Hoffman, 1974). This framework leads to important research projects which can be retranslated into measures by which the strengths of the motives can be compared. After analysis of the motives, one may find substitute paths toward the same goal. Thus there can be ways, other than becoming a parent, of asserting one's sexual identity in our society, or new ways of compensating for the failure to achieve one's own life goals. In addition, this method provides a way of comparing reasons for having children *within* societies. Variability in the number of children wanted *between* societies is not only a very rough measure but does not show differences between most groups. However, the pattern of motives for having children does vary from group to group within a society and also from society to society. Studies done in both the United States and the Pacific area compare the patterns of motives and values about fertility. The findings hold great promise for future population research (East-West Center, 1975–1979).

Another new approach to family relations centers on the question of decision making. Theoretical developments about how families make decisions on family size (or at least about the next pregnancy) have raised interesting methodological issues. A detailed analysis of theoretical issues such as are posed by exchange theory in family decision making must precede research in the field (Beckman, 1977, 1978). Models have been proposed which show that this decision-making process must be analyzed at key points. The process may change from a general idea to definite decisions after conception, and change again during pregnancy. The decision on eventual family size is the sum of all these decision points, child after child (Hass, 1974). This analysis also shows how the problem could be approached in extensive research on how these decisions are really made. Here simulations such as role playing become difficult and may have to be adapted to different decision points. Participant observation is impractical. Substitutes such as interviews in rapid succession—for instance, spaced a week apart—have been proposed (Mellinger, 1974).

The spread of contraceptive information can be seen as a diffusion of innovation, and the interaction of mass media and interpersonal communication can be studied. In contrast to other innovations, such as agricultural techniques, fertility control is more private, and its effects are perceived much later. In this case, misunderstanding may derive from indiscriminate mass propaganda. Detailed analysis of understanding and of communication across cultures has become a new and important application of social psychology in family planning (Rogers, 1973).

Conclusion: Diffusion of social psychology

The practical impact of social psychology on family planning research is encouraging or disappointing, depending on one's point of view. It may be typical of the history of any application of one science to a complex problem where definite results are expected. The concerns of social psychology are only part of the picture of human behavior. But if these concerns are omitted, only biological and permanent social structures are considered. A new look at interpersonal behavior may suddenly give new insight and hopes of finally solving the problem. A new field also gives new scope to the talents of individual social psychologists, who can then apply laboratory theories to real situations. However, after this first insight, further advances become rare and comparatively trivial. The work of the social psychologist leads typically to miniature theories and small interventions, which can be unimportant compared with the broad social trends. Overall, one must admit that no single approach of social psychology has had lasting success in the work on population control.

We can be satisfied with more modest aims. What the social psychologist does is to direct attention to certain aspects of the situation which have been overlooked, interpersonal relations, setting of goals, providing of information, and achieving continued action. This general framework has been transmitted to new generations of demographers so successfully that many workers in the population field do not recognize the changes achieved. In my informal survey of the practitioners' attitudes toward psychology, I found that the people who were further away from the research were much more prone to acknowledge its influence. Although their own research could not pinpoint any particular theory, they believe that the pioneering work of social psychologists made their own work possible. The directing of attention to the decisions of individuals, the couple, the community, and—hopefully—the policy maker has probably saved population control from being an empty exercise. It should not be surprising that theories which had to be teased out from precise experiments have little direct application in a complex field of social life. The great value of social psychology, and the real meaning of its initial successes, was to reorganize the field in such a way that personal relations could and would be considered. After the first enthusiasm came the first disappointment, which has now passed. Currently we find researchers taking these orientations as a matter of course; they are now general principles in approaches to the issue of population control.

In this history of information transmission, this point of view should not be surprising to social psychologists. After all, our own research has shown that no knowledge is transferred by introducing single items into a cognitive framework. Changes occur by changing the frame of reference and reorganizing one's cognitive organization and by restructuring the field. This means that the processes we have been studying will also apply to the understanding of social psychology's influence on other social sciences.

3

Fifty Years of Conflict

MORTON DEUTSCH

Introduction

The aim of this chapter is to consider what progress, if any, has been made during the past fifty years or so in the social psychological study of conflict. Conflict, of course, was not discovered by social psychologists. It is a pervasive fact of human experience which has been discussed throughout recorded history by social philosophers and others who have reflected on social life. I shall not review here the writings about conflict of the social philosophers, limiting myself to the era of modern social psychology. However, it is my impression that a careful reading of their work would leave most of us with a sense of humility and also a feeling of pride: humility at the recognition that few of our ideas are new; pride at the realization that, unlike the social philosophers, we are part of a scientific tradition which tests its ideas through research in order to eliminate those that cannot survive a rigorous, empirical examination.

Indicators of scientific progress

What indicators can we use to assess whether or not there has been scientific progress in the study of conflict? Progress could occur in such areas as the methodological, conceptual, empirical, and technological. Some of the questions that could be asked in each of these areas are listed below:

The writing of this chapter has been supported, in part, by a National Science Foundation Grant, BNS 77-16017.

The methodological. Have better methods of investigating the phenomena one seeks to observe, to record, to analyze, and to understand been developed? Do the methods make the phenomena more accessible and more open to experimentation? Are the techniques of observing, recording, and analyzing data more precise, objective, reliable, and valid?

The conceptual. Have new ideas been introduced which lead one to observe new phenomena which had previously been unnoticed or whose significance had been ignored? Have new ideas been developed which interrelate phenomena not previously seen as connected? Have ideas which were previously regarded as untestable been reformulated in a way which makes them testable or, if not, shown to have no empirical content? Have the existing ideas in the field been systematically integrated into a more coherent, consistent, aesthetically pleasing theory? Do we understand the phenomena of interest more fully, more deeply?

The empirical. Have new, surprising facts or phenomena been discovered? Have ideas which were once widely believed to be true been demonstrated to be false? Have regularities between phenomena been newly established so that reliable predictions or postdictions can be made?

The technological. Have methodological, conceptual, or empirical advances led to or stimulated the development of new or modified technologies, social institutions, social practices, educational procedures, and so on which affect individual, group, organizational, and/or societal well-being?

It is evident that any thorough attempt to assess progress in the social psychological study of conflict would necessarily be book length. I shall not attempt to answer all of the questions that have been detailed above. My focus will be primarily on the conceptual and the empirical and secondarily on the methodological or technological. The study of conflict informs and is informed by research on power, social influence, group formation, distributive justice, and many other related topics. Thus, it will be difficult to isolate the progress or lack of progress in the study of conflict from the associated progress or lack of it in other areas.

The meaning of the social psychology of conflict

There are various definitions of the term "conflict." A simple one, which I prefer (Deutsch, 1973, p. 10) is that: "A *conflict* exists whenever *incom-*

patible activities occur"; a conflict is potential to the extent that incompatible activities are likely to occur. An action that is incompatible with another action prevents, obstructs, interferes, injures, or in some way makes the latter less likely or less effective. Incompatible actions may originate in one person, group, or nation; such conflicts are called *intra*personal, *intra*group, or *intra*national. Or they may reflect incompatible actions of two or more persons, groups, or nations; such conflicts are called *inter*personal, *inter*group, or *inter*national.

The social psychological study of conflict is not characterized so much by the nature of the conflicting units it studies (although interpersonal and intergroup conflict are investigated most commonly) as by its approach to conflict. Its approach is distinguished by its focus on the interplay between psychological and social processes. It is concerned with the perceptions, beliefs, and values of the conflicting parties as well as their actualities; these may or may not correspond. It is concerned with how the social realities of the parties in conflict affect their perceived and experienced realities and how the psychological realities of the conflicting parties affect the development of their social realities.

The social psychological perspective on conflict highlights the possibility of discrepancy between the objective and the perceived state of affairs. Recognition of this possibility suggests a typology of conflicts (Deutsch, 1973, Ch. 1) which emphasizes the relationship between the two. Such an emphasis leads to specification of the types of distortion which can occur, including the nonrecognition of real conflicts of interest as well as their displacement and misattribution. This emphasis, in turn, leads to a consideration of what activates the sense of injustice and what turns a latent into a veridical conflict (Deutsch, 1974). This focus also suggests examination of the social and psychological determinants of the readiness to cope with real conflicts in an undistorted way. The study of the power, internal cohesion, and structure of the parties as they affect and are affected by the course of conflict between them are inherent concerns in this perspective.

Although intrapsychic, interpersonal, and social conflict are interrelated—and it is my view (Deutsch, 1973) that similar concepts and theories may be applicable to all levels of conflict—I shall not be able to consider the voluminous work that has been done on intrapsychic conflict here. Thus, it is beyond the scope of this chapter to consider the many valuable contributions arising from the research and theorizing on intrapsychic conflict done in the context of psychoanalytic theory, learning theory, field theory, dissonance theory, decision theory, or role theory.

My personal bias

In writing this chapter, I have not attempted to present a well-rounded survey of progress in the study of conflict. I have not taken the perspective of an objective "outsider"; I have been too much of an "insider" to present an overview which is not strongly colored by my personal orientation and work. From early in my career, I have thought of conflict in the context of competition and cooperation. I have viewed these latter as idealized psychological processes which are rarely found in their "pure" form in nature but, instead, are found more typically mixed together. I have also thought that most forms of conflict could be viewed as mixtures of competitive and cooperative processes and, further, that the course of a conflict and its consequences would be heavily dependent upon the nature of the cooperative-competitive mix. These views of conflict lead me to emphasize the link between the social psychological studies of cooperation and competition and the studies of conflict in my assessment of this latter area.

At the beginning . . .

Although its ancestry in social philosophy can be traced back to ancient times, modern social psychology was born in the first decades of the twentieth century. It is a child of psychology and sociology, having been conceived in the ambivalent mood of optimism and despair which has characterized the Scientific Age. The rapidly expanding knowledge, the increasing confidence in scientific methods, the ever quickening technological change with its resulting opportunities and social problems, the development of new social organizations and of social planning, the social turmoil, the repeated disruption of communities and social traditions—all of these helped to create both the need for social psychology and the awareness of the possibility that scientific methods might be applied to the understanding of social behavior.

The writings of three intellectual giants—Darwin, Marx, and Freud—dominated the intellectual atmosphere during social psychology's infancy. Each of these major theorists significantly influenced the writings of the early social psychologists on conflict as well as in many other areas. All three theorists developed broad, encompassing theories, and this stimulated early social psychological theorists such as McDougall (1908) to make programmatic statements which were grandly ambitious in scope but meager in their detail. In addition, all three theorists appeared—on a *superficial* reading—to emphasize the competitive, destructive aspects of conflict.[1] Darwin stressed "the competitive struggle for existence" and "the survival of the fittest." He wrote (quoted in Hyman, 1966, p. 29): ". . . all nature is at war, one organism with another, or with external nature. Seeing the contented face of nature, this may at first be well doubted; but reflection will inevitably prove it is too true." Marx emphasized "class struggle," and as the struggle proceeds, "the whole society breaks up more and more into two great hostile camps, two great, directly antagonistic classes: bourgeoisie and proletariat." He ends *The Communist Manifesto* with a ringing call to class struggle: "The proletarians have nothing to lose but their chains. They have a world to win. Working men of all countries, unite." Freud's view of psychosexual development was largely that of constant struggle between the biologically rooted infantile id and the socially determined, internalized parental surrogate, the superego. As Schachtel (1959, p. 10) has noted:

> The concepts and language used by Freud to describe the great metamorphosis from life in the womb to life in the world abound with images of war, coercion, reluctant compromise, unwelcome necessity, imposed sacrifices, uneasy truce under pressure, enforced detours and roundabout ways to return to the original peaceful state of absence of consciousness and stimulation. . . .

Thus, the intellectual atmosphere prevalent during the period when social psychology began to emerge contributed to viewing conflict from the perspective of "competitive struggle." Social conditions too—the intense competition among businesses and among nations, the devastation of World War I, the economic depression of the 1920s and 1930s, the rise of Nazism and other totalitarian systems—reinforced this perspective. Darwin's and, to a lesser extent, Freud's emphasis on biological determinism also helped to foster the view that the species who survived the competi-

---

1. I emphasize that this is a superficial reading of Darwin, Marx, and Freud but it was, I believe, the most prevalent one, especially after the destructiveness of World War I. Each of these dialectical theorists had a vision of a harmonious utopia which would be reached through the stimulus of conflict; this conflict-free utopia would result from the emergence of a new, cooperative synthesis or integration between the formerly opposed units.

tive struggle had developed, through natural selection, the competitive, aggressive instincts necessary to enable them to win the struggle for survival.[2]

The vulgarization of Darwin's ideas in the form of "social Darwinism" provided an intellectual rationale for racism, sexism, class superiority, and war. Such ideas as "survival of the fittest," "hereditary determinism," and "stages of evolution" were eagerly *mis*applied to the relations between different human social groups—classes and nations as well as social races— to justify existing exploitative social relations and to rationalize imperialist policies. The influence of evolutionary thinking was so strong that, as a critic suggested, it gave rise to a new imperialist beatitude: "Blessed are the strong, for they shall prey upon the weak" (Banton, 1967, p. 48). The rich and powerful were biologically superior; they had achieved their positions as a result of natural selection. It would be against nature to interfere with the inequality and suffering of the poor and weak. Imperialism was patriotism "in a race endowed with the genius for empire" or the "manifest destiny" of those superior peoples meant to lead inferior peoples. Blacks were slaves as a result of their being at a lower stage of evolution, closer to the apes than whites, who presumably were at the highest evolutionary stage. As Kamin (1974) has noted, in his description of the orientations of the early leaders of the mental test movement, some of the leading figures in American psychology during the 1910s and 1920s advocated what we would today consider to be racist views as though they were well-established scientific truths.

Social Darwinism and the mode of explaining behavior in terms of innate, evolutionary derived instincts were under challenge and in retreat by the mid-1920s. The prestige of the empirical methods in the physical sciences, the point of view of social determinism advanced by Karl Marx and various sociological theorists, and the findings of cultural anthropologists all contributed to their decline.[3] Since the decline of the instinctual mode of explaining such conflict phenomena as war, intergroup hostility, and human exploitation, two others have been dominant: the "psychological" and the

2. Darwin's theory, of course, indicates that the competitive struggle is between rather than within species. Hence, his theory, if correctly interpreted, would not lead to the conclusion that humans, having successfully survived *inter*species struggle, would be characterized by *intra*species competitive or aggressive instincts.

3. This is a decline, not a disappearance. The explanation of social phenomena in terms of innate factors justifies the status quo by arguing for its immutability; such justification will always be sought by those who fear change.

"socio-political-economic." The "psychological" mode attempts to explain such phenomena in terms of "what goes on in the minds of men" (Klineberg, 1964) or "tensions that cause war" (Cantril, 1950); in other words, in terms of the perceptions, beliefs, values, ideology, motivations, and other psychological states and characteristics that individual men and women have acquired as a result of their experiences and as these characteristics are activated by the particular situation and role in which people are located. The "socio-political-economic" mode, in contrast, seeks an explanation in terms of such social, economic, and political factors as levels of armaments, objective conflicts in economic and political interests, and the like. Although these modes of explanation are not mutually exclusive, there is a tendency for partisans of the psychological mode to consider that the causal arrow points from psychological conditions to socio-political-economic conditions and for partisans of the latter to believe the reverse is true. In any case, much of the social psychological writing in the 1930s, 1940s, and early 1950s on the topics of war, intergroup conflict, and industrial strife was largely nonempirical, and in one vein or the other. The psychologically trained social psychologist tended to favor the psychological mode; the Marxist-oriented or sociologically trained social psychologist more often favored the other mode.

The decline of social Darwinism and the instinctivist doctrines was hastened by the development and employment of empirical methods in social psychology. As Murphy, Murphy, and Newcomb (1937, p. 16) in their classic work, *Experimental Social Psychology,* pointed out, social psychology was defined as "the study of the way in which the individual becomes a member of, and functions in, a social group." This early empirical orientation to social psychology focused on the socialization of the individual; this focus was, in part, a reaction to the instinctivist doctrine. It led to a great variety of studies, including a number investigating cooperation and competition. These latter studies are, in my view, the precursors to the empirical, social psychological study of conflict. They will be discussed briefly in the next section.

Early studies of cooperation and competition

Two outstanding summaries of the then-existing research on cooperation and competition were published in 1937. One was in the volume of Murphy, Murphy, and Newcomb referred to above; the other was in the monograph *Competition and Cooperation,* by May and Doob (1937). Both of these works are worth reading in the original; each contains reports of investigations which bear upon a wide range of topics in social psychology. It is not my intention here to repeat these summaries but rather to give you my sense of the state of the research and theorizing on cooperation-competition in the 1920s and 1930s. My view is based upon reading a number of the individual studies cited in May and Doob and in Murphy, Murphy, and Newcomb, as well as upon these two volumes themselves.

My impression is that practically none of the earlier research on cooperation and competition would be acceptable in current social psychological journals because of methodological flaws in the studies. Almost all of them suffer from serious deficiencies in their research designs. There are too few subjects; possible experimenter effects are abundant; systematic comparisons between major experimental conditions (such as cooperation and competition) are often nullified because there is an unwitting confounding with other variables (such as probability of reward); subjects who are nested within groups within treatments are treated statistically as though they are independent of one another; and so on. In addition, there is little conceptual clarity about some of the basic concepts—"competition," "cooperation," "self-orientation"—that are used in the studies. As a result, the operational definitions used to create the differing experimental conditions have no consistency from one study to another or even within a given study.

Apart from these methodological and conceptual difficulties, the early studies on cooperation and competition suffered from a narrownesss of scope. They focused almost exclusively on the effects of "competition" versus "cooperation" on individual task output; individuals worked separately and had no interaction and no interdependence with one another in terms of their activities. There was no investigation of social interaction, communication processes, problem-solving methods, interpersonal attitudes, attitudes toward self, attitudes toward work, attitudes toward the group, or the like in these early investigations of cooperation-competition. In essence, there was no investigation of the intrapsychic, interpersonal, and social processes associated with cooperation and competition. The focus was narrowly limited to work output. The simplistic assumption was made that output would be an uncomplicated function of the degree of motivation induced by competition as compared with cooperation. The purposes of most of these early investigations appeared to be to support or reject a thesis inherent in the American ideology: namely, that competition fosters greater motivation to be productive than other forms of social organization.

Maller (1929), in his doctoral dissertation written at Teachers College, Columbia University, fifty years ago, describes one of the best and most comprehensive early studies of cooperation and competition. A brief summary of its main features and results follows.

The test material he employed consisted of forty pages of simple additions. This material was used to measure speed of work under the following forms of motivation:

1. Practice work: The children did not write their names on paper. They were told that score would not "count," that they should do the examples just for practice at their usual speed.
2. Competition: A speed contest was arranged. Children were told that a list would be prepared showing the rank of each child in speed, and they were urged to try to attain a high rank. Prizes were promised to those scoring high.
3. Cooperation: A contest was staged between two parallel classes. Children were not to write their names but only the numbers of their classrooms on the papers. A prize was promised to the group having the higher total score.

The practice work was done first. Then the work for self and the work for group were alternated, and each was repeated six times.

The scores for cooperativeness were derived as follows: The difference between the two scores of work for self and for group was taken as a score of cooperativeness (Efficiency Cooperation). Children were also given the alternative of continuing work either for themselves or for their group. This test was repeated seven times. The number of times a child chose to work for the group was another score of cooperativeness (Choice Cooperation). The two scores, which had a correlation of .23, were combined into one total score of cooperativeness. The total score equaled the "efficiency" score plus twice the "free choice" score.

The major results were:

1. The efficiency of work under competition was found to be consistently and significantly higher than under cooperation. The average child did 32.4 examples *more* in twelve minutes of work for self than in twelve minutes of work for his group. In terms of increment above the "unmotivated level" of practice work, the group motive was only .45 as potent as the self motive.

2. As the goal of work, the group was chosen in 26 percent and self in 74 percent of the total number of choices. The choices for group decreased with progress of the choice units.

3. Cooperation with an organized team (in which the two team captains were elected by the children), cooperation with self-selected partners against other partners, and cooperation of a team of boys against a team of girls, in each case, resulted in even greater efficiency than work for self, while cooperation with an arbitrary group, chosen by the examiner, resulted in lower efficiency than work for the class.

Although Maller's findings are consistent with other similar but less well-done studies of the early 1920s and 1930s, a little thought makes it evident that one cannot draw any general conclusions from his study about the relative strengths of individual motivation to work under cooperation as compared with competition. Too many important variables which may affect or be affected by cooperation and competition were allowed to vary unsystematically, including: the probability of obtaining a prize; the attractiveness of the prize; the significance of "winning" or "losing"; the attraction of the other children with whom one was cooperating or competing; the costs of failure; the confounding of ingroup cooperation and outgroup competition; and others. Nevertheless, Maller's (1929, p. 163) basic conclusions—that cooperativeness and competitiveness are "influenced by environmental factors" and are "habit patterns acquired in accordance with the general laws of learning"—appear to be safe and sound. His attempts to establish the validity of his measure of cooperativeness and to find personality and other correlates of cooperativeness, which I have not described, were impressive in scope and went considerably beyond the attempts of more recent investigators.

By comparison with then-existing research, the 1930s theorizing on cooperation-competition, as exemplified by May and Doob, was considerably more sophisticated. May and Doob (1937, pp. 17–18) presented a theory whose major ideas as they bear upon cooperation and competition are expressed in their following postulates:

Postulate 5. On a social level, individuals compete with one another when: 1. they are striving to achieve the same goal that is scarce; 2. they are prevented by the rules of the situation from achieving this goal in equal amounts; 3. they perform better when the goal can be achieved in unequal amounts; and 4. they have relatively few psychologically affiliative contacts with one another.

Postulate 6. On a social level, individuals cooperate with one another when: 1. they are striving to achieve the same or complementary goals that can be shared; 2. they are required by the rules of the situation to achieve this goal in nearly equal amounts; 3. they perform better when the goal can be achieved in equal amounts; and 4. they have relatively many psychological affiliative contacts with one another.

The theory of May and Doob is essentially centered on the social and psychological factors initiating cooperation or competition. It is not concerned with the social psychological processes which result from cooperation and competition, nor with the effects of these resulting processes upon individuals and groups. Thus, their theory has a narrow focus, but within its focus, its postulates have been supported reasonably well by subsequent research.

Field theory, conflict, and cooperation-competition

During the 1920s, 1930s, and 1940s, quite independently of the work being conducted in the United States on cooperation-competition, Kurt Lewin and his students were theorizing and conducting research which profoundly affected later work in many areas of social psychology. Lewin's field theory—with its dynamic concepts of tension systems, "driving" and "restraining" forces, "own" and "induced" forces, valences, level of aspiration, power fields, interdependence, overlapping situations, and so on—created a new vocabulary for thinking about conflict and cooperation-competition.

As early as 1931, employing his analysis of force fields, Lewin (1931, 1935) presented a penetrating discussion of three basic types of psychological conflict: *approach-approach*—the individual stands between two positive valences of approximately equal strength; *avoidance-avoidance*—the individual stands between two negative valences of approximately equal strength; and *approach-avoidance*—the individual is exposed to opposing forces deriving from a positive and a negative valence. Hull (1938) translated Lewin's analysis into the terminology of the goal gradient, and Miller (1937, 1944) elaborated upon it. Theoretical analysis, verified by experimental evidence, has shown (Miller, 1944) that: 1. *Approach-approach* conflict will be resolved quickly without vacillation unless contaminated by latent avoidance. 2. *Avoidance-avoidance* conflict will be characterized by compromise resolutions; the individual will escape both negatives unless restrained by physical barriers or other sources of avoidance. When escape is impossible, vacillation and blocking will occur. 3. In *approach-avoidance* conflict no barriers will be needed to hold the subject in the conflict situation; the approach tendency will bring him into it. As long as the goal gradients cross, the subject will remain trapped partway to the goal, unable either to achieve or leave it.

Although Lewin's contribution to the understanding of three basic types of intrapsychic conflict are well known, it is not so well recognized that Lewin's concept of tension system has led to a series of investigations having much relevance to the processes involved in cooperation and competition. Lewin postulated that a tension for which there is a cognized goal leads not only to a tendency to actual locomotion toward the goal but also to thought about this type of activity: the force toward the goal exists not only on the "reality" level of doing but also on the "irreality" level of thinking. From the foregoing assumptions, it follows that the tendency to resume or recall interrupted activities should be greater than the tendency to resume or recall completed ones. Zeigarnik (1927) and many others, including Marrow (1938a, 1938b), conducted experiments in which subjects were given a series of tasks to perform and then prevented from completing half of them. Later, the subjects were asked to recall what tasks they had performed. The results of these experiments indicate that, as Lewin's tension system theory would predict, the subjects recall more of the interrupted than the completed tasks except when task completion is viewed as a personal success and lack of completion is viewed as a personal failure.

Ovsiankina (1928) studied the resumption of task activity and, as predicted, found that interrupted tasks were almost always resumed when the subjects were left free to do as they wished. Lissner (1933), Mahler (1933), and many others have investigated the conditions under which one activity can substitute for and, hence, release the tension connected with another, interrupted activity. The substitute value is measured by the amount of decrease in resumption or recall of the interrupted original activity after a substitute activity has been completed. Elsewhere (Deutsch, 1968) I have summarized the results of this important line of research. Here, I want to point up the significant new directions initiated by Helen Block Lewis and her associate in two pioneering papers (Lewis, 1944; Lewis and Franklin, 1944).

Lewis, drawing upon Lewinian concepts, developed ideas which started to give fundamental insights into the nature of the psychological processes involved in cooperation and competition. She wrote (Lewis, 1944, pp. 115–116):

> Satisfaction in work should be obtainable from the cooperating person's activities as well as from one's own. Since the objective situation is focal, rather than the ego, the actual agent in dealing with the objective world need not necessarily be one's self. What the other person does may be as important, as satisfying as one's own activities.

In a series of experiments, Lewis and Lewis and Franklin essentially used Zeigarnik's experimental procedure of interrupting the subjects on half their assigned tasks and allowing them to complete the other half. Their research demonstrated that cooperative work which is interrupted and not completed can lead to a persisting force to recall which is not much different from the pressure to recall induced by interrupted individual work. In other words, in cooperative relations, a co-worker's activity can substitute for similarly intended activities of one's own.

My own initial theorizing on cooperation-competition (Deutsch, 1949a) was influenced by the Lewinian thinking and research on tension systems which culminated in Helen Block Lewis's work. But even more, it was indebted to the ideas which were "in the air" at the M.I.T. Research Center for Group Dynamics. Ways of characterizing and explaining group processes and group functioning, employing the language of Lewinian theorizing, were under constant discussion among the students and faculty at the M.I.T. Center for Group Dynamics. Thus, it was quite natural that when I settled on cooperation-competition as the topic of my doctoral dissertation, I should employ the Lewinian dynamic emphasis on goals and how they are interrelated as my key theoretical wedge into this topic. Even more importantly, the preoccupation with understanding group processes at the Center pressed me to formulate my ideas about cooperation and competition so that they would be relevant to the psychological and interpersonal processes occurring within and between groups. This pressure forced my theory and research (Deutsch, 1949a, 1949b) to go considerably beyond the prior social psychological work on cooperation-competition. My theorizing and research were concerned not only with the individual and group outcomes of cooperation and competition but also with the social psychological processes which would give rise to these outcomes.

My theorizing and research have been published (Deutsch, 1949a, 1949b, 1958, 1962, 1973, 1979) and widely referred to, so there is little need here for more than a brief summary. To oversimplify it somewhat, my theory has two basic ideas; one relates to the type of interdependence among goals of the people involved in a given situation and the other to the types of actions by the people involved. I identify two basic types of goal interdependence: *promotive interdependence,* in which the goals are positively linked in such a way that the amount of his goal a person obtains or the probability of obtaining his goal is positively correlated with the amount of their goals that others obtain or the probability of obtaining their goals; and *contrient interdependence,* in which the goals are negatively linked in such a way that the amount or probability of one's own goal attainment is negatively correlated with the amount or probability of the others' goal attainments. I also characterize two basic types of actions by an individual: *effective actions,* which improve the actor's chances of obtaining his goal, and *bungling actions,* which worsen the actor's chances of obtaining his goal. (For purposes of simplicity, I use dichotomies for my basic concepts; the dichotomous types of interdependence and the dichotomous types of actions are, I assume, polar ends of continua.) I then combine types of interdependence and types of actions to posit how they jointly will affect three basic social psychological processes: "substitutability," "cathexis," and "inducibility." Thus, my theory predicts that when you're in a promotively interdependent relationship with someone who bungles, his bungling will not be a substitute for effective actions you had intended, and the bungling will be cathected negatively. In fact, when your net-playing tennis partner in a doubles game allows an easy shot to get past him, you will have to extend yourself to avoid being harmed by the error. On the other hand, if your relationship is one of contrient interdependence and the other bungles (as when your tennis opponent double-faults), your opponent's bungle will substitute for an effective action on your part and will be cathected positively or valued. The reverse is true for effective actions: An opponent's effective actions are not substitutable for yours and are negatively cathected or valued; a teammate's effective actions are substitutable and are positively valued. A teammate can induce you to help him make an effective action, but you are likely to try to prevent or obstruct a bungling action by your teammate. In contrast, you will be willing to help an opponent bungle, but your opponent is not likely to induce you to help him make an effective action (which, in effect, would harm your chances of obtaining your goal).

My theory of cooperation and competition, then, goes on to make further predictions about different aspects of intrapersonal, interpersonal, in-

tragroup, and intergroup processes from the predictions about substitutability, cathexis, and inducibility. Assuming that the individual actions in a
group are more frequently effective than bungling, among the predictions
which follow from the theory are that cooperative groups (i.e., those more
promotively interdependent) as compared with competitive groups will
show the following characteristics:

1. More effective intermember communication. More ideas will be ver-
   balized, and members will be more attentive to one another, more accepting of the ideas of other members, and more influenced by them.
   They will have fewer difficulties in communicating with or understanding others.
2. More friendliness, more helpfulness, and less obstructiveness will be expressed in the discussions. Members will also be more satisfied with the
   group and its solutions and more favorably impressed by the contributions of the other group members. In addition, members of the cooperative groups will rate themselves higher in desire to win the respect of
   their colleagues and in obligation to the other members.
3. More coordination of effort, more division of labor, more orientation to
   task achievement, more orderliness in discussion, and higher productivity will be manifested in the cooperative groups (if the group task
   requires effective communication, coordination of effort, division of
   labor, or the sharing of resources).
4. More feeling of agreement and similarity in ideas and more confidence
   in one's own ideas and in the value that other members attach to those
   ideas will be obtained in the cooperative groups.

The above predictions, which are described more fully in my article
"A Theory of Cooperation and Competition" (Deutsch, 1949a), have been
supported by my own research (Deutsch, 1949b) as well as by the studies
of many other investigators (Back, 1951; Berkowitz, 1957; Gerard, 1953;
Gottheil, 1955; Grossack, 1954; Levy, 1953; Margolin, 1954; Mintz, 1951;
Mizuhara and Tamai, 1952; Raven and Eachus, 1963; Thomas, 1957;
Workie, 1967). More recently, research done in classrooms, reported by
Johnson and Johnson (1979), Slavin (1977a, b, c), and Aronson, Bridge-
man and Geffner (1978), have provided further support for the theory.

All these studies except Workie's, however, were confined to comparisons of competitive and cooperative relations among individuals. Workie
studied intergroup as well as intragroup cooperation and competition. His
research indicates that whether the units being looked at are groups or

individuals, the same basic findings are obtained. The total productivity of a system of interdependent groups is smaller when the reward structure orients the groups toward intergroup competition rather than cooperation. Not surprisingly, more intergroup goal blocking and deceptiveness occur between groups that are in competition with one another than between groups that are cooperatively interdependent. Workie's results are consistent with the earlier field investigations of intergroup cooperation and competition in a summer camp, the classic "Robbers Cave" study by Muzafer Sherif and by Blake and Mouton (Blake and Mouton 1961a, 1961b, and 1962a, 1962b; Sherif, 1966; Sherif et al., 1961). There is a marked parallel in the results of the research on both cooperation and competition within groups and between groups; the same theory appears to be applicable to the relations between individuals and the relations between groups.

Game theory and games

In 1944, Von Neumann and Morgenstern published their now-classic work, *Theory of Games and Economic Behavior*. Game theory has made a major contribution to social scientists by formulating in mathematical terms a problem which is central to the various social sciences: the problem of conflict of interest. However, it has not been either its mathematics or its normative prescriptions for minimizing losses when facing an intelligent adversary that have made game theory of considerable value to social psychologists. Rather, it has been its core emphasis that the parties in conflict have interdependent interests, that their fates are woven together. Although the mathematical and normative development of game theory has been most successful in connection with pure competitive conflict ("zero-sum" games), game theory has also recognized that cooperative as well as competitive interests may be intertwined in conflict (as in "coalition" games or "non-zero-sum" games).

The game theory recognition of the intertwining of cooperative and competitive interests in situations of conflict (or in Schelling's [1960] useful term, the "mixed motive" nature of conflict) has had a productive impact on the social psychological study of conflict, theoretically as well as methodologically. Theoretically, at least for me, it helped buttress a viewpoint that I had developed prior to my acquaintance with game theory— namely, that conflicts were typically mixtures of cooperative and competitive processes and that the course of conflict would be determined by the nature of the mixture. This emphasis on the cooperative elements involved in conflict ran counter to the then dominant view of conflict as a competitive struggle—an orientation that was prevalent in the social as well as the biological sciences. Methodologically, game theory had an impact on an even larger group of psychologists. The mathematical formulations of game theory had the indirect but extremely valuable consequence of laying bare some fascinating paradoxical situations which were presented in such a way that they were highly suggestive of experimental work.

Thus, when Howard Raiffa acquainted me with the Prisoners Dilemma game early in the 1950s, I immediately realized that it would be an enormously useful tool for the study of some of the interpersonal phenomena of trust and suspicion in situations of mixed-motive conflict. I had come to believe that trust and suspicion were central to the development of cooperation or competition as a result of further theoretical analysis subsequent to my dissertation work on the effects of cooperation and competition. Similarly, as other social psychologists became aware of the rich experimental possibilities in the matrices of game theory, there was a mushrooming of experimental studies of conflict employing such matrices.

Game matrices as an experimental device are popular because they facilitate a precise definition of the reward structure encountered by the subjects, and hence of the way they are dependent upon one another. Also, as Pruitt and Kimmel (1977, p. 366) indicate:

> A. They yield behavioral, as opposed to questionnaire, measures and hence appeal to the desire for objective observations shared by most experimental psychologists. B. They permit precise measurement of such elusive variables as "extent of cooperation" and "coalition composition." C. They are usually easy to employ and economical. D. Many sources of variance found in more naturalistic settings are absent to experimental games, enhancing the power of tests of significance. E. Heavy competitive or hostile behavior can be manifested without injury to people or their relationships—one might say that these games permit conflict without tears.

Partly stimulated by and partly in reaction to the research using game matrices, other research games for the study of conflict have been developed. Siegel and Fouraker (1960) developed a bilateral monopoly, "buyer-seller" negotiation game; Vinacke and Arkoff (1957) invented a three-person coalition game; Deutsch and Krauss (1960) constructed a "trucking game"; Deutsch (1973) employed an "allocation" game; and many other investigators have developed variants of these games or new ones. Pruitt and Kimmel (1977) estimate that well over 1,000 studies have been published based on experimental games. Much of this research, as is true in other areas of science, was mindless—being done because a convenient experimental format was readily available. Some of it, however, has, I believe, helped to develop more systematic understanding of conflict processes and conflict resolution. Nevertheless, it seems likely that the predominant reliance on experimental games in the social psychological study of conflict has led to a neglect and underemphasis of important aspects of conflict. The short time spans involved in most experimental games, the tendency to use individuals rather than groups as the parties involved in conflict, and the structuring of the issues in conflict for the experimental subjects have led to the neglect of the study of the processes involved in the development of conflict, to inadequate characterization of the different phases of conflict, and to insufficient investigation of the processes involved in conflict group formation and mobilization. Fortunately, in recent years, experimental gaming has been supplemented by other experimental procedures and by field studies which have overcome some of the inherent limitations of experimental gaming.

Themes in contemporary social psychological research on conflict

Social psychological research on conflict during the past twenty-five years or so has largely taken the form of experimental gaming and has mostly been identified as research on bargaining and negotiation. Research in this area has been primarily addressed to three major overlapping questions: 1. *What are the conditions which give rise to a constructive or destructive process of conflict resolution?* In terms of bargaining and negotiation, the emphasis here is on determining the circumstances which enable the conflicting parties to arrive at a mutually satisfactory agreement which maximizes their joint outcomes. In a sense, this first question arises from a focus on the cooperative potential inherent in conflict. 2. *What are the circumstances, strategies, and tactics which lead one party to do better than another in a conflict situation?* The stress here is on how one can wage conflict, or bargain, so as to win or at least do better than one's adversary. This second question emerges from a focus on the competitive features of a conflict situation. 3. *What determines the nature of the agreement between conflicting parties, if they are able to reach an agreement?* Here the concern is with the cognitive and normative factors that lead people to conceive a possible agreement and to perceive it as a salient possibility for reaching a stable agreement: an agreement which each of the conflicting parties will see as "just" under the circumstances. This third question is a relatively recent one and has been addressed under the heading of research on the social psychology of equity and justice. In the next three sections, I shall attempt to describe the tentative answers which social psychological research has given the foregoing three questions.

Many other important questions and topics have been investigated. These include: coalition formation (Komorita and Moore, 1976; Sauermann, 1978; Stryker, 1972); the influence of third parties, such as mediators (Rubin, 1979); the effect of the personalities of the conflicting parties (Terhune, 1970); strategies for deescalating conflict (Lindskold, 1978); the nature of the issues in conflict (Morley and Stephenson, 1977; Rubin and Brown, 1975); and the nature of the bargaining setting (Druckman, 1973; Rubin and Brown, 1975). It will be impossible to discuss these topics in this chapter.

What are the conditions which give rise to a constructive or destructive process of conflict resolution?

In social psychology this question has been most directly addressed in the work of my students and of myself. My book *The Resolution of Conflict: Constructive and Destructive Processes* (Deutsch, 1973), summarizes much of this work. People who have worked with me in this research include, in a temporal ordering: Leonard Solomon, Robert M. Krauss, Harvey A. Hornstein, Peter Gumpert, David Johnson, Barbara Bunker, Donnah Canavan, Jeffrey Rubin, Bert Brown, Roy Lewicki, Yakov Epstein, Lois Biener, Madeline Heilman, Katherine Garner, Kenneth Kressell, Rebecca Curtis, Charles Judd, and many others. In our research, we have employed a variety of experimental games: the Prisoners Dilemma, the Acme-Bolt trucking game, the Allocation game, the Siegel-Fouraker buyer-seller game, and several intergroup situations. In addition, some exploratory field research was done on the mediation process in labor-management conflict and in divorce.

Our research started off with the assumption that if the parties involved in a conflict situation had a cooperative rather than competitive orientation toward one another, they would be more likely to engage in a constructive process of conflict resolution. In my earlier research on the effects of cooperation and competition upon group process, I had demonstrated that a cooperative process was more productive in dealing with a problem that a group faces than a competitive process. I reasoned that the same would be true in a mixed-motive situation of conflict: A conflict could be viewed as a mutual problem facing the conflicting parties. Our initial research on trust and suspicion employing the Prisoners Dilemma game strongly supported my reasoning, as did subsequent research employing other experimental formats. I believe that this is a very important result with considerable theoretical and practical significance.

At a theoretical level, it enabled me to link my prior characterization of cooperative and competitive social processes to the nature of the processes of conflict resolution which would typically give rise to constructive or destructive outcomes. That is, I had found a way to characterize the central features of constructive and destructive *processes* of conflict resolution; doing so represented a major advance beyond the characterization of *outcomes* as constructive or destructive. This was not only important in itself but it also opened up a new possibility. At both the theoretical and practical levels, the characterization of constructive and destructive processes of conflict created the very significant possibility that we would be able to develop insight into the conditions which initiated or stimulated the development of cooperative-constructive versus competitive-destructive processes of conflict. Much of the research of my students and myself has been addressed to developing this insight.

Much of our early research on the conditions affecting the course of conflict was done on an ad hoc basis. We selected independent variables to manipulate based on our intuitive sense of what would give rise to a cooperative or competitive process. We did experiments with quite a number of variables: motivational orientation, communication facilities, perceived similarity of opinions and beliefs, size of conflict, availability of threats and weapons, power differences, third party interventions, strategies and tactics of game playing by experimental stooges, the payoff structure of the game, personality characteristics, and so on. (I shall not give the specific results of our various experiments here.) The results of all of these studies fell into a pattern which I slowly began to grasp.

All of these studies seemed explainable by the assumption, which I have labeled "Deutsch's crude law of social relations," that *the characteristic processes and effects elicited by a given type of social relationship (cooperative or competitive) also tend to elicit that type of social relationship.* Thus, cooperation induces and is induced by a perceived similarity in beliefs and attitudes; a readiness to be helpful; openness in communication;

trusting and friendly attitudes; sensitivity to common interests and deem-
phasis of opposed interests; an orientation toward enhancing mutual power
rather than power differences; and so on. Similarly, competition induces
and is induced by the use of tactics of coercion, threat, or deception; attempts to enhance the power differences between oneself and the other;
poor communication; minimization of the awareness of similarities in
values and increased sensitivity to opposed interests; suspicious and hostile
attitudes; the importance, rigidity, and size of the issues in conflict; and
so on.

In other words, if one has systematic knowledge of the effects of
cooperative and competitive processes, one will have systematic knowledge
of the conditions which typically give rise to such processes and, by extension, to the conditions which affect whether a conflict will take a constructive or destructive course. My early theory of cooperation and competition
is a theory of the *effects* of cooperative and competitive processes. Hence,
from the crude law of social relations stated earlier, it follows that this
theory provides insight into the conditions which give rise to cooperative
and competitive processes.

The crude law is *crude*. It expresses surface similarities between "effects" and "causes"; the basic relationships are genotypical rather than
phenotypical. The surface effects of cooperation and competition are due
to the underlying type of interdependence ("promotive" or "contrient")
and type of action ("effective" or "bungling"), the basic social psychological processes involved in the theory ("substitutability," "cathexis," and "inducibility"), and the social medium and social context through which these
processes are expressed. Thus, how "positive cathexis" is expressed in an
effective, promotively interdependent relationship will depend upon what
is appropriate to the social medium and social context; that is, presumably
one would not seek to express it in a way which is humiliating or embarrassing or likely to be experienced negatively by one's partner. Similarly,
the effectiveness of any typical "effect" of cooperation or competition as an
initiating or inducing condition of a cooperative or competitive process is
not due to its phenotype but rather to the inferred genotype of type of
interdependence and type of action. Thus, in most social media and social
contexts, "perceived similarity in basic values" is highly suggestive of the
possibility of a promotive linkage between oneself and the other. However,
we are likely to see ourselves as contriently linked in a context which leads
each of us to recognize that similarities in values lead us to seek something
which is in scarce supply and available for only one of us. Also, it is evi-

dent that while threats are mostly perceived in a way which suggests a contrient linkage, a threat that is perceived as intended to compel you to do something that is good for you or that you feel you should do is apt to be suggestive of a promotive linkage.

Although the crude law *is* crude, it is my impression that it is reasonably accurate; phenotypes are often indicative of the underlying genotypes. Moreover, it is a synthesizing principle which integrates and summarizes a wide range of social psychological phenomena. Not only do the typical effects of a given relationship tend to induce that relationship, but also it seems that any of the typical effects of a given relationship tends to induce the other typical effects. For example, among the typical effects of a cooperative relationship are positive attitudes, perception of similarities, open communication, and an orientation toward mutual enhancement. One can integrate much of the literature on the determinants of positive and negative attitudes in terms of the other associated effects of cooperation or competition. Thus, positive attitudes result from perceptions of similarity, open communication, and so on. Similarly, for "effectiveness of communication," many of its determinants can be linked to the other typical effects of cooperation or competition. And so on.

The crude law is crude, but it can be improved. Its improvement requires a linkage with other areas in social psychology, particularly social cognition and social perception. Such a linkage would enable us to view phenotypes in their social environments in such a way as to lead us to perceive correctly the underlying genotypes. We would then be able to know under what conditions "perceived similarity" or "threat" will be experienced as having an underlying genotype different from the one that is usually associated with its phenotype.

I wish to make one further brief point about the crude law: From this law, one would expect that any relationship would normally intensify— e.g., if a relationship were more cooperative than competitive, it would move increasingly in a cooperative direction and the intensity of cooperation would increase. Undoubtedly, this intensification does occur to some extent, but it tends to be limited. What are the influences restricting such a process? It seems likely that there are both external and internal constraining factors. Externally, the involvement and pull of other simultaneous relationships and overlapping situations tend to prevent or contain what might be termed an obsessive intensification of any particular relationship. Internally, there seem to be normal pathologies that develop in most types of relationships; these appear to curb the unceasing intensification of the relationship. Elsewhere (Deutsch, 1973), I have indicated such pathologies for cooperation, and it may well be generally true.

What are the circumstances, strategies, and tactics which lead one party to do better than another in a conflict situation?

Most of the important theoretical work by social scientists in relation to this question has been done not by social psychologists but by economists, political scientists, and those concerned with collective bargaining. Some of the most notable contributions have been made by Chamberlain (1951), Schelling (1960, 1966), Stevens (1963), Walton and McKersie (1965), Kahn (1965), Jervis (1970, 1976), and Snyder and Diesing (1977). Machiavelli (1950) and Stephen Potter (1965) earlier had described useful strategies and tactics for winning conflicts: Machiavelli's emphasis was on how to use one's power most effectively so as to intimidate or overwhelm one's adversary; Potter's, on how to play upon the good will, cooperativeness, and politeness of one's opponent so as to upset him and make him lose his "cool." More recently, Alinsky (1971) has described a "jujitsu" strategy that the "have-nots" can employ against the "haves" and described various tactics of harassing and snarling the "haves" in their own red tape by pressuring them to live up to their own formally stated rules and procedures.

Social psychologists have just barely begun to tap and test the rich array of ideas about strategies and tactics for winning conflicts or for increasing one's bargaining power and effectiveness that exist in the common folklore as well as in the social and political science literature. Summaries of the relevant social psychological research on bargaining and negotiation can be found in Deutsch (1973), Druckman (1973, 1977), Tedeschi, Schlenker, and Bonoma (1973), Krivohlavy (1974), Rubin and Brown (1975), Chertkoff and Esser (1976), Morley and Stephenson (1977), and Magenau and Pruitt (1978). This research has provided some support and qualification of preexisting ideas about bargaining strategy and tactics. I shall briefly discuss research relating to "being ignorant," "being tough," "being belligerent," and "bargaining power."

"Being ignorant"

Common sense suggests that one is better off if one is informed rather than ignorant. Schelling (1960) has, however, advanced the interesting idea that in bargaining it is sometimes advantageous to be in a position where you are or appear to be ignorant of your opponent's preferences; similarly, it may give you an edge to be in a situation where you could inform your opponent of your preferences but the other could not so inform you. Research (Harnett and Cummings, 1968; Harnett, Cummings and Hughes, 1968; Cummings and Harnett, 1969) provide experimental support for Schelling's idea. In several different bargaining situations, it was demonstrated that a bargainer who did not have complete information about the bargaining schedule of his opponent began bargaining with higher initial bids, made fewer concessions, and earned higher profits than bargainers with complete information. Being ignorant of what the other wants, or appearing so, may justify to oneself and to the other a relative neglect of the other's interests in one's proposals; neglecting the other's interests when they are known is a more obvious and flagrant affront.

The bargaining tactic of "ignorance," as well as other tactics, such as "brinkmanship" and "appearing to be irrational," can be characterized in terms of the bargaining doctrine of "the last clear chance." The basic notion here is that a bargainer will gain an advantage if he can appear to commit himself irrevocably so that the last clear chance of avoiding mutual disaster rests with his opponent. A child who works himself up to the point that he will have a temper tantrum if his parents refuse to let him sit where he wants in the restaurant is employing this doctrine. So is the driver who cuts in front of someone on a highway while appearing to be deaf to the insistent blasts of the other's horn. Such tactics do not always work. They seem most apt to do so when the situation is asymmetrical (you can use the tactic but your opponent cannot) and when your opponent does not have a strong need to improve or uphold his reputation for "resolve" or "toughness."

"Being tough"

"Bargaining toughness" has been defined experimentally in terms of setting a high level of aspiration, making high demands, and offering fewer concessions or smaller concessions than one's opponent. It is a widely held view, to quote Leo Durocher, that "nice guys finish last." The results of many experiments (see Magenau and Pruitt, 1978) support a more complex conclusion, stated by Bartos (1970, p. 62): "toughness plays a dual role and has contradictory consequences. On the one hand, toughness *decreases* the likelihood of an agreement, while on the other hand, it increases the payoffs of those who survive this possibility of a failure." A relentlessly tough approach throughout bargaining appears to result in worse outcomes than a more conciliatory approach (Hamner and Baird, 1978; Harnett and Vincelette, 1978). There is, however, some evidence to suggest that initial toughness in terms of high opening demands, combined with a readiness to reciprocate concessions, may facilitiate a fuller exploration of the alternative possibilities of agreement and lead to the discovery of an agreement which maximizes payoffs to the bargainers (Kelley and Schenitzki, 1972): premature tendencies to reach an agreement without full exploration of the possibilities may be prevented by tough, initial positions (Deutsch, 1973).

"Being belligerent"

Since the initial research of Deutsch and Krauss (1960) demonstrated the deleterious effects of threat upon bargaining, there have been a deluge of bargaining experiments bearing upon the use of weapons, threats, fines, punishments, rewards, promises, and the like. Tedeschi, Schlenker, and Bonoma (1973, p. 141) have summarized the results of this research as follows: "Threats seldom improve and almost always decrease a bargainer's outcomes if his adversary is similarly armed and the values are important to both parties. Yet when threats are available, bargainers are tempted to use them." Research (see Deutsch, 1973) also demonstrates that threats have considerable reputational costs: a "threatener" as compared to a "promiser" is viewed much more negatively and is much less likely to get compliance.

Although belligerent, coercive tactics usually impair negotiation, it is evident that one is apt to yield to an adversary when there is a gun pressed against one's head. Coercion can be successful, especially when the power of the conflicting parties is unequal. The effectiveness of a threat or promise in affecting the behavioral and attitudinal response of the person being subjected to the attempted influence, as well as the likelihood that a threat or promise will be employed, will be determined by the characteristics of the available threats and promises. Elsewhere (Deutsch, 1973) I have discussed how the following characteristics affect the use and effectiveness of threats and promises: 1. legitimacy; 2. credibility; 3. magnitude; 4. kinds of values appealed to; 5. targets of threat or promise; 6. time perspective; 7. clarity and precision of the contingencies involved; 8. style; 9. costs and benefits to user.

"Bargaining power"

Common sense would suggest that a bargainer is likely to be better off if he has more power than the adversary. The results of social psychological research indicate that the situation is more complex than it first seems. Experimentally, bargaining power is sometimes defined as the relative power of each of the bargainers to inflict harm upon one another; the relative desirability of the alternatives to bargaining that are available to each of the bargainers; the relative time pressure on each bargainer to reach an agreement; and so forth. The research evidence (Magenau and Pruitt, 1978; Rubin and Brown, 1975) indicates that when bargaining power is equal, agreement is relatively easy to reach and the outcomes to the parties are high. When bargaining power is somewhat unequal, a power struggle often ensues as the bargainer with more power tries to assert superior claims and as these are resisted by the bargainer with lesser power; the result of this struggle is that agreement is difficult to reach and the bargainers have low outcomes. When bargaining power is markedly unequal, the differences in power are more likely to be accepted as legitimate and lead to quick agreement, with the advantage going to the more powerful bargainer. However, if the differences in power are not viewed as providing a legitimatization of relatively low outcomes to the low-power bargainer, he will resist what he considers to be greed and exploitation; agreement here also will be difficult, and outcomes will be low. Differences in bargaining power may lead the bargainer with greater power to make claims which he feels are legitimate but which he cannot force the other to accept; the bargainer with lesser power may resist the claims as being exploitative and illegitimate and as a way of asserting his equal status as a person. His resistance causes the low-power bargainer to suffer relatively more than the high-power bargainer, but the high-power bargainer also suffers. In essence, the bargaining research demonstrates that having higher power than one's bargaining opponent may be less advantageous than having equal power if your fellow bargainer is apt to resist any greater claims that you might make as a result of your greater power.

From this brief and very incomplete survey of some of the experimental research bearing on the strategy and tactics of waging conflict, it is evident that social psychological research has given some support for surprising tactics ("being ignorant") and has raised some doubts about common assumptions relating to the advantages to be obtained from "toughness" as a strategy, from "coercive tactics," and from "superior bargaining power."

Although the experimental research on bargaining has produced some interesting results, social psychologists have not yet developed a systematic theory of social influence. We have not yet developed a set of descriptive categories for classifying the various strategies and tactics that are employed in competitive bargaining that goes beyond the excellent early work of Walton and McKersie (1965). Nor have we anything like miniature theories of seduction, coercion, blackmail, or bluffing, nor sufficient empirical knowledge of these "black arts" to provide a curriculum for a school for scoundrels. In part our deficiency in these respects results from our insular tendency to ignore related work in other areas of social psychology—e.g., Jones' (1964) work on ingratiation, Freedman's (1966) work on "the foot-in-the-door" technique, French and Raven's (1959) work on social power, and Moscovici's (1976) approach to social influence. In part it reflects a tendency to neglect theorizing and to favor research—a tendency which is characteristic of much of social psychology.

What determines the nature of the agreement between conflicting parties if they are able to reach an agreement?[4]

A bargain is defined in *Webster's Unabridged Dictionary* as "an agreement between parties settling what each shall give and receive in a transaction between them." The definition of "bargain" fits under common social science definitions of the term "social norm." What determines the agreement or social norm for settling the issues in conflict? Two compatible ideas have been advanced in answer to this question, one related to "perceptual prominence" and the other to "distributive justice."

Schelling (1960) has suggested that perceptually prominent alternatives serve a key function in permitting bargainers to come to an agreement. He has pointed out (1960, p. 70): "Most bargaining situations ultimately involve some range of possible outcomes within which each party would rather make a concession than fail to reach agreement at all.

4. This question suggests a consideration of the factors influencing the creativity of group problem solving: In a cooperative context, a conflict can be viewed as a common problem requiring a mutually satisfactory solution. Elsewhere (Deutsch, 1969, 1973) I have discussed some of the factors affecting the development of creative solutions to conflict. It is evident that the social psychological literature on factors influencing group productivity is directly relevant. Here, however, I do not wish to discuss the relevant research on small group processes but instead want to focus on the *normative* aspects of conflict resolution and bargaining agreements.

. . . The final outcome must be a point from which neither expects the other to retreat; yet the main ingredient of this expectation is what one thinks the other expects the first to expect, and so on. . . . These infinitely reflexive expectations must somehow converge on a single point, at which each expects the other not to expect to be expected to retreat." A perceptually prominent agreement—e.g., "a 50–50 split," "equal concessions"— provides an obvious place to converge and to stop making or expecting further concessions. Research has provided some support for Schelling's idea (see Magenau and Pruitt [1978] for a summary).

Homans (1961, 1974) has suggested that the principle of distributive justice would play a role in determining how people would decide to allocate the rewards and costs to be distributed between them. Although Homans was not primarily concerned with conflict or bargaining, it is evident that his conception of distributive justice does not exclude them. In his discussion, Homans has emphasized one particular canon or rule of distributive justice, that of "proportionality" or "equity": In a just distribution, rewards will be distributed among individuals in proportion to their contributions. "Equity theorists" such as Adams (1963, 1965, 1976) and Walster, Walster, and Berscheid (1978) have continued Homans' emphasis on the rule of proportionality and have elaborated a theory and stimulated much research to support the view that psychological resistance and emotional distress will be encountered if the rule of proportionality is violated. In recent years, other social psychologists—Lerner (1975), Leventhal (1976), Sampson (1969), and myself (Deutsch, 1974, 1975)—have stressed that proportionality is only one of many common canons of distributive justice. Amplifying a list of Rescher's (1966), the moral philosopher, I (Deutsch, 1979) have recently described eleven rules of distributive justice that are widely used in different contexts.

We know very little about what makes a given rule of justice stand out as saliently appropriate in a given situation of conflict. However, a number of us (Deutsch, 1975; Lamm and Kayser, 1978a,b; Lerner, 1975; Leventhal, 1976; Mikula and Schwinger, 1978; Sampson, 1975) have begun to articulate hypotheses about factors favoring the selection of one or another rule and to do related experiments. It seems evident that if a conflict is experienced as having been resolved unjustly, it is not likely that the conflict has been adequately resolved; similarly, a bargaining agreement that is viewed as unjust is not apt to be a stable one. "Justice" and "conflict" are intimately intertwined; the sense of injustice can give rise to conflict, and conflict can produce injustice.

Social psychological research on justice and conflict is too new to have led to any definitive results. However, let me note the direction of my thinking in this area. I have applied and elaborated my crude hypothesis of social relations (the typical consequences of a given type of social relation tends to elicit that relation) so as to be relevant to the question of what rule of justice will predominate in a group or social system. I (Deutsch, 1975) have developed rationales to explain the tendency for economically oriented groups to use the principle of equity; for solidarity-oriented groups to use the principle of equality; and for caring-oriented groups to use the principle of need. I have then characterized typical effects of economically oriented relations, solidarity-oriented relations, and caring relations and have hypothesized that these different kinds of typical effects will elicit different principles of distributive justice.

Thus, among the typical consequences of an economic orientation (Diesing, 1962) are: 1. the development of a set of values which includes maximization, a means-end schema, neutrality or impartiality with regard to means, and competition; 2. the turning of man and everything associated with him into commodities—including labor, time, land, capital, personality, social relations, ideas, art, and enjoyment; 3. the development of measurement procedures which enable the value of different amounts and types of commodities to be compared; and 4. the tendency for economic activities to expand in scope and size. The crude hypothesis advanced above would imply that an economic orientation and the principle of equity are likely to be dominant in a group or social system if its situation is characterized by impersonality, competition, maximization, an emphasis on comparability rather than uniqueness, largeness in size or scope, and so on. Specific experimental hypotheses could readily be elaborated: The more competitive the people are in a group, the more likely they are to use equity rather than equality or need as the principle of distributive justice; the more impersonal the relations of the members of a group are, the more likely they are to use equity; and so forth.

Preliminary results in my laboratory, as well as in the laboratories of other investigators, are consistent with my crude hypothesis. It seems likely that the reason "equity" has been the central principle of distributive justice to social psychologists is that there has been an unwitting acceptance of the view that the dominant orientation of American society, a competitive-economic orientation, is a universally valid orientation. This is too parochial a perspective. Equity is only one of many principles of distributive justice. It is evident that questions of justice may arise in noneconomic social relations and may be decided in terms that are unrelated to input-output ratios.

Evaluation of progress in the social psychological study of conflict

I now return to the question posed at the beginning of this chapter: What progress, if any, has occurred during the past fifty years or so in the social psychological study of conflict? I have no yardstick by which to evaluate whatever progress has been made. It would be difficult to assess whether progress has been more or less rapid in this area than in other areas of social psychology or to assess whether the social resources (the personnel, funds, space, equipment, etc.) expended in support of this area of research would have been better spent elsewhere. I am a biased observer but, even taking my bias into account, I am strongly inclined to believe that significant scientific progress has been made and that important contributions to society are being derived from the scientific study of conflict. Let me briefly characterize the nature of the progress in the methodological, conceptual, empirical, and technological domains.

Methodological

As in every area of social psychological research, there have been major methodological advances during the past fifty years in the study of cooperation-competition, conflict, bargaining, and negotiation. New and better techniques for studying these phenomena in the laboratory and also in the field have emerged. The development of experimental gaming and simulations by social psychologists has helped to provide many of the other social sciences with research tools not previously available to them. Experimental economics and experimental political science owe much of their impetus to the research tools developed by social psychologists studying conflict and bargaining. These fields are now, in turn, refining social psychological methodologies and advancing them in a way which should be of value to social psychologists.

Conceptual

In the course of this chapter, I have outlined some of the conceptual developments that have taken place in my work on cooperation and competition; on understanding the nature and determinants of constructive and destructive processes of conflict resolution; and on understanding some of the determinants and consequences of different systems of distributive justice. This represents significant theoretical progress and a more systematic integration of our knowledge of the social psychological aspects of conflict and distributive justice. I believe I have found a simple but deep answer to the question which my work has addressed over the years ("What determines whether a conflict will take a constructive or destructive course?"), an answer which proliferates into rich detail even though its basic idea is quite simple.

Conceptual progress on questions related to bargaining strategy and tactics in competitive contexts has not yet been marked. However, economists, political scientists, and sociologists appear to be developing conceptual models of conflict at the macro and micro levels which should be of great intellectual interest to social psychologists. Many of their models are employing social psychological variables such as "level of aspiration," "relative deprivation," "level of information," and "attraction" (Sauermann, 1978a). Although I have not systematically reviewed recent social psychological work on coalition formation, my impression is that there has been significant conceptual progress in this area in recent years (see Sauermann, 1978b).

Empirical

We know a great deal more, with considerable more certainty, about the empirical regularities associated with conflict. Thus, we know how such psychological processes as "autistic hostility," "self-fulfilling prophecies," "unwitting commitments," and "biased perceptions" operate to produce an escalation of conflict (Deutsch, 1973). We know the social psychological correlates of intensifying conflict and of deescalating conflict. Thus, as conflict escalates there is an increased reliance upon a strategy of power and upon the tactics of threat, coercion, and deception. Also, there is increased pressure for uniformity of opinion and for leadership and control to be taken over by those elements organized for waging conflict. Deescalation of conflict is characterized by graduated reciprocation in tension reduction (Osgood, 1959, 1962, 1966); tactics of conciliation; accentuation of similarities; and enhancement of mutual understanding and goodwill. We are increasingly aware of the social psychological regularities associated with benign and malevolent conflict. We are reasonably sure of the typical effects of certain forms of bargaining strategies and tactics and can reliably conclude that many commonsense beliefs about bargaining are much too simple part-truths.

Technological

There have been many significant social consequences of the scientific study of conflict; not all of these can be attributed to the work of social psychologists. Social psychologists have been important contributors to some changes in thinking about conflict at the national level—as exemplified in Kennedy's American University speech and in the Kerner Commission reports. Also, in recent years, many of the ideas generated in the social psychological study of conflict have been employed in training administrators and negotiators, in schools, labor unions, industry, government, and community organizations how to deal with conflict more effectively. "Conflict," "negotiation skills," and "mediation skills" workshops are now common features of training for work in organizations in the United States, Europe, and Japan. Osgood's (1959, 1962, 1966) strategy for deescalating conflict—"graduated and reciprocated initiatives in tension reduction" (GRIT)—has received considerable experimental support (Lindskold, 1978), has been widely discussed in international and national meetings, and appears to have been the basis for the "Kennedy experiment" (Etzioni, 1967) to end the cold war.

Let me conclude by stating that although there has been significant progress in the study of conflict, the progress does not yet begin to match the social need for understanding conflict. We live in a period of history when the pervasiveness and intensity of competitive conflict over natural resources are likely to increase markedly. We also live in a period when hydrogen bombs and other weapons of mass destruction can destroy civilized life. The social need for better ways of managing conflict is urgent. In relation to this need, it is my view that too few social psychologists are working on the scientific issues which are likely to provide the knowledge that will lead to more constructive conflict resolution of the many intensive conflicts which await us all.

4

The Causes of Behavior:
Their Perception and Regulation

HAROLD H. KELLEY

The person exists and acts within a complex context of causes—a tangled web of opportunities, instigations, goals, dangers, obstacles, and so on. This context is determined by both the objective environment and personal properties. The context, in turn, determines the person's behavior, beliefs, and feelings. This chapter reviews some of what we presently know about these matters. Particular attention is given to the person's understanding of the causal context and the possibilities that this understanding provides for the person to play a deliberate role in structuring the context. We will see that there is a sound psychological basis for treating persons as responsible, to some degree, for their views of their causal worlds and, therefore, for their actions and feelings.

Many psychologists have written about the causal context of behavior. One thinks, for example, of Tolman's analysis of the determinants of behavior at a choice point (1938) and his general conception of learning as the acquisition of hypotheses about what behaviors have what consequences. In their paper "The Organism and the Causal Texture of the Environment," Tolman and Brunswik (1935) described how the success of an organism depends on its ability correctly to determine how proximal events are coupled causally with distant means and goals. Perhaps no psychologist of this century has written more perceptively about the causal context than Kurt Lewin (1935, 1946). From his writings and motion pic-

The preparation of this paper was supported by a grant from the National Science Foundation, BNS 76-20490.

tures, one suspects that as he watched a child at the seashore vacillating about retrieving a toy swan from the waves or a youngster being induced to eat a spoonful of disliked spinach, Lewin virtually saw the invisible configurations of causal forces that he later used to conceptualize such situations. Though rarely drawn today, the life space, with its paths, goals, barriers, force fields, and social power fields summarizes many important facts about the person's causal context and its effect on behavior.

This chapter summarizes some of what we have learned about the causal context in the several decades since Lewin and others wrote about it. Inasmuch as all psychological knowledge pertains to this context, this summary will necessarily be selective, representing those facts with which the author is most familiar. The picture will be painted in broad strokes, with omission of many qualifying details. It is hoped that the reader will find the overall portrait to be recognizable and accurate, and will forgive a degree of imprecision in the brush work.

The general line of thought to be developed can be outlined by reference to a simple example. Consider a situation in which a colleague makes a critical comment to me about an article I have recently published. I then reply to his comment. The causal context of my reply comprises a vast array of features, such as the nature of the colleague's comment, the antecedent emotional state, circumstances, intentions, etc.; my own state and circumstances at the time and their antecedents, such as other recent provocations, arousal from a toothache, etc.; what I hear and understand him to say; and my repertoire of possible reactions, with their various habit strengths, anticipated consequences, etc. This list is intended to illustrate that the term "cause" is being used liberally, to refer to any event or factor, internal or external, that directly or indirectly affects the focal behavior.

In what follows, we will see that the effective causes of my reply, the subset that determines my reply, depends on such general factors as intellectual ability, motivation, and available information. Depending upon these, my reply may be governed by a limited, simple subset of the total context or by a broad, complex subset. In the course of this incident, I will perceive, accurately or inaccurately, various causes. Some of these perceptions will be in my awareness and subject to verbalization and report. For example, I may be aware of the causes for my colleague's comment and some of the reasons why I feel the way I do about it. As we will see, these perceptions of causes may also be simple or complex, depending on the general factors of intellectual ability, motivation, information, and so on.

We will then examine evidence that my perception of the causes is likely to have some effect upon my behavior. For example, my understanding of the reasons for my colleague's comment is likely to be among the determinants of what I say or do in response. The fact that causal perceptions play a causal role in behavior raises the possibility that through management of these perceptions, behavior itself can be managed. We will review some of the evidence that reveals the operation of such management and examine the details of the management process. This sets the stage for examining data showing that common people have a considerable degree of explicit understanding of the facts outlined above. This raises the possibility that people can and do exercise a degree of deliberate self-regulation over their behavior, and has implications for their being regarded, by themselves and others, as responsible beings.

The causes of behavior

For a small child, the causes of behavior tend to be limited to a small number of events, conditions, and other factors that are close, immediate, frequent, and similar to prior events, conditions, and so on. The same tends to be true for an adult who is undermotivated (unconcerned, lazy); overmotivated (anxious, aroused; cf. Easterbrook, 1959); acting out of habit in a familiar situation (Langer, 1978); or dealing with an information-sparse environment. In contrast, for an adult who is optimally motivated, is well informed, and has time to think, the causes of behavior tend to be more inclusive and complex. As a preliminary to our considerations, it is necessary here briefly to amplify this difference. The relevant facts are quite familiar to us as psychologists, but their present review serves two purposes: 1. It makes explicit some of the things that common people can and should learn about the causes of their own and others' behavior. Some understanding of these facts is important if people are to gain control over their own behavior out of awareness of its causes. 2. It reveals what proves to be some of the major causes of the perception of causation. This will be made explicit in the subsequent section.

The causes of the child's behavior

Spatial proximity. Lewin (1946) postulated that the strength of the force a goal object exerts upon a person decreases as the person's distance from the goal increases. He summarized some evidence in support of this hypothesis, and it has been well confirmed in subsequent research (e.g.,

Losco and Epstein, 1977). The closer a goal, either positive or negative in valence, the greater its effect on such things as speed, force, and persistence of locomotion. Inasmuch as the effect is obtained for animals and children, we may assume that it reflects a basic way in which the causal world operates. Lewin also suggested that the same is true of the power field of one person over another. The ability of one to influence the other decreases with distance. Wiehe's research (described in Lewin, 1935) also indicated that the power field is generally stronger and extends farther in front of the "power" person, in the direction of that person's line of vision, than behind. Subsequent research on personal space (e.g., Sommer, 1969) shows that moving very close to another person, invading his space, has strong effects on inducing such reactions as flight, nervousness, or freezing. However, there are enormous variations in what constitutes an "invasion" of space, depending on such things as gender, nature of the relationship, and cultural background. The subsequent research also provides various indications of the special "power" that persons exert in the area of their visual fields.

Temporal precedence and contiguity. The learning of behavior is strongly governed by temporal relations between events. In classical conditioning, the conditioned stimulus must precede the unconditioned stimulus, and the latter must follow after only a short delay. At this simple level of functioning, the organism learns to use as signals (for engaging in appropriate preparatory behavior) primarily those stimuli that are closely antecedent to the forthcoming significant events. Instrumental learning is also promoted by temporal contiguity between a response (necessarily prior) and the subsequent effect. Reward delivered after delay is less effective in bolstering the response than immediate reward, and delayed punishment is less effective in suppressing a response than immediate punishment. The steepness of the delay curve may vary (e.g., Garcia, Ervin, and Koelling, 1966), but in general, instrumental behavior is ruled by its consequences to the degree that they follow the behavior closely. Lewin (1946) noted that one consequence of the temporal contiguity effect is that the tension associated with waiting for a desirable outcome tends to mount as the time of attaining it approaches. Another consequence is that behavior may be more strongly controlled by a small imminent incentive than by a large delayed one (Ainslie, 1975).

Frequency and consistency. Other things being equal, behavior is controlled by present events according to the frequency and consistency of their causes and/or effects in the past. In the simple learning experiment, the unconditioned stimulus regularly follows the conditioned stimulus or a particular action regularly has a certain consequence. With increasing frequency of experience, the person's behavior becomes increasingly under the control of the situation.

Similarity. A basic tendency is to act as if similar events have similar implications for behavior and similar behaviors have similar consequences. This is manifested in the stimulus generalization that occurs in both classical conditioning and instrumental learning. Events similar to the stimulus used in earlier conditioning subsequently elicit the unconditioned response. The response found earlier to be rewarding under certain stimulus conditions will be repeated later under different but similar ones. In the instrumental situation, if the action that was effective at an earlier time is no longer possible, a different but similar action will now be taken.

Simplicity and assimilativeness. The preceding properties of the child's causal context are not independent or mutually exclusive. Spatial effects are often entangled with temporal ones (things at a distance are also often removed from the person's present commerce), and stimulus generalization may underlie both the spatial and temporal gradients associated with goals. Jointly, the various properties result in the simplicity and assimilativeness of the child's causal construction. Given a focus on the frequent and the similar, the causes reflect only the major differentiations that occur in the external world. Generalization gradients are broad, with the result that many different events are treated as equivalent in their causal significance. The corollary to treating only frequent and consistent events as important is that they provide the structure within which rare and inconsistent ones are assimilated. Evidence of such assimilation is found in the consistency young children show in the evaluative content of their descriptions of liked and disliked acquaintances. They tend to give mainly favorable items for the former and unfavorable items for the latter, a tendency that decreases with age.

The causes of adult behavior

The preceding summarizes the basic way young children respond to their causal worlds. However, with growth and intellectual development, their behavior may come under the control of a broader range of causes. As

Lewin (1946) described the development of the life space, there is an increase in its scope, including the breadth of the present and the extension of time perspective into both the past and the future, and an increasing differentiation accompanied by an increasing organization among the parts. This suggests that under the optimal conditions mentioned earlier (motivation, information, time), the causes operating to determine the adult's behavior are quite extensive, highly differentiated, and complexly interconnected. The relevant evidence comes mainly from studies of development but also from observations of adult behavior occurring under nonoptimal versus optimal conditions.

Social and spatial perspective. One consequence of development is that the person becomes aware of the distal consequences for other people of his own behavior and begins to act out of consideration of these consequences. This provides the basis for the comparison of one's own outcomes (success, rewards, costs) with those of others (Ruble, Feldman, and Boggiano, 1976), and this comparison underlies both achieving-competitive motivation (McClintock, Moskowitz, and McClintock, 1977; Veroff, 1969) and concerns about the fair allocation of rewards (Nelson and Dweck, 1977). Also, of course, awareness of the distal consequences of one's own behavior provides a basis for the development of cooperation and altruism. Hoffman (1979) observes that independent moral behavior is fostered by the parents' teaching the child about the harmful consequences for others of its behavior. A common feature of adult life is that people take cognizance of other persons' outcomes and respond to them in both prosocial and egoistical ways (Kelley, 1979; McClintock, 1972).

Characteristic of much adult behavior is its conformity to social norms in the absence of social surveillance. Recalling Wiehe's description of the spatial configuration of the social power field, we may say that the adult often acts under the influence of social agents even when at great distances from them or when behind their backs. In some cases, merely a minimal reminder, which makes salient the distant power field, serves to arouse conforming behavior (Kelley, 1955).

Time perspective. As noted above, Lewin (1946) suggested that one consequence of development is an increasing time perspective, present behavior becoming affected by more distant events in both the future and the past. Consistent with this idea is Mischel's (1974) evidence that with increasing age, children become increasingly able to resist the temptations of immediate rewards in the interest of later obtaining greater ones. Mischel also reports that the ability to delay gratification in this manner is related positively with intelligence, achievement orientation, and social responsibility. Here, as noted above, the latter two are viewed as aspects of social perspective.

Change and chance. The person is able to break with what has been frequent and consistent in the past by means of principles associated with the concepts of change and chance. An example is the Principle of Exhaustible Supply. If one has repeatedly drawn on a given supply of rewards, it is desirable to shift to a new one. More generally, an action previously rewarded will not be repeated if the person has reason to believe the causal system has changed (Estes, 1972). Breaks with the past are difficult if the past has not been very consistent. Thus, behavior that has been consistently rewarded is quickly given up when reward is no longer forthcoming, whereas intermittently rewarded behavior tends to persist. In the first case, the person readily sees the causal properties as having changed; in the second case, the inconsistency makes it difficult to detect the change (Rest, 1976). Given proper motivation and information, adults have considerable ability to deal with inconsistency, analyzing it in a quasi-statistical manner in order to detect average differences between different sets of events (e.g., Irwin, Smith, and Mayfield, 1956). Yet, even adults seem to have their limitations in dealing with inconsistency in events. There seems to be a bias toward assuming that the world is characterized by order and predictability. This is suggested by the strong tendency of subjects in probability learning experiments to match their choice rates to the reinforcement rates, a matching that would result from their doggedly pursuing fruitless hypotheses about the patterning of successive events. This bias may also underlie the success of Langer's procedures (1975) in inducing people to treat chance tasks as if they involved a skill component.

Differentiation and labeling. With continued experience in an environment, the stimulus generalization gradients usually become narrower, and behavior becomes more differentiated and geared to specific occurrences and circumstances. This is based on training in perceptual discrimination and on the tendency of behavior to develop toward more efficient forms. Making such discriminations is enormously affected by learning to use language. Upon learning to apply verbal labels to causes and effects, the person is able to break loose from being wholly controlled by superficial, phenotypic similarity. Generalization becomes mediated by similarity of meaning. Things differing in appearance can elicit similar behavior if they have labels with common semantic components. This is illustrated by shifts with age in the generalization of conditioned responses to words. Children usually show more generalization to words that sound like the training word, whereas adults show more generalization to words related to the training word by meaning (Miller, 1951).

Complexity and organization. With development and learning, the person understands not only that the causal world is highly differentiated but that it is interconnected in complex and systematic ways. Behavior becomes multiply contingent, as it is conditioned to patterns of cues and as instrumental acts are shaped to take account of combinations of cues and conditions. With cognizance of things that are temporally and spatially distant, behavior becomes organized both serially and in parallel lines. Long sequences of behavior are directed toward distant ends, and a number of goals are pursued simultaneously.

Implications

The foregoing are some of the facts a person may learn about the causes of behavior. For children and even, under certain conditions, for adults, behavior is controlled by a narrow range of simple considerations, being responsive to what is close, frequent, familiar, and so on. In contrast, for optimally motivated and informed adults, behavior may be controlled by broad and complex considerations, such as distant consequences, changing circumstances, and multiple contingencies. Equipped with an understanding of these facts, an adult may be able to gain some skill in managing the causes that affect his own behavior, such as by taking steps to create optimal conditions for himself. We will return to this possibility later. Presently, we must examine people's understanding of these matters, i.e., their perceptions of the causes of behavior.

The perception of the causes of behavior

We will now consider differences between children and adults (and between adults under nonoptimal conditions and those under optimal conditions) in their perception of the causes of behavior. In general, these differences closely parallel the above differences in the actual causes of their behavior. This is not surprising. The perception of causes to some extent reflects the actual causes, both because people experience the causes and are able to report them and because what they believe to be the causes determines in part what the causes actually are (see next section). Furthermore, perception of causation, requiring the enactment of certain cognitive behaviors, is affected in the same way as are other behaviors by the factors of intellectual maturity, motivation, experience, and others. That is to say, the causes of the perception of the causes of behavior are to some degree also the causes of behavior itself.

The child's perception of the causes of behavior

Spatial proximity. In research on perceived causes of behavior, there are a number of parallels to the proximity effects noted above for behavior. If what is seen as causal is what is close to an effect, an observer of another person's action, seeing the action as close to him, should attribute the behavior to that person. Heider (1944) suggested exactly this: that although persons' acts almost always operate in combination with other factors to cause changes, "the tendency exists to ascribe the changes entirely to persons" (p. 361). There are several kinds of relevant evidence. Children tend to judge a person according to the consequences of the person's actions, without taking full account of intentions or circumstances (e.g., Shaw and Sulzer, 1964; Weiner and Peter, 1973). Under sparse information conditions, adults have been found to draw some conclusion about a person's evidence of compelling situational causes for those statements (Jones, 1979).

If what is causal is what is close, then actors might be expected to attribute their own behavior to what is close to them—namely, the immediate stimulus or situation. Again, Heider (1958) proposed a similar hypothesis, that people tend to attribute their own reactions to the "object world." Evidence of this tendency comes from research showing that people often assume that their own reactions are shared by others, doubt evidence to the contrary, and attribute reactions divergent from their own to personal characteristics of the divergent persons (Ross, Greene, and House, 1977; Wells and Harvey, 1977).

The notion that the actor is close to the behavior for an observer but the situation is close for the actor is similar to an argument Jones and Nisbett (1972) presented for their hypothesis about attributional divergence between actors and observers: For the actor, the salient feature relevant to the behavior is the situation, but for the observer, the salient feature is the actor. The evidence is generally consistent with the hypothesis. The actor tends to attribute behavior to the situation, and the observer tends to attribute it to the actor. There is some evidence that the actor can be encouraged to make self-attributions by arranging with mirrors or video playback for the self to be visible to him (Arkin and Duval, 1975; Storms, 1973). These procedures might be interpreted as means of inducing the actor to see that the self is close to the behavior. In a similar vein, observers' attributions for the relative causal efficacy of two interacting persons have been manipulated by selectively focusing their attention on one person or the other. An actor viewed frontally is seen as more influential than one viewed from the rear (shades of Wiehe!), and an actor closely attended to is similarly seen (Taylor and Fiske, 1975). It is perhaps not too fanciful to assume that focusing on a particular causal agent in a complex web of causes and effects has the consequence of making that agent appear close to what is going on.

Temporal precedence and contiguity. The basic role of these factors in the perception of causality is shown clearly in Michotte's (1963) classic work on the "launching effect." Again, the situation is one of sparse information. Object A is observed to move from left to right toward a stationary object B. On reaching B, A stops and B moves off toward the right. For the observer to have the impression that A caused B's movement, A's motion must be prior to B's and the temporal delay between A's reaching B and B's subsequent movement must be small. In recent work (Kun, 1978; Mendelson and Shultz, 1976), temporal precedence and contiguity has been shown to play an important role in young children's perceptions of causality. If they have little else to go on, adults will also use this cue, as shown by Strickland, Gruder, and Kroupa (1964) in an interpersonal setting.

Frequency and consistency. The governance of behavior according to what has been frequent and consistent in the past is quite appropriate as long as the environment can be depended upon to be stable. In their perceptions of the causes of behavior, observers reveal in various ways their beliefs in such an environment, apparently assuming that both its personal and impersonal occupants are stable. Thus, observers treat the consistency of a person's answers to a problem (e.g., a judgmental task) as evidence that the answers are controlled by the problem, i.e., that they are correct (Harvey and Kelley, 1974; Nemeth, Swedlund, and Kanki, 1974). Individuals are assumed to have certain stable properties, such as abilities. Consequently, a few initial observations serve to form a judgment of these properties, and subsequent information is disregarded (Jones and Goethals, 1972). When behavior occurs that is different from what has been consistent for the person, it is not taken as a sign of change but as reflecting the particular situation surrounding the behavior.

Similarity. In the course of interacting with the causal world, the person learns that the nature of a cause often bears some resemblance to the nature of its effect. Thus, the magnitude of an unconditioned stimulus is roughly correlated with the magnitude of the unconditioned response, the weight of an object is correlated with the effort required to move it, or with the damage it does when thrown, and so on. Accordingly, there exists a tendency to identify causes and effects on the basis of similarity. Duncker (1945) described this tendency in these terms: ". . . properties of form, character, direction, material, etc., pass right before our eyes from the cause into the effect" (p. 68, italics omitted). Shultz and Ravinsky (1977) find strong evidence that children make causal inferences on the basis of similarity between cause and effect. Adults use this principle too when they have little else to go on, as in attributing skillful performance to a stranger's ability when he has earlier shown polite and agreeable behavior toward them (Regan, Straus, and Fazio, 1974). Further evidence of this tendency comes from Chapman and Chapman (1969), who find that the symptoms people expect to be indicators of various personal problems often have some resemblance to those problems.

Simplicity. With its focus upon the spatially and temporally proximal, the child does not achieve much complexity of causal understanding. Each event identified as an effect tends to be linked in one-step fashion to a single cause. The attributed causes for observed effects are simple as the child settles for a "sufficient" explanation rather than a complete one. The expected consequences of observed causes are limited in their temporal scope, as the child appreciates only the immediate effects and not the delayed ones. In the extreme case, the constricted perspective leaves events without any causal connections to other events. They are simply isolated occurrences with neither detectable antecedents nor observable consequences. Thus, young children describe their acquaintances in terms of peripheral characteristics and make little reference to the inner dispositions that lie behind behavior (Livesley and Bromley, 1973; Peevers and Secord, 1973).

The adult's perception of the causes of behavior

Social and spatial perspective. The older child and the adult know that a cause may have an effect at some distance. Shultz[1] presents evidence that by age five or six, children explain events in terms of energy transmitted over a distance and do so despite a conflicting cue of spatial contiguity. Piaget (1974) describes the development of the notion of mediate transmission. For example, the child becomes able to predict that a rolling marble that strikes the end of a row of marbles will act at a distance and set in motion the marble at the other end of the row.

Important in the adult understanding of causes is the wisdom that their effects on other people are not identical with their effects on oneself. A simple instance of this is awareness of how the world appears to other people. Flavell and his colleagues (e.g., Lempers, Flavell, and Flavell, 1977) have identified several successive stages in the development of this understanding. The child is first able to infer what another person can or cannot see, and only later is able to infer how an object appears to another person. These investigators' studies of the development of ability to show and hide an object are interesting in suggesting the early awareness of the function of the other person's eyes in relation to distance, barriers, and direction of gaze.

Very young children exhibit empathic response to another person's distress. Hoffman (1979) suggests that initially the child is not aware of who is in distress and has no inkling from its own response of the other person's inner feeling. With maturity, the distal causal connections become understood, the older child knowing that it is responding to what is happening to the other person, having a sense of what the other is feeling, and even attributing that feeling (if appropriate) to life experiences of the other person that lie beyond the present situation.

Adults are able, to some degree, voluntarily to adopt the perspective of another person, as when instructed to do so. In several studies on causal attribution, this has been found to lead observers of actors to give explanations for behavior similar to those given by actors themselves (Galper,

1. T. R. Shultz, "The Principles of Causal Inference and Their Development." Unpublished manuscript. McGill University, 1979.

1976; Gould and Sigall, 1977; Regan and Totten, 1975). Unfortunately, there are doubts that these results reflect putting oneself in the actor's position rather than merely predicting how he will react to the situation.[2] Part of our extended understanding of the causal structure of the world is how people will react to certain situations. We can undoubtedly make these predictions without having to imagine what the other person experiences or feels.

Time perspective. In their perceptions of other persons' actions, children increasingly take account of causal factors that have occurred in the past and recognize the control of behavior by the actor's orientation to future ends. Thus, they may interpret and evaluate another person's behavior in light of the provocations and social influence that preceded it (e.g., Baldwin and Baldwin, 1970) and the ends to which it is directed (e.g., Robertson and Rossiter, 1974). The adult repertoire of causal explanations is replete with concepts referring to temporally distant factors, including both history-oriented notions such as background and upbringing and future-oriented notions such as intentions and indirect consequences (Orvis, Kelley, and Butler, 1976). The imputation of such causes as intentions, attitudes, and goals requires integrating information that is often diverse in nature and distributed unevenly over time. As Heider (1958) points out in his discussion of the equifinality of means, the perceiver must be able to detect the invariant end or purpose served by a variety of superficially different actions. The adult also often perceives a present event as being the final effect in a chain of cause-effect relations. As Brickman, Ryan, and Wortman (1975) show, earlier causes in the chain may be regarded as more important than later ones.

A look at oneself from the perspective provided by time may help one to understand the self in the same way that others understand you. This is consistent with evidence from Lenauer, Sameth, and Shaver (1976) and Moore, Sherrod, Liu, and Underwood (1979). As noted earlier, observers tend to interpret an actor's behavior in dispositional terms (as reflecting the actor's properties), whereas actors tend to interpret their own behavior in situational terms. Both of the above sets of investigators found that actors' explanations for their past behavior are less situational and more dispositional than their explanations for present behavior. As we gain tem-

2. V. Melburg and P. Rosenfeld, "Empathy, Role Playing, and Attributions of Outcomes." Paper presented at Annual Convention of the American Psychological Association, September 1979, New York.

poral distance from certain situations, our own causal role in our actions seems to become more apparent.

Chance. The major investigation of the development of the concept of chance is that of Piaget and Inhelder (1975). Their general conclusion is that the understanding of chance develops as a differentiation between chance and nonchance domains. Younger children fail to make this distinction and are little surprised by either regularity or randomness. The older child clearly identifies random versus nonrandom occurrences (as in the stopping of a wheel of fortune) but knows only that the former are characterized by uncertainty. At a still later stage, the child understands how to interpret random events by means of the Law of Large Numbers. Multiple observations or their symbolic equivalents are used to aid in characterizing regularities in the randomness, e.g., relative proportions of various events. Thus, where the original differentiation of the domain of random events leaves it as merely something about which one can only guess, the final understanding establishes "probability" in place of total uncertainty.

We may note in passing that luck or chance are not as common in people's spontaneous explanations for events as one might suppose (Elig and Frieze, 1979). There is also evidence of a tendency to see the past as more determined than it probably was (Fischoff, 1975).

Differentiation and labeling. As its causal understanding develops, the child's earlier global conceptions become differentiated into more specific ones. Thus, psychological causality is distinguished from physical causality (Berzonsky, 1973). The broad notion of competence becomes differentiated into the concepts of ability and effort. Heckhausen[3] observes that the idea of effort seems to develop first, probably because the child can easily make discriminations between the presence and absence of effort, both in its own direct experience and in observing others. The concept of ability requires distinguishing stable individual differences in the midst of performance varability due to shifting effort, task difficulty, and other factors.

Important for the person's conceptual repertoire is the fact that words and other symbols are used to portray causes and causal processes that are

3. H. Heckhausen, "Developmental Steps in the Causal Attribution of Action Outcomes." Unpublished manuscript. Psychologisches Institut der Ruhr-Universität Bochum, German Federal Republic, 1979.

largely outside of one's own experience. The adult learns numerous theories about causal agents such as bacteria, genes, and atomic particles, and about the media by which the effects of such agents are transmitted (exotic hosts, vectors, radiation, etc.). These theories provide examples of causation at a distance; significantly, they repeatedly illustrate that a cause may bear little resemblance to its effects. The learning of this last lesson may begin in the early school years. At least, that is the implication of evidence presented by Shultz and Ravinsky (1977). They found that similarity was a potent cue for causal inference between ages six and twelve. However, the older children were readier to set similarity aside when it conflicted with the cues of covariation or temporal contiguity.

Complexity and organization. The ability to assemble information about events scattered over an extended time and space enables the person to shift from the use of simple cues of causation, such as temporal contiguity and similarity, to a reliance on more complex ones involving temporal and spatial distributions of events (see footnote 1). Organized patterns of information are used to distinguish among different possible causes for an event (McArthur, 1972). Idealized conceptions of these patterns, based on the more commonly occurring ones, serve as templates against which observed patterns are interpreted (Orvis, Cunningham, and Kelley, 1975). These idealized patterns (causal schemata) provide the basis for various inferential rules that are used in sorting out the interactive effects of multiple concurrent causes and in judging the importance of particular ones (Kelley, 1972).

Developmental studies of the attribution process clearly show the child's growth in the use of information and causal schemata. For example, as effort and ability are differentiated, they can be used jointly for prediction or for attribution. In their joint consideration, effort and ability seem first to be regarded as combining additively, and only later is it understood that they operate multiplicatively (Kun, Parsons, and Ruble, 1974). With a development in the use of information about the outcomes of various different people, the youngster also differentiates between ability and task difficulty as causes bearing on success (see footnote 3). Even preschoolers show some ability to take account of task difficulty, indicated by other children's success, in explaining a target child's success or failure (Shultz and Butkowsky, 1977). Similarly, Karniol and Ross (1976) show that many though not all kindergartners can take account of the presence or absence of extrinsic incentives for behavior in order to infer whether another child is really interested in what it is doing.

Adults, of course, can carry out these predictive and attributional operations with ease. They discount the role of a particular cause if other causes are known to have contributed to the effect, and they augment their judgment of the potency of a cause if its effect occurs in the face of other, counteractive causes. Research to date has barely scratched the surface of the adult's understanding (in his more thoughtful moments) of the causal web. This understanding certainly includes not only notions relating to multiple causes for a given effect, as above, but also notions relating to multiple effects of a given cause (Jones and Davis, 1965). Causes that serve to provide the energy for change are distinguished from those that merely trigger the release of energies previously latent within the changed entity (Michotte, 1963). Effects that serve to mediate other effects are distinguished from effects that are mere epiphenomena (e.g., symptoms). Taken for granted are circular causal processes in which early, seemingly insignificant causes set in motion sequences that have effects of snowballing magnitude.

Implications

Just as the behavior of the child and, often, that of the adult is subject to proximal and simple causation, their perceptions of cause are often governed by cues of proximity and similarity, and the perceived causes are, therefore, simple events or conditions that are close or similar to observed effects. On the other hand, just as adult behavior is sometimes based on broad and complex considerations, adult causal explanations are sometimes based on extensive and complex sets of information, and events are understood as being controlled by causes that bear little resemblance to them and are distant and complex. To some degree, the broader basis of the control of adult behavior reflects this broader construction of the causal world (Hoffman, 1979; Kurdek, 1978). Thus, to encourage "adult" behavior, it is important to promote a broad understanding of the causal context. An important point here is that the adult's understanding of causes is subject to great variation, depending upon fluctuations in motivation, information, and so on. Insofar as the perception of causes enters into the determination of behavior, these variations in the conditions governing perception introduce concomitant variations in the quality of the behavior itself.

The effects on behavior of perceived causes

The preceding sections, showing a developmental parallel between the causes of behavior and the perception of causes, suggests indirectly that causal perception affects how the person feels and acts. Here we consider more direct evidence on this point. This evidence has recently been reviewed elsewhere (Kelley and Michela, 1980), so the present summary will be brief and little documented. There is considerable research indicating what everyone knows: that another person's intentional behavior, whether harmful or beneficial, is reacted to more extremely, either aggressively or benevolently, than a similar behavior that is perceived to be caused by external circumstances. Similarly, persuasive communications perceived to be delivered by a person in performing a job (e.g., as a radio announcer) have less influence on an audience than communications the audience attributes to the person's genuine opinions or expertise. People undoubtedly enjoy more the activities they do out of intrinsic interest than those they do in order to obtain other ends. In part, these perceptions of the reasons for an activity are subject to external management, as shown in recent research on intrinsic versus extrinsic motivation (Lepper and Greene, 1978).

A great deal of research shows that the effect of a person's physiological arousal—its effect on evaluations, behaviors, and subjective feelings—depends on the person's perception of its source. Stemming from Schachter's (1964) theory of emotion, this work indicates that arousal caused by an unperceived cause will heighten the reactions to plausible perceived instigations. It also appears that people are rather easily misled about their states of arousal. This has the consequence that through provision of false information about arousal in association with various arousal-relevant causes, the evaluative reactions to these causes can be changed or at least put in question.

The effects of causal perceptions have been most fully explored in relation to success and failure in academic and athletic performance. Weiner (1979) finds that the perceived causes for an outcome determine feelings of pride or shame and the degree of persistence after failure. Similar effects are found in realms of social success and failure where, for example, perceiving one's loneliness as caused by one's inadequate social skills results in few efforts to correct the situation.

In short, attributional research has shown that the perceived causes of events "affect our feelings about past events and our expectations about future ones, our attitudes toward other persons and our reactions to their behavior, and our conceptions of ourselves and our efforts to improve our fortunes" (Kelley and Michela, 1980, p. 489). Pretty much the same conclusions are indicated by evidence from clinical psychology, where patients' reports of their causal interpretations have proven useful in understanding pathological behavior and in designing therapeutic interventions (Kendall and Hollon, 1979).

The management of the causes of behavior

We have seen that causal perceptions affect behavior. This raises the possibility that through managing those perceptions, behavior itself can be affected. Thus, a more awkward but accurate title for this section might have been "Managing behavior through modifying perceptions of its causes." We will now consider evidence pertaining to such management. These are instances in which behavior and/or affect seem to be shaped or changed by modifications in perceptions of relevant causal factors. We will examine these instances for what they suggest to be the details of the management process. Furthermore, recalling the earlier evidence about the important role that motivation, information, and other factors play in both behavior and causal perception, we will want to see if and how the management process takes account of these factors.

For this problem, as for many of those we have already considered, some of the basic thinking can be traced back to Lewin. He was deeply interested in the structuring and restructuring of the life space. He gave particular attention to the restructuring that occurs when a person takes up (*Vornahme*) a task with the intention of completing it. From his 1926 analysis of intentional action (translated in Rapaport, 1951, pp. 76–153), Lewin concluded that an intention arises only when the person foresees a future situation in which the forces will be such that they will not bring about an action the person desires. "Due to the act of intending, at some subsequent time a psychological field appears which otherwise would not have existed, or at least not in the same form. Forming an intention creates conditions which allow us to abandon ourselves to the effects of the field . . . , or permit a field to be so transformed, or so supplied with additional forces, that a controlled action becomes feasible or easier" (p. 148, italics omitted). Often concomitant to the act of "intention" is a process of decision. In a context where initially several causes act simultaneously but in opposing directions on the person, a decision creates a final situation in which a more or less unitary causal system controls the action. According to Lewin, this is brought about through reconciling the opposing causes or isolating one and suppressing the others.

Beyond the above, Lewin had little to say about exactly how these restructurings—the one to facilitate a desired behavior and the other to promote unidirectional behavior in a context of conflict—are brought about. He was more interested in the consequences of intentions and decisions than in their detailed workings. However, in later writings on group decision (e.g., 1946), he mentioned several mechanisms by which a decision could "freeze" behavior in a desired direction. One mechanism involves commitment to a group, i.e., publicly saying or doing things at the time of decision that make it costly later to depart from the promised line of action. Another mechanism consists of making an external arrangement (e.g., an automatic savings plan at a bank) that eliminates further decisions and is not subject to later whimsies.

What is important for our present purposes are the broad implications of Lewin's observations. They clearly imply that the person's causal context—the configuration of causes that affect behavior and feelings—is subject to management. The person thinks about the causes, judges their implications for behavior, and then, if necessary reconceptualizes them or says or does things that modify his subsequent perceptions of them. This management is not always carried out as explicitly or as self-consciously as this description implies but, as we will see, it is sometimes performed in this manner. Nor may we assume that life is one continuous process of such management. To the contrary, Lewin asserts that "acts of intending" are very rare in daily life.

The argument here follows very closely the above implications of Lewin's analysis. The causal context is, to a degree, managed by the person's cognitive processes—by attention, memory, and thought. It is, to be sure, partly a product of such obvious other factors as the external environment, the person's needs and abilities, and the person's cognitive development and prior experience. However, these factors permitting, the way the person structures the causal world is partially managed by the person's cognitive processes. One is tempted simply to say "by the person himself." In the next section of this chapter, we will consider the sense in which this characterization is, according to present evidence, probably justified.

Let us now consider the operation of these management processes in several common causal contexts.

Making a choice

Problems relating to the management of the causal perceptions in choice situations have preoccupied social psychologists during the past thirty years more than any other comparable topic. Festinger (1957, 1964), Brehm and Cohen (1962), Kiesler (1971), and Janis and Mann (1977) provide a small sampling of the relevant research. The basic situation is one in which a choice must be made between two or more courses of action. The time at which choice is required is specified in some way, as by external circumstances. The person must choose at or before that time and then live with the consequences. This is to be distinguished from the situation described below as "maintaining a resolve." In the latter case, the person embarks upon one or another course of action (as in the decision to diet or give up smoking), and from that time on, until the resolve is broken, the person is faced with the problem of persisting in the chosen behavior. Many of life's problems, of course, involve mixtures of choice making and resolve maintenance, as illustrated by decisions relating to careers and interpersonal relationships.

The perceptions of the causes involved in the choice situation (e.g., the perceptions of the relative consequences of two courses of action) should be managed so as to provide a basis for 1. an objectively *good* choice—a course of action with good consequences, and 2. a psychologically *comfortable choice*—a choice one can later "live with," not have disturbing second thoughts about, and so on. The perceptual management necessary to satisfy the first criterion is something with which we all have a basic familiarity. The problem is to ensure that, to as great a degree as possible, the causes are perceived as an adult might see them and not in a childlike manner. The causal analysis must be extensive: All possible courses of action must be identified and their consequences, both immediate and remote, must be weighed, and this assessment must be made in relation to a broad survey of the person's goals and values. For such extensity, a search must be made for complete information pertaining to the alternatives, and this information must be integrated without contamination by the person's preconceptions or initial preferences. These and other details of the management strategy are spelled out by Janis and Mann (1977) in their criteria for effective decision making.

The strategy of stop, look, and think will sometimes enable the person confidently to differentiate the alternatives and to make a choice that is likely to give rise to few second thoughts. However, if the alternatives are not clearly differentiated (as when they are complex and incommensurable), external constraints may require that a choice be made nevertheless; then the second criterion, its psychological comfort, becomes problematic. At that point, it becomes desirable for the person to manage the post-choice perceptions of the relevant causes in a manner such that disturbing second thoughts will be at a minimum.

The post-choice management has been theorized by Festinger (1957) to involve a special post-decision motivational state created by the chosen action being dissonant with relevant cognitions. Jones and Gerard (1967) discuss this same management process in terms of the cognitive work that the person must do in order to come to terms with the chosen act during its enactment and not be "forced to listen to the babble of competing inner voices" (p. 181). In either case, the management has the same end—namely, to enhance the perception that all the causes in the situation indicated the chosen action and contraindicated the rejected alternatives. In a sense, the person desires to believe that there were very good reasons for the choice. Research has provided much evidence about the effect of the post-decision process. The chosen action and the rejected alternatives become evaluatively more differentiated, the first becoming more favorably regarded and/or the latter less so. The differentiation is said to proceed by "thinking about, considering and reconsidering, and re-evaluating [the] dissonant cognitions until adequate reinterpretations are invented or discovered" (Festinger, 1964, p. 157). The differentiation seems also to be managed by selective attention to relevant information. From these comments, it will be seen that the post-decisional processes may generate causal perceptions similar to those characteristic of a small child, these being based on limited information and providing a simple and unconflicted account of the chosen action.

Some theorists, especially Janis and Mann (1977), have given particular attention to the motivational state of the person prior to making the decision and have indicated the risks that this state may not be optimal for an adultlike causal analysis. Along with others before them (Brown and Farber, 1951; Lewin, 1946), Janis and Mann find evidence that decisional conflicts create stress. This is especially true when there is risk of suffering serious losses no matter what action the person chooses. This conflict-generated stress interferes with working out a sophisticated analysis of the causal structure of the choice problem. The person either becomes "defensively avoidant," with lack of information search, selective attention and memory, and distorted reasoning, or "hypervigilant," with extreme cognitive constriction, reduction in memory span, and simplistic thinking. Janis and Mann describe some interventions that a "decision counselor" can take to improve the quality of the causal analysis. These are designed to reduce the stress itself and to promote better management. For example, the person is encouraged to discuss the choice with others who have different perspectives on it, is guided to new information sources, and is helped in arranging for more time before the choice deadline. Janis and Mann emphasize that to pursue these activities, the decision-stressed person must have some hope of finding a good course of action among all the objectionable ones. In other words, as is true in other areas that engage one's skills, one's confidence in one's own causal analytical abilities affects the persistence with which the necessary management activities are pursued.

Maintaining a resolve

Lewin described how the act of "intending," with its internal commitment to complete some action, affects not only the subsequent behavior but produces sensitization to and selective memory for goal-related stimuli. It now seems reasonable to view these perceptual and memory effects not merely as the consequences of an intention but as manifestations of the cognitive processes that serve to sustain the intended activity. Attention to and thought about things related to an ongoing activity support its continuation, whereas attention to and thought about competing activities threaten its disruption. Accordingly, to promote their effective work on a complex problem, impulsive children are taught to remind themselves (at first, aloud, and later, covertly) to sit still and scan the problem, to think about it and identify an approach to it, and to focus their attention on this approach and where it leads them (Kendall and Finch, 1979). In short, they are taught a strategy for engaging the causal structure of the problem so that it sustains their efforts on it. They are also taught self-statements that help them cope with experienced difficulties and enable them to reward themselves for task completion.

In a different domain, that of maintaining a resolution to lose weight (Leon, 1979), training in self-management has encouraged such cognitive activities as planning ahead as to what one will eat at special dinners (in restaurants, at Christmas), recognizing the stimulus to eating that is provided by such states as emotional arousal and boredom, developing alternative and distracting activities for these occasions, and visualizing how the self now appears unclothed in front of a mirror. Additionally, there is emphasis on management of the environment so as to reduce the number of cues for eating and to make it less convenient. To a considerable degree, this program is oriented toward heightening people's awareness of the causal network in which their eating is located, e.g., the instigations to eating, the opportunities for and obstacles to eating, and the consequences of eating as compared to alternative activities. The assumption is that this explicit and sophisticated causal analysis helps people control the causes that act upon them, enabling them, through thought, attention, and environmental arrangements, to restructure the situation so that it stably supports the desired eating patterns.

A general problem with maintaining one's resolve to pursue a course of action is the shift in preferences with time. When all goals are rather distant in the future, the truly more important ones are preferred. At a distance from both, the overweight person prefers a slender figure to a piece of pie. However, as time passes and the less important goal-object becomes immediately available, it often becomes preferred. One implication of this phenomenon is that a person will be able to maintain a resolve to gain a distant but important reward if he can maintain a psychological distance from both it and the competing lesser ones that become available meanwhile. Examples of such distancing are provided by Mischel's work (1974, 1979) on delay of gratification. A child is faced with a choice between a less attractive reward it can have anytime it wishes and a more attractive reward it can have only after a considerable wait. The child is found to be able to wait longer if it cannot see the two rewards or if they are represented by pictures rather than by the real objects. Illustrative of the important role of thought in this process, children encouraged to think about absent rewards are as little able to delay as if the rewards are present. Finally, delay is promoted by instructing the children to think about the nonconsummatory qualities of the rewards (e.g., the resemblance of marshmallows to puffy clouds or round moons) rather than about their consummatory qualities (the chewy, soft sweetness of the marshmallows). The former seems to be a way for a child to "distance" itself from the rewards.

Out of recognition that the relative effectiveness of alternative goals may shift with the passage of time, Ainslie (1975) describes some of the methods that can be used to modify the perceived causes so that transient small rewards will be bypassed in favor of larger but later ones. At the time of the initial resolve, a side bet can be made with other persons whereby something valuable will be forfeited unless the preference for the large late reward is maintained. A public commitment, noted by Lewin

(1946) as "freezing" a change in behavior, has the effect of a side bet: One loses social standing unless one carries out resolutions publicly made. Ainslie describes the side bets that can be made with oneself in order to promote self-control of impulses. These amount to self-imposed rules (Kanfer, 1979) which specify contingencies between behavior and consequences and which are enforced by self-monitoring and self-provision of reward or punishment. This is the epitome of the process described by Lewin (see earlier quotation). As a consequence of foreseeing a situation in which a desired action will not occur, the person actively creates conditions which make that action more probable. In the present terms, the individual manages the causal structure, with the aid of causal understanding, in the interest of insuring adherence to a resolution.

Coping with fear and anger

As noted earlier, attributional research shows that the effect of physiological arousal depends to a considerable degree upon the person's perception of its cause. This phenomenon provides a basis for helping people deal with fear, anger, and other states of arousal by modifying their causal attributions. As an example, Langer, Janis, and Wolfer (1975) were able to improve patients' coping with major surgery by providing training in how to reperceive the causes for the stress they were feeling. The patients were told that the stress resulted more from their own thoughts than from the external events (which could be viewed in a variety of ways) and that they could control their own thoughts in ways that would reduce their discomfort. It was then shown how they might focus on the benefits to be gained from undergoing surgery in a good hospital (improved health, the care and attention they would receive, an opportunity to relax and be free of outside pressures, etc.), and it was suggested that they think about these aspects of the situation when they began to feel upset about the unpleasant features.

In these situations, there exists the particular problem that sophisticated causal thinking is likely to be impaired by the person's high level of arousal. The procedure above is intended to get the reassuring reappraisal underway at the first sign of arousal before it mounts too high. In other cases, special additional measures may be taken to deal with the arousal separately. An example is provided by Novaco's (1979) program for preparing law enforcement officers to deal with provocations and their own resulting anger. The trainees are instructed and rehearsed in monitoring their arousal and controlling it with pauses and relaxation procedures. Additionally they are helped to develop an explicit understanding of the causes of anger, both in general and in their own experiences. This involves their recognition that anger depends on their causal interpretations of provocations, that they can make alternative interpretations (e.g., that provocations are to be expected and should not be attributed to intentions directed at them personally), and that anger often has undesirable distal consequences. The provocation situation requires not only self but also social control, so the program also involves training in verbal and problem-solving skills. For our purposes, the program is important in suggesting how own responses to a situation can be managed through developing a detailed causal understanding of it.

Reactions to success and failure

Lewin (1946) postulated that when a person has an intention to carry out a certain task, if interrupted before its completion the person will tend to continue to think about the task and will later resume it if the occasion arises. Research soon showed that this does not occur if the interruption is interpreted as a personal failure (Rosenzweig, 1943). Recent research interprets this phenomenon in terms of perceived causes. Reactions to failure depend upon the cause(s) to which the failing person attributes the event. Attribution of failure to own ability, which is a stable property of the self about which little can be done, tends to result in feelings of shame and lack of persistence on the task (Weiner, 1979). Some people tend to perceive lack of ability as the main cause for their failure when, in fact, other causes such as their own effort are important. Their persistence on the task and even their performance can be improved by inducing them to perceive the failure in a different causal context. For example, Dweck (1975) was able to show that certain children with poor reactions to failure (decreased rate of work, increased errors, tendency to withdraw) could be greatly improved by attributional retraining. This consisted simply of providing occasional failures (as part of a string of successes) that were explained by the trainer as being due to insufficient effort. This method assumes, of course, that the child's subsequent efforts prove to be effective. Bandura (1977) emphasizes this point. The effectiveness of verbal persuasion in changing the person's perception of causes is sharply limited by the person's own prior inconsistent experiences and subsequent disconfirming ones. More generally, although Bandura's self-efficacy theory emphasizes the necessity of changing performance, it is entirely consistent with the present view in its insistence that the effects of performance changes are mediated by the cognitive interpretation (here, perception of causes) made of them.

As noted above, the belief that one's failures are due to lack of ability leads to withdrawal from the relevant class of tasks. The belief is then likely to be self-maintaining because opportunities for disconfirming experiences are precluded. Various cognitive approaches to behavior change emphasize methods for dealing with this problem. For example, Hollon and Beck (1979) describe methods for training people to verbalize their causal beliefs and to subject them to unbiased prospective tests through a comparison of explicit predictions with objective outcomes.

If people understand that their causal attributions for success and failure affect their subsequent feelings, and if they know something about their own processes for perceiving causes, they have the means for controlling their feelings through managing the evidence relevant to their causal perceptions. Several recent lines of work show this management in action. Frankel and Snyder (1978) show that subjects will exert little effort on an ego-threatening task in order to avoid the perception, if they fail, that they have low ability. This occurs for problems of moderate difficulty but not for very difficult ones, presumably because the subjects realize that failure on the latter can be attributed to the tasks, so they run no risk of a negative self-attribution by trying their hardest on them. A related management strategy, described as "self-handicapping," is proposed by Jones and Berglas (1978). If a person is uncertain about the causes of past success and worried about not being able to repeat it, the introduction on later attempts of a performance-interfering cause, such as alcohol or lack of sleep, offers a solution. This creates a situation in which it is possible to excuse failure but take credit for success. Thus, the self-handicapper sets a causal context in which a depressing self-attribution is avoided and a pleasing one is possible. Berglas and Jones (1978) offer some evidence in support of their reasoning.

Summary

We have considered some of the settings in which behavior and feelings are managed by means that involve modifying perceptions of relevant causes. These means prominently include attention, thought, and reasoning. In some cases, these processes operate in a focused way (as in emphasizing the good consequences of certain actions and the bad consequences of others); in other cases, they operate with a broad scope (as in thinking about a more extensive set of causes and consequences, conceiving of alternative causal scenarios for an event, and connecting an action to additional goals and properties of the self in order to create self-commitment). The means of causal perception management also include manipulations of the environment and of other causes over which one has control (e.g., effort), these serving to change the actual causes and thereby, the perceived ones. In some of the instances reviewed above, the causal perceptions are modified spontaneously by the person (as in post-decision re-evaluation of alternatives) and in other instances, the management procedures are acquired through special training. However, in all cases the modifications take account of both 1. the antecedents of causal perceptions and 2. their effects on behavior and affect.

To apply the term "management" to these processes is to imply that they are used deliberately and self-consciously with a realization of their consequences. This is probably not the case in many instances (as in dissonance reduction), but it may be true in some cases (as in not exerting effort on a risky task in order to avoid a self-attribution of low ability). We now turn to evidence which suggests that people do have some understanding of these processes and are probably able voluntarily to use them for the purposes of self-regulation.

Metacognition and self-regulation of behavior

During the last few years, John Flavell (1979) has opened up an area of research dealing with metacognition. This concerns people's "knowledge and cognition about cognitive phenomena." As Flavell describes it, "Metacognitive knowledge consists primarily of knowledge or beliefs about what factors or variables act and interact in what ways to affect the course and outcome of cognitive enterprises" (1979, p. 907). In the present context, we are interested in the existence of knowledge about the antecedents of causal perceptions and their consequences. Flavell suggests that on the antecedents side, a person acquires knowledge of the factors that decrease the accuracy of understanding, such as one's biases, intense affect, and mental or physical illness. This is essentially knowledge about what makes the difference between a childlike and an adult understanding of the world. On the consequences side, Flavell's research shows that people learn to monitor their understanding of material and recognize when it will be adequate, as for a forthcoming test in school. In other words, a person can know that his current causal analysis may have good or bad behavioral consequences.

The general implication of Flavell's work is that a person can and does examine his current causal construction; consider antecedent variables that possibly jeopardize its quality; survey its contents and assess their coherence and plausibility; and anticipate its consequences for the attainment of his goals. If the examination raises doubts about the construction, the person's store of metacognitive knowledge about the antecedents of causal analysis provides a repertoire of cognitive strategies (e.g., rehearsing current information, acquiring new information, seeking out knowledgeable advisors) by which it can be improved.

Along much the same lines, Mischel (1979) finds that with increasing age, there is increasing awareness of effective strategies for self-control—as, for example, in the delayed gratification situation described earlier. Most preschoolers do not have effective strategies. Given the opportunity, they choose to view the real stimuli during the waiting period—which, as research shows, is detrimental to waiting for the large, delayed reward. By the third grade, most children know such strategies as 1. to avoid looking at the rewards, 2. to keep reminding themselves that "If I wait, I'll get the big one," 3. to distract themselves by thinking about other things, and 4. to think about the rewards in ways that make them less appealing. By the sixth grade, most children recognize the advantage of "cool" rather than "hot" ideation about the rewards (i.e., to focus on the abstract or nonconsummatory qualities rather than the consummatory ones). "These developmental shifts seem to reflect a growing recognition by the child of the principle that the more cognitively available and hot a temptation, the more one will want it and the more difficult it will be to resist" (1979, p. 751).

Mischel presents similar evidence about the development of understanding of how to make and carry out "plans," i.e., intentional activity. At older ages, children are aware of such strategies as "elaborate mental rehearsal, public commitment, externalizing the plan by sharing it with others, rearranging and 'marking' the environment, [and] using mnemonics" (p. 749). Significantly, Mischel observes that "the gist of natural plans" is quite congruent with behavior modification procedures, which give the person "controlling responses that are incompatible with the to-be-avoided behavior, and . . . a focus on the negative consequences of transgressions plus the positive consequences of self-control" (p. 749). Thus, youngsters apparently learn a good deal about the causes of behavior, in-cluding knowledge about how causal thinking (e.g., thoughts about actions and their consequences) enters into it.

Further evidence on metacognitions, as they relate to self-control of eating, is provided by Leon (1979). Persons report that they have restrained themselves by engaging in behaviors that distract them from eating or remove them from the places associated with eating, and by covert activities that include visualizing positive or negative self-images and subvocal self-instructions to refrain. Apparently this management of behavior through modifying causes and their perceptions is not wholly successful, because these accounts come from a sample of obese people. We must not assume that such management will always be successful or even make a noticeable difference. The metacognitive knowledge may feature less effective strat-egies rather than better ones; high arousal levels may exist too often to permit causal analysis that is consistently high in quality; and the more potent causes of particular behaviors may simply not be susceptible to cog-nitive control. Yet, the existence of metacognitive knowledge opens the door to some degree of self-regulation, and the potential extent of this regulation will be known only when the functioning of this knowledge has been fully investigated. It is at least possible that, as Mischel observes, "Once people recognize how their own ideation makes self-control either hard or easy, the option to delay or not to delay becomes truly their own: They know how to delay effectively and must merely choose whether or not they want to" (1979, p. 750).

Conclusion

Certain implications of the material reviewed above can be summarized in the form of a logical argument relating to an everyday person P who acts in some common situation S.

1. One of the determinants of P's behavior is P's perception of the causes in S. P's perception is not necessarily accurate and, to repeat, it is only *one* of the determinants of P's behavior.

2. The causal role of P's perception of causes, its effect on P's behavior, is something P can perceive. As one facet of P's perception of causes, P can understand the causal role of such perceptions.

3. P can also come to understand the factors that affect his perception

of causes. This is another product of P's ability to perceive cause and effect relationships.

The perception and understanding described in (2) and (3) above are plausible inasmuch as his causal perceptions often enter P's awareness, and P can verbalize them to himself and report them to other persons. Thus, P has opportunities, in observing both himself and others, to infer what factors underlie various perceptions and to recognize the difference those perceptions make in behavior. This understanding of the antecedents and consequences of causal perception is part of what Flavell (1979) refers to as "metacognition."

4. Provided with the understanding described above (P's metacognitions), to some degree P can control his perception of causes (through controlling some of its antecedents) and can thereby exercise some degree of regulation over the causes of his behavior.

To extrapolate beyond these "facts" just a bit (they have already been stretched rather far), several other points can be suggested:

5. It is likely that the common person has metametacognitions. That is, P not only understands that his causal construction affects his behavior and knows some ways to manage this construction, but he also understands that this insight into the management process has its potential consequences for self-regulation. In other words, on the basis of his experience (though perhaps with a bit of coaching), our everyday person, P, might have written Flavell's or Mischel's paper, or at least an essay that captures their essential points.

6. This likelihood, that P has metametacognitions (and the reader will immediately understand that the papers by Flavell and Mischel constitute metametacognitive materials), has an important consequence. Our everyday person, P, is likely to paraphrase for himself what Mischel wrote about him: "Now that I recognize that my own thoughts make self-control either hard or easy, and now that I know something about how to control my thoughts, the choice to control myself or not is truly my own."

7. Not only will P recognize the cognitively based possibilities for self-regulation, but other persons will understand that he is capable of such. In fact, during P's lifetime, other persons' recognition of P's self-regulatory potentialities will have preceded his own, and very likely will have been communicated to P. Furthermore, other persons' modeling of behaviors that manifest their own self-regulatory processes and show P effective means of managing perceived causes will have been influential in

both his understanding and his skill (Bandura, 1977; Meichenbaum and Asarnow, 1979).

8. Given the above conditions, P will be held responsible to some degree, both by others and by P himself, for his behavior and feelings. The question of how responsible P can legitimately be considered to be will probably always be subject to debate. The ambiguity here corresponds to our current and probably continuing empirical uncertainty about the efficacy of the self-regulatory processes outlined here. Despite this ambiguity, self and social evaluations of P will be rendered on the basis of the degree of self-regulation P shows. Other persons will tend to evaluate P in terms of how much his behavior, in adultlike fashion, is responsive to broad and complex considerations. However, P will not necessarily use the self-regulatory powers for prosocial purposes. P may employ these powers to narrow his causal construction in order to justify self-serving behavior, or to broaden the construction in order more effectively to compete with or exploit others, or to modify the construction for other egoistic ends.

The social psychological aspects of these phenomena have only been alluded to in the foregoing. Much careful analysis is required of such matters as the use of socially derived information in managing the causal analysis, the role of modeling and other social influence methods in self-regulation training (Bandura's analysis is an excellent beginning), and the consequences for interpersonal relations of various modes of self-regulation. It is hoped that this chapter, in its attempt to identify some relevant connections between social psychology and current thought in developmental and clinical psychology, will stimulate research on the social psychological aspects of self-regulation.

5

The Trait Construct in Lay
and Professional Psychology

RICHARD E. NISBETT

In the first third of this century, it was possible to believe that social be-havior was best understood in terms of personality traits—that is, best understood by knowing people's locations on nomothetic dimensions de-fining individual differences in general tendency to display a given type of social behavior. Thus the best way to *predict* a person's behavior in a particular situation would be to examine the primary trait which the situa-tion taps, note the person's level on the relevant trait, and make predic-tions accordingly. Similarly, the best way to *explain* behavior of a given type would be to call on a personality trait corresponding to the behavior.

This model of behavior had much to recommend it early in the cen-tury. It was extremely close, if not identical, to the commonsense lay view of behavior. The literature of every era is replete with trait terms and with plot developments dictated by the traits of the central characters. In daily life, the layperson uses a wide variety of trait terms in discussing other people and often speaks with confidence of the honesty, aggressive-ness, or dependency of other people—that is, the degree to which they possess a chronic disposition to behave in a particular way. In addition to its congruence with commonsense views, this conception was essentially identical to the formal model of abilities, which was gaining empirical

The writing of this article was supported in part by grants BNS 75-23191 and BNS 79-14094 from the National Science Foundation. I am indebted to Walter Mischel for comments on an earlier draft.

support through the early part of the century and which indeed remains largely unchallenged today. This model is nomothetic, in that it assumes that it is meaningful to assign a score to each person, relative to everyone else, on each variable. The model also assumes that the best way to predict the behavior (or rather, performance) of a given person on a given task is to determine what ability or abilities the task primarily taps, note the person's level on the relevant ability or abilities, and make predictions accordingly.

It is the thesis of this chapter that the trait conception of the determinants of social behavior, or at least this particular trait conception, is largely wrong. I will argue that, over the last forty or fifty years, empirical and theoretical work increasingly has called into question this trait conception of social behavior. I will argue specifically: (1) The empirical evidence indicates that only very weak predictability is possible using traditional trait constructs. (2) People—both laypeople and psychologists—have exaggerated the degree to which behavior can be predicted by traits because they are subject to certain perceptual and judgmental illusions first identified by Lewin and Heider and well documented by research conducted over the last twenty years. Finally, I will speculate that (3) whatever the scientific utility of the nomothetic social trait construct, its personal utility, for predictions about social behavior in everyday life, may be so low that any reliance on it by the layperson may be quite disadvantageous.

Before discussing the empirical evidence on the power of the trait construct, it will be helpful to review briefly the theoretical work over the last half-century which leads to the expectation that people might overemphasize the role of stable dispositions in producing social behavior.

The critique of naive trait psychology

Lewin believed that the psychology of his day overemphasized the role of presumed dispositions of the person in explaining behavior. Naive psychology, he believed, shared with what might be called "naive physics" a preoccupation with the nature of the object. Progress in psychology, like progress in physics, would come with the recognition that behavior is best understood in terms of the field of forces operating at the time the behavior occurs. It is instructive to consider Lewin's view of the error in ancient conceptions of the physical world, because it is so similar to what social psychologists have claimed is the fundamental error in naive conceptions of the social world.

. . . the kind and direction of the physical vectors in Aristotelian dynamics are completely determined in advance by the nature of the object concerned. In modern physics, on the contrary, *the existence of a physical vector always depends upon the mutual relations of several physical facts,* especially upon the relation of the object to its environment. (Lewin, 1935, p. 28; italics in original)

In other words, in ancient physics, the behavior of objects was understood exclusively in terms of the object itself: A stone sinks when placed in water because it has the property of "gravity"; a piece of wood floats because it has the property of "levity." In modern physics, in contrast, an understanding of the behavior of objects requires a simultaneous specification of the environmental forces, the properties of the object, and the relation between the environmental forces and the properties of the object. A stone sinks when placed in water because of the existence of a field of forces in which the most relevant are the earth's gravity, the mass and surface area of the stone, and the density of the intervening medium, namely water. There are no properties inhering in objects such as gravity or levity.

Lewin argued that a transition similar to that for conceptions of the physical world would have to take place in psychology, that a tendency to explain the behavior of people largely or exclusively in terms of enduring properties of individuals would have to give way to a recognition of the need for specifying simultaneously in concrete detail the relevant properties of the environmental forces and of the individual. And, Lewin emphasized, the relevant properties of the individual for the purposes of a given prediction might or might not be ones of historical significance. That is, they might or might not involve such enduring properties of the individual as could be called "traits," but might instead be purely transient properties induced by immediately preceding situations.

Perhaps the next fundamental contribution to the critique of naive trait psychology was made by Heider, who explicitly articulated the present thesis that the layperson errs in presuming more individual consistency in behavior from one situation to another than is warranted. Heider also proposed a basis for people's tendency to inflate the presumed contribution of enduring dispositional factors:

. . . behavior . . . has such salient properties that it tends to engulf the field rather than be confined to its proper position as a local stimulus whose interpretation requires the additional data of a surrounding field—the situation in social perception. (1958, p. 54)

In other words, the actor's behavior is so salient, relative to the situation in which it occurs, that the behavior is attributed largely to the actor himself rather than to the situational factors he confronts. This tendency has been called the "fundamental attribution error" by Ross (1977).

Heider's explanation for the fundamental attribution error is largely perceptual, and it rests on the assumption that causal attribution follows attention—that people are inclined to attribute causality to those factors which are most salient perceptually. There is by now a great deal of evidence indicating that people are indeed inclined to attribute causality to those factors that happen to enjoy the greatest perceptual salience. This evidence has been reviewed by Taylor and Fiske (1978) and by Nisbett and Ross (1980). People attribute causality more to those persons, or to those environmental factors, toward which their attention is directed. Simple manipulations involving seating arrangement or lighting can alter causal attributions dramatically by influencing which factors are perceptually salient to the observer. One of the most interesting implications of the findings on the importance of salience in causal attributions is that the tendency to attribute behavior to dispositional properties of the person should be reduced in magnitude for the actor himself, since it is not his own behavior that is likely to be most salient to him, but rather the environmental factors toward which he directs his behavior. This hypothesis was proposed by Jones and Nisbett (1971) and has been supported by much subsequent research. Work done by Jones and his colleagues (e.g., Jones and Harris, 1967) indicates that the fundamental attribution error is indeed an error. Even when it is made quite clear to subjects that actors were literally forced by circumstances to engage in some behavior, subjects are still inclined to presume that the actor has dispositions that correspond to the behavior that he has witnessed. Thus an actor who was required by a debate coach or political science instructor to write an essay favoring Castro's Cuba is presumed by subjects who read the essay to have a favorable attitude toward Castro's Cuba.

An additional logical link is still required, however, between Heider's salience hypothesis and the thesis that people overemphasize presumed *enduring dispositions* of the actor. Heider himself supplied this link:

> . . . Man is not content simply to register the observables that surround him; he needs to refer them as far as possible to the invariances of his environment. Second, the underlying causes of events, especially the motives of other persons, are the invariances of the environment that are relevant to him; they give meaning to what he experiences. . . .

As applied to the actions of another person, the depth dimension of relevant invariances is often of the following order: There is first the raw material which provides the information that change X occurs or has occurred and that O causes or has caused X (though this can already be a further level of interpretation). Then, further meaning is given to these facts when, relating them to certain dispositional properties of the person and of the environment, we conclude that O can do X, O is trying to do X, O likes to do X, etc. These conclusions become the recorded reality for us, so much that most typically they are not experienced as interpretations at all. (1958, pp. 81–82)

Thus the actor's salience prompts the observer to look to properties of the actor to explain the actor's behavior, and the search for "invariances" results in attributing the cause of the behavior to inferred dispositions of the actor. These *inferred* dispositions, as we shall now see, are both broader and more powerfully determinative of behavior than are any *true* dispositions which social scientists have been able to measure. It should be noted in passing, however, that Heider's perceptual account provides a plausible interpretation of the error of ancient physicists as well as of the error of modern laypeople and professional psychologists. The behavior of objects, like that of people, is more salient than the properties of the field in which the behavior takes place. Since attention, and thus attributions, are focused on the object, the "relevant invariances" are seen to inhere largely or exclusively in the dispositions of the object itself—that is, in properties such as gravity, levity, and so on.

Personality traits and the prediction of behavior

We may now turn to the question of the degree of predictability of social behavior that can be attained by use of traditional trait constructs. The evidence on the question has been slowly accumulating over the last fifty years. It was last reviewed by Walter Mischel (1968) and also by Donald Peterson (1968). Both authors concluded that the evidence indicated that traditional trait constructs have little predictive power. This conclusion produced angry protests from personologists, which continue to this day. We may now re-review the most telling of the evidence that prompted their conclusion, as well as some new evidence, and some very old evidence, by Newcomb (1929), that has only recently been rediscovered.

An answer to the question of the predictability of behavior by trait constructs requires data of a very simple type: Objective measures of behavior in one situation, for a given sample of subjects, are correlated with objective measures of behavior in another situation which the investigator believes to tap the same personality trait—either a personality trait of the sort common in everyday parlance or a trait construct originated by the investigator or some other professional psychologist. For reasons that should be clear (but which, in any case, will be spelled out later), data on self-reported behavioral consistency along trait lines, and data on peer reports of behavioral consistency, are not relevant to the question of objective predictability of behavior from one situation to another.

Despite the importance of objective data of the sort required for answering our question, twentieth-century psychology has produced only a very few studies meeting the above requirements, plus the additional requirements that 1. more than two behavioral measures were used, 2. at least twenty subjects were examined, enough to give at least moderate stability to correlation coefficients, and 3. the traits and behavior under examination were at least minimally socially relevant and observable in everyday life (a criterion which excludes studies of, for example, "cognitive style" variables, such as field dependence as measured by performance in tilting rooms and chairs and spatial relations tasks). These studies may be briefly described, in the order in which they were conducted.

1. A study by Hartshorne and May (1928) in which the honesty of elementary and secondary school children was examined in a wide range of classroom and nonclassroom situations (e.g., willingness to steal, willingness to lie to avoid getting another child into trouble, willingness to cheat by adding false scores to a classroom test).

2. A study by Newcomb (1929) of "problem" adolescent boys at a summer camp, in which a total of nine personality traits (e.g., talkativeness, dominance, independence) were examined. Counselors kept daily behavioral records on each boy and reported on two to five behaviors tapping each trait. It should be noted that this is the study for which the claim of "objectivity" is weakest, since the measure of behavior was the retrospective judgment of a single individual. Newcomb's measure, however, seems to be clearly less subject to distortion (by mechanisms to be discussed later) than reports which are retrospective over a time period much exceeding Newcomb's sixteen hours and which ask for judgments of much less specificity than Newcomb's typical report—e.g., "How much of the time did he talk at the table?" "Did he get into scraps with other boys?"

3. A study by Sears (1963) of preschool children's dependency on peers, teachers, and mother, measured in classroom situations and in the

laboratory by such variables as frequency of attention seeking, frequency of requests for reassurance, and frequency of touching or holding a teacher or another child.

4. A study by Bem and Allen (1974) of conscientiousness in college students, in which three behavioral measures were examined. These were average promptness in returning four course evaluation forms, reported completion of assigned course readings, and a summed measure of judged neatness of subjects' hair, clothing, and nine aspects of neatness in their living quarters. Bem and Allen also examined two behavioral measures of the trait of friendliness. These were A. a summed measure of the frequency and duration of contributions in a group discussion, plus ratings of the subject's friendliness provided by his or her peers in the discussion, and B. the latency to begin a conversation with a confederate sitting in a waiting room.

5. A study by Epstein (1979) of college students in which two "traits" which are difficult to label were examined. One of these might be called "tendency to initiate and receive indirect social contacts." It consisted of four variables—number of telephone calls made, number of calls received, number of letters written, and number of letters received. These variables were all self-reported, but the extent of inference necessary to report on such variables (and the consequent low probability of error or distortion) and the brevity of the retrospective period (a few days) suggest that there is no reason to deny them objective status. The resulting "trait" is of course a very narrow one and does not really capture a social construct that either laypeople or professional psychologists use. A second "trait" measured a number of classroom behaviors that are hard to label but clearly would be highly related in the minds of most people. These were "borrowing of a Number 2 pencil routinely made available to students who had forgotten to bring their own, number of minutes late to class, number of errors and omissions in providing information on the answer sheet, and number of erasures in filling in the spaces for recording answers. In addition, the instructor kept records throughout the semester of number of absences, number of papers turned in late, and number of papers not turned in at all" (p. 1113). Most undergraduates of the author's acquaintance would have a ready label for this package of variables—"degree to which the student has his act together." For brevity, however, let us call the trait "organization."[1]

1. It should be noted that in describing Epstein's, and Bem and Allen's results, I will focus on different aspects of the data than did the investigators themselves.

A summary of the empirical findings of these studies is simple and noncontroversial, and not essentially different from the conclusions reached by Mischel and Peterson. Predictability from one situation (or from one type of behavior) presumed by the investigator to tap a particular trait, to another, phenotypically different situation (or behavior) presumed to tap the trait, virtually never exceeds .30, rarely exceeds .20, and most typically is in the range from .10 to .15. Let us be clear about what is meant by "phenotypically different." I mean by that term that at least one plausibly important element of the stimulus situation or behavioral setting, or of the "morphology" of behavior, is different from one test or behavior occurrence to another. Thus, copying from an answer key on one classroom test and adding scores onto another classroom test I regard as phenotypically different. (Clearly, however, it is not very different with respect to the full range of possible behaviors measuring classroom cheating, not to mention cheating generally, let alone dishonesty generally.) Copying from an answer key on one type of classroom test and copying from an answer key on another type of classroom test I regard as phenotypically the same because no important element is different. The only change is that the particular type of classroom test is different across the two occasions, a stimulus difference which I arbitrarily define as too small to be a plausibly important difference. With this definition in mind, we may review the evidence.

1. In the Hartshorne and May study of honesty, the average correlation between any two even minimally phenotypically different behaviors was .23. Some of these behavioral tests were based on three to six different measures of the same behavior on different occasions. Thus the .23 value is a very liberal estimate of "average correlation of one behavior with another," since there is much more stability in some of the measures than would be expected for measures based on only one test of the behavior. The .23 value actually refers to a mixture of single behaviors and repeated measures of behavior of a given type.

2. In Newcomb's study, the average correlation between any two behaviors presumed to tap the same trait (e.g., among any two of the behaviors "telling of his own past, or of exploits he had accomplished," "giving loud and spontaneous expressions of delight and disapproval," "confining his conversations with counselors to asking and answering necessary questions," degree of talk and noisiness during "quiet hours," and "amount of time spent talking at table," to tap the trait of "talkativeness" or "volubil-

ity") was .14. This correlation, it should be noted, is based on the sum of the daily records over *twenty-four days,* so that it is actually a very much more liberal measure of predictability from one situation or behavior to another than would be expected from simply correlating level of one type of behavior on *one* day with level of another type of behavior on *another* day.

3. In the Sears study of dependency, the average correlation between any two behaviors was .11.

4. In the Bem and Allen study, the average correlation among the three conscientiousness measures—which, it will be recalled, were not single-situation measures but sums over several occasions—was actually negative, −.19. For the two friendliness measures (one of which was a summed measure), the *r* was .30.

5. In the Epstein study, we find our only exception, if such it is, to our generalization. For the trait of initiation and receipt of indirect social contact, the average *r* between any two variables was in excess of .30 in every case, though only just in excess of that level for the four "cross-modality" (letter versus phone) correlations, for which the average *r* was .38. This is a very narrow trait indeed. Also, it should be noted that, as for the Newcomb and the Bem and Allen correlations, the criteria are very liberal, since the correlations are based on the sum of telephone calls and letters initiated and received over a considerable time period—half a semester.

Epstein's other trait is somewhat broader—"organization shown in class-related behavior"—although even this broad label should probably not be allowed because the behavior in question was measured in only a single class. However, quibbles about breadth are not in order, because the median *r* of any two behaviors (again, where these were defined liberally as sums over half a semester) was quite low. Only four of fifteen correlations were higher than .30.

It is important to note that not a single one of these studies was conducted by an investigator who was in any way "antitrait." Indeed, investigators in the first three studies were all as surprised by the low correlations as the layperson would be expected to be, and both Bem and Allen and Epstein conducted their studies with the intent of salvaging the trait construct from the Mischel and Peterson attacks.

It is equally important to note that the studies as a group do not rule out the possibility that some traits, as traditionally defined, do actually exist. First, all of the findings, except for Bem and Allen's on conscientiousness, indicate that there may be a very weak tendency for a given behavior tapping a particular trait to be associated with another given behavior. The only study which is at all persuasive on this possibility, however, is the Hartshorne and May study of honesty, where a persistent though weak association was found among nearly all the behaviors studied, and the measures, moreover, were impeccably objective.[2]

Still more encouraging from the standpoint of the scientific viability of the trait construct is the finding, in the Hartshorne and May study, that when it is *tests* of honesty—that is, sums over several "items" of behavior—which are correlated with other *tests,* the degree of predictability is substantial. This result is an inevitable consequence of conventional measurement theory considerations, as many writers have noted recently, and it was shown to be empirically the case in the Hartshorne and May data. When those investigators pooled all of their nine measures, most of which were summed observations, into a single "honesty test," they achieved a scale with a reliability of .75, corrected for attenuation. (The correction means that the .75 figure is the reliability estimated for a test of eighteen items, twice the length of the actual nine-item scale.)

The magnitude of the test-test correlation quite properly gives comfort to personality theorists who wish to believe in the scientific viability of the trait construct. Indeed, when it is a Hartshorne and May-type test, based on many observations, that is correlated with a single behavior, the predictability can be quite respectable—in the vicinity of .4 or higher. The magnitude of the correlation also raises the possibility that the layperson might actually benefit by using trait constructs for predicting behavior, *if the layperson uses a "test score," rather than an "item," to predict behavior, and if the layperson is capable of constructing such "test scores" from many observations of disparate behaviors of another person.*

We will examine these two large *ifs*. First, however, we will examine

---

2. It is sometimes argued by personologists that situation-situation correlations are not good indicators of the consistency to be found in everyday life because people normally create their own situations rather than find themselves "pushed up against" situations devised by an experimenter. This criticism has an intuitive plausibility, but the study which is most subject to this criticism is clearly the Hartshorne and May study. Here all observations were made in situations created by an experimenter and in situations, in fact, which the child might very well never have encountered before or since. Yet it is the Hartshorne and May study which finds the highest average correlations between measures (except for Epstein's narrow trait of indirect social contact).

the question of whether the layperson's beliefs about the predictive power of trait constructs are based on empirical observation of the behavioral evidence.

The basis of the layperson's beliefs in traits

Was the flap produced in 1968 by the Mischel and Peterson reviews just a misunderstanding—caused by the reviewers' failure to understand the measurement theory requirement that item-item correlations of .20 can parlay themselves into item-total correlations of .40 and split-half reliabilities of .75? An answer to this question depends on whether the degree of empirical predictability at the trait level corresponds well to people's beliefs about predictability at the trait level. Most personologists of this writer's acquaintance, as well as most laypeople exposed to the critique, responded to it by asserting that the argument of little or no validity for traits is manifestly false because the experience of daily life gives proof of the existence of traits. Thus the question is whether the .10–.20 behavior-behavior correlations can be reconciled with convictions about the validity of traits stemming from daily life experience. That is, is it correlations of .10–.20 that we are seeing in daily life, and is it this level of perceived correlation that gives rise to the widespread belief in traits? If so, the conflict is at an end: The same correlations that give rise to people's beliefs in traits are the ones detected in the literature. Everyone is agreed.

In order to approach this question, let us take as our estimate of the actual item-item (single behavior-single behavior) correlation something approaching the maximum that has been found in literature—.20—a figure close to that reported by Hartshorne and May, and substantially higher than the .10–.15 we would obtain by averaging the values of all the pertinent studies. And in considering the behavioral evidence available to the layperson, let us also look at a near-optimal case. Let us take a sorority woman, call her Jane, who has lived with twenty or thirty other women at a small college for a period of two years or so, and has observed each of these women repeatedly in a very wide range of situations—mealtimes, parties, classrooms, informal conversations, and so on.

Taking the Hartshorne and May values as our estimate for behavior-behavior correlation values, could Jane's belief in the power of traits be based on observations of the sort that, say, the degree of talkativeness displayed by her sisters at meals is correlated .20 with the degree of talkativeness displayed by them at parties, or the degree of dominance displayed by them in classroom situations is correlated .20 with the degree of dominance displayed in bull sessions?

The answer seems to be quite clearly "no." Nisbett and Ross (1980) have reviewed the body of evidence on people's ability to detect covariation. (This includes work by the Chapmans [1967, 1969]; D'Andrade [1974]; Golding and Rorer [1972]; Hamilton and Gifford [1976]; and Jennings, Amabile, and Ross [1980]). This work indicates that people's ability to detect covariation is astonishingly poor. In a word, if people expect to see a given covariation in a data set, they tend to see it even if it is not present, and sometimes even if the *opposite* relation to that expected is present. In contrast, if people do not expect to see a given covariation, they tend not to see it, unless the degree of covariation is quite large by the standards of social science. Jennings, Amabile, and Ross (1980) found that correlations of .60 were necessary in order for people to detect associations for which they had no strong a priori covariation expectations one way or the other. Correlations below that range were not seen as significantly different from zero. Thus it seems quite out of the question that Jane's belief in personality traits could be based on accurate observations of behaviors correlated even at Hartshorne and May levels.

There is another plausible route, however, by which accurate observations of data might conceivably produce the belief in traits. In making predictions about behavior in a given situation, Jane has available to her much more information than just the behavior of her sisters in a single other situation which she believes to tap the same trait. She has available, for each woman, *repeated* observations of *many* phenotypically different behaviors which she believes to tap the given trait. She can add together her various observations of Lisa's degree of dominance—at parties, at bull sessions, in one-to-one conversations, at sorority meetings, in classrooms, and so on—to arrive at an omnibus "dominance score." In principle, in other words, she has the same kind of data from which Hartshorne and May constructed their honesty scores. If she can construct scores for each of her sisters with the same reliability and validity achieved by Hartshorne and May, and from approximately the same number of observations, then for any trait with the construct validity that Hartshorne and May showed for honesty, she can, by conventional computational formulas, be expected to predict behavior in a given, single situation with a correlation as high as .40. Unfortunately, however, this degree of association is still too low for her to detect. Thus the signal coming from feedback about the correlation between the scores she has assigned to her sisters, and their behavior in any given situation, is so feeble that, were she to use this evidence about the predictability of behavior from her trait scores, she would have to conclude that it was negligible. Again, it is hard to see how people's belief in traits could be based on accurate observation of behavioral evidence.

One remaining way in which Jane's belief in traits could be empirically based lies in the possibility that the evidence she uses is that coming from the correlation of a test with another test, a form of split-half reliability in which, for example, she observes the covariation between her test scores for her sisters based on the first year of her acquaintance with them with her test scores for the second year. If we make the extremely dubious assumption that the one set of scores does not in any way contaminate the other set, we at last have an empirical correlation that is within the region of the detectable, again using the maximum figure from the literature— the .75 reliability estimated by Hartshorne and May.

Thus it appears that people's beliefs in the predictive power of traits could have an empirical basis under one set of circumstances: 1. if the Hartshorne and May data are taken as the best estimate of the predictability values to be obtained for traits and 2. if people are capable of assigning "test scores" with something approximating the accuracy achieved by Hartshorne and May. The answer to 1. must await the collection of more data by people as ambitious and energetic as Hartshorne and May. A tentative answer to 2. lies closer at hand.

Can people assign accurate personality scores to their peers?

Nisbett and Ross have written a book about the errors that people make in their judgments about other people. The book summarizes the research on such errors conducted over the last half century and categorizes the sources of such errors under approximately two dozen major headings. The body of research may be described succinctly as demonstrating that there are many different types of error which produce large distortions in judgments about other people. These errors have been demonstrated in settings which are for the most part ecologically representative but which place, in general, *fewer* demands upon people's information-processing and judgmental capacities than do most everyday inferential contexts. We will briefly summarize just four of these sources of error, with the intention of suggesting that any assumption that people are capable of assigning accurate trait scores to their fellows may lie in the realm of fond hopes and wishful thinking. Other more extended reviews of the sources of error may be found in work by Mischel (1968), Jones and Nisbett (1971), D'Andrade (1974), and Shweder (1977).

Prior expectations and theories

We have prior expectations about many of the people that we meet, based on secondhand descriptions of them or on sexual, ethnic, occupational, or role stereotypes. The literature indicates that the effect of such expectations can be very great. To take just one example, Kelley (1950) showed that the single adjectives "warm" or "cold," provided in a description of a speaker subjects were about to hear, were capable of greatly biasing people's evaluations of the speaker when they actually encountered him.

Primacy effects

One of the more powerful phenomena in the cognitive literature is the influence of early-encountered data on the interpretation of later-encountered data. Even when people approach another person with minimal preconceptions, they are at the mercy of the representativeness of the first sample of behavior they encounter. As Jones and his colleagues have shown (e.g., 1968, 1972), people persist in attributions of ability and other dispositions made on the basis of small, misleading samples of initial behavior. This appears to occur because people form theories on the basis of early-presented information which serve to distort all the subsequently presented information. They do this, in fact, even when they are required to attend closely to the later-presented information, something they would not be expected to do very often in real life.

Perseverance of judgments

Ross and Lepper and their colleagues (e.g., Ross, Lepper, and Hubbard [1975]; Ross, Lepper, Steinmetz, and Strack [1977]) have shown that even when the entire evidence base for an initial impression has been completely discredited, people will persist in the judgment formed on the basis of that evidence. The "discrediting" manipulations employed by Ross and Lepper and their colleagues were, moreover, far more decisive and unequivocal than those that could be expected to occur with any frequency in real life (for example, the experimenter's admission that he lied about the initial evidence). Perseverance of belief appears to occur because, prior to the discrediting manipulations, subjects recruit additional facts, consistent with the alleged evidence, from their memories, and because they fabricate causal explanations for the alleged evidence which remain plausible to them even after they are told that the evidence is false.

Halo effects

Among the most massive effects in the entire psychological literature is the so-called halo effect. If a rater gives a desirable rating to another individual on a given dimension, it is highly likely that the rater gives desirable ratings on most other dimensions to that individual. The same strong association is found for undesirable ratings. Recently it has been established that these associations are not due to a grossly inequitable distribution by nature of desirable and undesirable traits, or to the possibility that differential criteria are employed by different raters, but instead are due to a distortion in trait judgments because of affective "spillover" from evaluation of traits or from global evaluations (Landy and Sigall, 1974; Nisbett and Wilson, 1977).

This selected bouquet of judgmental errors should be sufficient to make the point that our judgments about other people, including specifically the trait scores we assign to them, are riddled with opportunities for bias and distortion. If people's beliefs about the predictive power of traits are based on "data" at all, there is good reason to doubt that they are based on an *accurate reading* of data. Instead, the data probably have been "doctored" in just such a way as to produce an appearance of far more consistency than exists in reality. We have seen that the only apparent way people's beliefs in traits could be produced by an accurate reading of covariation would be if they could assign trait scores based on many diverse observations and then note the covariation of these scores with the next batch of scores based on diverse observations. But accuracy in assigning these trait scores seems highly unlikely; thus an accurate empirical basis for people's beliefs in traditional, nomothetic, social behavior traits seems equally unlikely.

The sources of judgmental error also make it clear why self-report and peer report data cannot be taken seriously as evidence for the validity of trait constructs. Even when convergence of data is demonstrated, this provides evidence for nothing more than the *possibility* that peers are accurately assigning trait scores on the basis of behavioral data observed without inferential bias or distortion. Such convergence could equally well be evidence of shared bias and distortion in processing the behavioral evidence. In fact, however, the evidence suggests that convergence in peer reports is usually weak, and thus that people are not only invalid judges of their fellows but also idiosyncratically invalid judges (Dornbusch, Hastorf, Richardson, Muzzy, and Vreeland, 1965; Mischel, 1968; Norman and Goldberg, 1966).[3]

The personal utility of the trait construct

Based on the maximum values in the literature, the highest degree of predictability that people could attain for single behaviors is in the range corresponding to a correlation of about .40. If people could attain this level, it would probably be useful for them to employ trait scores when predicting the behavior of other people. It appears, however, that the .40 figure is likely to be far above that realistically attained by use of nomothetic trait scores, both because it is the ceiling found in the literature and because the likely invalidity of people's assignment of such scores would have to lower the actual predictability to a substantial degree.

Let us assume a more modest range of predictability, say, .15 to .30. Would people be aided in their daily lives by using their trait scores for others to predict behavior? Quite possibly not. Kahneman and Tversky (1973) have shown that people are highly "nonregressive" in their prediction strategies. That is to say, they tend to predict Y values that are as far from the mean of the (to-be-predicted) Y variable as the X value is from the mean of the X variable (from which the prediction is to be made). When the correlation between X and Y is low, such a strategy produces very large average prediction errors. Indeed, Ross, Amabile, and Jennings (1976) found that, at least when r is below .30, people's predictions may be *less accurate when they know a target's score on X than when they do not*. Most of the time, when making predictions, their subjects would have

---

3. Even the convergence of expert judges—clinicians—making their judgments from behavioral evidence collected at points widely separated in time (Block, 1971) does not establish the validity of trait constructs. Though such convergence is consistent with validity, it is also consistent with the possibility that people reliably behave in such a way as to produce the same (erroneous) trait impressions in such judges. For example, if judgments of shyness or dependency are erroneously based on decibel level of speaking voice, and decibel level of speaking voice is a lifelong trait, then judges widely separated in time might reach convergent impressions about shyness or dependency simply because the described level of speaking voice was the same over time.

reduced their average prediction errors by simply repeating their average Y score as their prediction for each target, rather than varying their prediction on the basis of their knowledge of the target's score on X. (The inefficacy of subjects' strategy of using the X score for prediction of the Y score would be even more dramatic if average *squared* deviations were considered.)

Thus it cannot be assumed that reliance on trait constructs could only be helpful, and helpful in proportion to the validity of the construct and of one's ability to assign accurate trait scores. If validity and scoring ability are low enough, predictions may literally be less accurate than if people did not rely on trait constructs at all.

There are, however, two fairly clear ways out of this dismal conclusion. People may not base their predictions on the equivalent of the personologist's traditional nomothetic scores. They may either "shrink" 1. the population about whom they make their predictions—that is, they may make predictions as if they were idiographic theorists, or they may "shrink" 2. the breadth of the trait constructs they employ, so that they refer only to behavior in a given type of situation. We now examine these possibilities.

The layperson: Nomothetic or idiographic trait theorist?

Bem and Allen (1974) have revived the idiographic position that used to be associated with Gordon Allport: the position that it may not be meaningful to characterize many if not most people on many if not most trait dimensions. In response to Mischel's contention that nomothetically conceived traits can account for only a very small portion of the variance in any given behavior, Bem and Allen attempted to isolate a group of people for whom a given trait designation might be meaningful and useful. They divided a group of Stanford undergraduates into high- and low-variability groups with respect to the two traits they examined. The subjects who were more variable from situation to situation (by self-report) were removed, and analyses were conducted using only the remaining half. Bem and Allen reasoned that it might be only the low-variability subjects for whom a trait designation was appropriate, and for whom strong cross-situational consistency might be found. The resulting intercorrelations among reports of the degree to which the subject possessed the trait of conscientiousness (reports by the subject, by his or her mother and father, and by a peer) were higher than for the sample as a whole. The correlations among the (summed) behavioral measures, however, still did not reach an impressive level. Indeed, none of the three behavioral correlations reached zero; all were slightly negative. (On the other hand, the mean correlation of the behavioral measures with all other measures, including reports of self and others, was .23.) For the two behavioral measures of friendliness, the correlation for the low-variability subjects went to .73. (Whether the measures of friendliness should actually be regarded as measures of behavior in two different situations is open to some debate, since one was a composite of talkativeness and rated friendliness by peers in a laboratory group discussion and the other was the latency to speak to a single other person in the waiting room of the laboratory immediately prior to the discussion. However, the fact that the two settings were different on one of at least two plausibly different dimensions—the number of people present and the task, to "have a discussion" in the one case and to "wait" in the other—would seem to place the two situations safely in my category of "phenotypically different.") The correlation of the two behavioral measures with all other measures of friendliness was also impressively high—above .50 for both.

The Bem and Allen study raises the possibility that people may suffer much less by using trait scores to predict behavior than was implied by the preceding discussion. 1. *If* they are idiographic theorists, or at least behave as if they were—that is, if they toss out, as did Bem and Allen, a sizable fraction of the people whom they know as simply not having a "scorable" value on the given trait dimension, and 2. *if* we take Bem and Allen's two behavioral measures of friendliness as an estimate of the predictability to be achieved, rather than their three behavioral measures of conscientiousness, *then* 3. they may do rather well by using trait constructs to predict the behavior of those people whose behavior they choose to predict.

These are two large "ifs." About the second "if," we can say nothing. The Bem and Allen type of research is difficult to do, and if there have been attempts to replicate it, they have not been published.

About the first "if," we can say a little more. I am aware of no evidence suggesting that laypeople are idiographic trait theorists, and there is a bit of evidence to suggest they are not. Nisbett, Caputo, Legant, and Maracek (1973) gave twenty trait adjective pairs (e.g. "conscientious–happy-go-lucky," "unassuming–self-asserting") to subjects and asked them to indicate for themselves, for their best friend, for a liked acquaintance, for their father, and for the television commentator Walter Cronkite whether one or the other trait was a good description of the person or whether the phrase "depends on the situation" was more applicable. For people other than themselves, subjects preferred a trait designation as the more accurate description for fourteen of the twenty options, on the average. If these data are taken literally, they imply that people think that most people can be described accurately as having a level on most trait dimensions, rather than not having the trait at all; thus people would not appear to be very idiographic in their theories. Of course, the data may not mean this, but may show merely that subjects felt that to be good sports they should pick a trait rather than "defaulting" all the time. Still, this study, and countless others in which subjects are asked to assess the traits of their fellows, provide no evidence that subjects find this sort of task at all arbitrary. Subjects seem to regard such tasks as an easy and natural one for most of the traits, and most of the people, that they rate.

Though the question, Are people more nearly nomothetic or more nearly idiographic trait theorists? must be regarded as open, my own suspicion is that they are strong nomothetic theorists, and do not regard personality traits as being distributed any differently in the population than are ability traits. Just as they believe it is meaningful to assign all people a score on running ability or mathematical ability, and just as traditional personologists do, they believe it is meaningful to assign all people a score on dependency, aggressiveness, or honesty.

Predictability at the level of the specific behavior category or situation type

There is still another way in which people might not actually suffer by using trait observations to predict social behavior. If, despite their expressed beliefs about broad trait constructs, people actually use behavior of a highly specific nature or behavior in a highly specific situation as the basis of their predictions, then individual difference data might be useful as a basis for predictions. They would be useful, that is, if predictability at the narrow, situation-specific level were high enough.

Is it high enough? Is there very substantial predictability at the level of specific behavior? Yes, in my view, at least for many behaviors. Again, the best evidence comes from Hartshorne and May. At the level of phenotypically identical behavior, even the correlation of behavior on a single occasion with that on another single occasion is often high. For example, copying from an answer key on one general information test in March correlated .79 with copying from an answer key on a parallel general information test in October. And in general, the correlations between behavior in identical situations were in the range .4 to .8, typically .5 to .6. Correlations were just as high between behavior in one situation and behavior in another phenotypically near-identical situation occurring at roughly the same time; an example is the correlation between copying from the answer key on a test of general information with copying from the answer key on a test of arithmetic.

Newcomb's less solidly objective data also include some highly pertinent evidence. The correlation between the sum of behavior of a given type on odd days with the sum for the same behavior on even days (e.g., "How much did he talk at the table?") was .78. This value is based on a correlation of the sum of behavior on twelve occasions with another sum over twelve occasions for behavior of a given type or behavior in a given situation. Thus the value is much higher than would be expected for the correlation of a single behavior with a single other behavior. The estimate for the latter correlation is not high enough to be useful (about .23), although the correlation of the sum of twelve observations with a single behavior might be high enough (in excess of .40) to be useful.

Some readers might prefer not to place much faith in Newcomb's data because of their relatively high degree of reliance on the rater's memorial and inferential capabilities. Despite my role as a cataloguer of inferential error, however, I am inclined to take the data seriously; on the face of it, such errors do not seem to be necessarily great in Newcomb's data. More importantly, some of Newcomb's additional evidence encourages us to take the data at face value. It will be recalled that, despite the very high correlation between the odd and even sums for a *given* type of behavior, the average correlation between any two *different* behaviors that Newcomb thought might tap the same trait was .14. In the *long-term retrospective* reports, however, where raters were asked to recall, over the entire period of the study, how much of the given behavior was shown in general ("Did he talk more than his share of the time at the table?"), these correlations—across behavior categories but still within a given trait—soared to .49. Newcomb's own interpretation of the discrepancy between the average correlation of .14 for the daily reports and the average correlation of .49 for the retrospective reports has been amply supported by research on people's ability to detect covariation: "this is presumably due more to habits of logical association in the minds of the raters than to actual behavior" (p. 56). If we assume that these "habits of logical association" were given much greater rein in the retrospective ratings than in the daily records (where its influence was at most sufficient to induce an average correlation of .14), this gives us license to presume that the daily records were relatively free of inferential and memorial distortion introduced by prior expectations and thus to take seriously the .78 estimate of correlations at the level of specific behavior.

The study by Epstein also provides evidence of fairly substantial predictability from one situation or behavior to another identical one. At this level (or rather, with sums over short time periods involving a few occasions), Epstein's correlations range from .3 to .4 for the "indirect social contact" behaviors and center on .5 for the "organization" behaviors. Summing these behaviors over the time period of half a semester provides reliability at the specific behavior level of a minimum of .60 and more typically .90.

Thus if people merely *believed* that they were able to predict across behaviors and situations but based their *actual* predictions only on near-identical behaviors and situations, they could attain substantial predictability, and, at the level of aggregated occasions, very substantial predictability. Do people so confine themselves, behaving circumspectly while making exaggerated boasts?

It seems quite likely that people often do base their behaviors on such a narrow and firm foundation. For example, "Harry always drones on at meetings, I hope he'll be absent today"; "Mary always apologizes when she feels she may have hurt someone's feelings." But there is no good reason to assume that people *habitually* base their predictions on so narrow a footing, and one provocative study suggests strongly that they often do not limit themselves in this fashion at all. Taylor and Crocker (1980) presented subjects with information about the behavior of a target person suggesting that, in several academic situations, or in several social situations, the person behaved in ways that could be described as either extroverted or introverted (or, for another set of subjects, as either dependent or independent). Subjects were then asked to make predictions about how the target person would behave in a variety of situations, some academic and some social. The predictions showed no indication that subjects paid even the slightest attention to situational context. If the subjects had read about extroverted behavior by the target in exclusively academic settings, they predicted extroverted behavior in both academic and social settings, and to the same degree for both. The same was true for subjects who had read about extroverted behavior in exclusively social settings.

As Heider put it, people are inclined to refer the observables "as far as possible to the invariances." The level at which people appear to refer the presumed invariances is the traditional trait level. The evidence is quite clear that this level is much too deep. So far from there being invariance at this level, the most optimistic evidence suggests that there is no more than trivial correspondence between single behaviors at the trait level. When we sum across many, many behaviors, the consistency *may* become impressive at the upper bound represented by Hartshorne and May, and thus *might* be useful for the layperson.

As we have seen, however, there is every reason to suspect that people cannot accurately perform the many information-processing and judgmental tasks necessary to arrive at trait scores for their fellows. The conclusion would appear to be that, except for those cases in which people predict behavior from observation of behavior in many identical past situations, they are ill served by using individual difference constructs for prediction. There is no reason to assume that constructs at the level of generality of nomothetic social traits could provide more than trivial increments over random predictions. And as three generations of social psychologists have observed, the strong preference for personal dispositions as a basis for prediction is likely to deflect people from attending to those factors that often *can* serve as a useful guide for predictions—that is, to situational factors, or as Lewin put it, the field of forces operating at the time the behavior takes place.

6

Non-psychological Explanations
of Behavior

STANLEY SCHACHTER

There was a time when graduate students in clinical psychology at the University of Minnesota were required to take a course in neuroanatomy. Since this was a course designed for students in physiology, the psychologists generally found it rough going; they moaned and groaned and bitched but, like it or not, generations of Minnesota clinicians took this year of neuroanatomy. Since Minnesota, at that time, was known for its work in clinical psychometrics and was also more than receptive to the principles of operant psychology and Mr. Skinner's black box, I, a new faculty member there, never quite understood what the fuss was all about. I finally decided that Paul Meehl and Stark Hathaway, at that time the intellectual leaders of the clinical wing of the department, had a suspicion that some day they and their kind were going to be wiped out by some smelly biochemist, for it was all going to turn out that schizophrenia and anxiety neurosis and paranoia and the like had nothing to do with Momma or impoverished environments or psychodynamic complexities of any sort but were due to an excess or a deficiency of some unpronounceable chemical in some inaccessible spot in the brain. And I suspect that Meehl and Hathaway simply wanted to be sure that their students, at least, could understand what had wiped them out even if they could do nothing about it.

The Minnesota clinicians' insecurities highlight one of the peculiarities

My thanks to Kathleen Redington and Michael Rennert for their considerable help in preparation of this chapter.

of the field. The psychologist's, indeed the social scientist's, subject is a machine—a biological machine of guts and glands and fluids—but, by and large, the social scientist's theories and explanatory concepts have almost nothing to do with the machinery. For many, perhaps most, areas of interest to social scientists, this is as it should be. Given the present state of biological knowledge, it would be pretentious and preposterous to attempt a biological explanation of a political preference or a sociometric choice or the reasons for the superiority of cooperatively over competitively structured groups. It is my observation, however, that in many areas we are considerably closer to a useful reductionism than most social scientists suspect, and I would suggest that the growth of knowledge in both the biological and social sciences has been such in recent decades that in some of the most surprising areas biological knowledge is already capable of revolutionizing our understanding of the nature of a presumably psychological or social phenomenon.

I shall attempt to document this contention by presenting three case studies from the recent history of social science—one from medical psychology, one from anthropology, and one from experimental social psychology in which the data are such that one can examine the relative power of socio-psychological versus biological explanations for a phenomenon.

I turn first to medical psychology, the field of obvious concern to the Minnesota clinicians—and for very good reason. The maladies that at some point in medical history have been considered of psychological etiology include not only such erstwhile psychosomatic classics as asthma, ulcers, colitis, neurodermatitis, dysmenorrhea, and the like but, astonishingly, maladies such as Parkinson's disease, tertiary syphilis, and tuberculosis as well.

Gilles de la Tourette syndrome

To illustrate the interplay of biological and psychological explanations in psychological medicine, I shall review the recent history of an exotic malady known as Gilles de la Tourette syndrome. I choose this particular malady because literature on the condition is readily accessible and still limited enough so that one feels some confidence that he has covered the literature and has a reasonably accurate picture of the current state of affairs.

Tourette syndrome is a condition characterized by multiple tics, both physical and vocal. Physically, virtually any part of the body may be involved in either simple tics such as eye or nose twitches or complex move-ment tics such as jumping, squatting, kicking, kneeling, and the like. Vo-cally, the condition is characterized by any of a combination of symptoms such as grunts, barks, whistles and, most bizarre of all, tics such as echola-lia—involuntary repetition of the words of others—and coprolalia—the compulsive repetition of obscene words.

This malady is a disease in transition. At one time, Tourette syndrome was generally considered a psychological condition, caused by profound psychological disturbances and treatable by psychoanalysis or by behavior therapy of one sort or another. More recently, the press of research has made psychological interpretation of the malady less and less plausible, and it seems increasingly evident that the disease is of purely biochemical or biological origin. The case is far from complete, but the drift of the data is such that it seems as inevitable that Tourette will prove to be of biological origin as it now does that Parkinson's disease, tuberculosis, and tertiary syphilis have proven to be biologically determined.

In my description of this malady, I rely heavily on the splendid book on this subject by Shapiro, Shapiro, Bruun, and Sweet (1978).

Historically, the condition was named by Charcot after Georges Gilles de la Tourette, who in 1894 and 1895 described nine patients with multiple verbal and physical tics. Though psychological medicine had long been interested in tics and compulsive movement, it was Ferenczi's 1921 paper that triggered what Shapiro et al. identify as the psychoanalytic period in the history of Tourette syndrome—a period that lasted from 1921 to roughly 1955, when drug rather than psychotherapy became the treatment of choice for the condition. Ferenczi suggested that tics may be the "ste-reotyped equivalents of onanism and that the remarkable connection of tics with coprolalia . . . might be nothing else than the uttered expression of the same erotic emotion usually abreacted in symbolic movements" (p. 1).

Abraham (1927), disagreeing, hypothesized that tics are of anal-sadistic rather than erotic origin and suggested that: "The tic which takes the form of making grimaces has an obvious hostile significance. . . . Other tics, particularly coprolalia show their anal origins quite clearly . . . some, for example, the whistling tic are derived directly from anal processes (flatus). Here the patient carries out his hostile and degrading purposes by anal means" (p. 324).

This theoretical opposition triggered a spate of conflicting observa-tions and theories, which are summarized by Shapiro et al. (1978) as variously identifying the etiology of Tourette tics as ". . . oral, anal, genital, narcissistic, obsessive-compulsive, psychotic, aggressive, hysterical or other pejorative unconscious psychological states" (p. 63). There is no need to elaborate further. The point is simply that for at least a thirty-five-year period, Tourette syndrome was considered almost exclusively a psychologically induced malady, and the major debate about the condition concerned the nature of the psychological causation.

It was probably the persistent failure of any form of psychotherapy or behavior therapy, plus the first indications that the phenothiazines could relieve the condition, that led to the increasing suspicion that the condition is organic rather than psychological in nature. Whatever the cause, it is probably reasonable to assess current interpretations of this disorder as considerably more biological than at any previous time in medical history. This assessment is based on the following facts:

1. Psychological test batteries including the WAIS or WISC, Bender-Gestalt, Rorschach, Draw-a-Person Test, TAT, and MMPI have failed to find any indications in Tourette patients of "schizophrenia, underlying psychoses, inhibition of aggression, obsessive-compulsive traits, hysteria, somatization, hypochondriases or other common psychopathological factors" that have been suggested by one theorist or another as causal or corollary with Tourette (Shapiro et al., 1978, p. 157).
2. Direct evidence of organic involvement is supplied by the following data from the Shapiro et al. studies. In all cases, the data for Tourette subjects are substantially and significantly greater than for control groups of psychiatric outpatients.

   a. EEG abnormalities are manifested by 47 percent of Tourette subjects (71 percent of children and 25 percent of adults).
   b. On the Bender-Gestalt test, 42 percent of Tourette patients manifest organic signs and 68 percent receive overall ratings of organicity on psychological testing.

3. Genetic involvement is suggested by the identification of eighteen families with Tourette syndrome, plus a relatively high frequency of tics in the families of Tourette patients.
4. Finally, we note that the condition is remarkably improved by administration of a drug called haloperidol—a strong dopamine blocker. Some 90 percent of patients show marked improvement when taking

this drug as compared with roughly 10 percent who improve when in psychological treatment.

Obviously, the case for an organic etiology of Tourette syndrome is still circumstantial. There is as yet no identified organic process or agent which has been proven responsible for the condition. Given the success of dopamine blocking agents in the treatment of the condition, it has been hypothesized that Tourette is due to a dopaminergic excess; so far, however, research has failed to support this guess. Nevertheless, it does seem to this author that the press of accumulating data almost relentlessly forces one to the conclusion that this is an organically, not a psychologically, induced condition and that it is simply a matter of time until research identifies the responsible biological agent. Probably the strongest barrier to accepting this conclusion is the weird symptom of coprolalia, for it seems somehow particularly unlikely that there could be a simple biochemical basis for compulsive cursing. However, it has been demonstrated that coprolalia does occur in proven organic conditions such as klazomania, a sequel of encephalitis (Benedek, 1925; Wohlfart, Ingvar, and Hellberg, 1961), and occasionally also in patients after cerebrovascular accidents or in those with general paresis.

Ethnic differences in drunken comportment

I turn next to the subject of ethnic differences in reaction to alcohol. In reductionistic terms, this is an area of great interest, for over time the biological and social sciences have articulated beautifully. In turn, the social scientists have corrected the naïveté of the pharmacologists, and the biologists have opened up totally new interpretive possibilities for what once appeared to be purely anthropological or sociological problems. The sequence is the following:

Classically, the pharmacologists have shared Western civilization's conventional interpretation of the effects of alcohol. As early as 50 A.D., Seneca wrote: "Drunkenness does not create vice; it merely brings it into view." The pharmacologist's version of this hypothesis can be found in virtually any older textbook treatment of ethyl alcohol. For example, in Drill (1958) one finds: "Alcohol, even in rather small amounts, causes loss of inhibitions and the individual responds to many impulses which are ordinarily repressed" (p. 199). Of course, the pharmacologists have tended to think about the effects of alcohol as they do about the effects of any other drug. Alcohol is a drug which has a particular set of effects on the central nervous system, and this results in a particular pattern of uninhibited behavior. As Greenberg (1953) described the process, "Alcohol . . . depresses the uppermost level of the brain—the center of inhibitions, restraint and judgment . . . the drinker feels that he is 'a free human being'; many of his normal inhibitions vanish; he takes personal and social liberties as the impulse prompts" (p. 88). Just as an injection of norepinephrine will depress heart rate, so an injection of alcohol will depress that portion of the central nervous system involved in self-control. That is the way the biological machinery is built, and that is the explanation for the effects of alcohol on the human species.

The difficulty with this view is that the human species appears to be far from uniform in its reaction to alcohol. In fact, as the anthropologists and sociologists have delighted in pointing out, there are societies which manifest virtually every conceivable reaction to alcohol. On the basis of a comprehensive cross-cultural survey of the effects of alcohol, MacAndrew and Edgerton (1969) conclude:

> (1) There are societies whose members' drunken comportment fails to exhibit anything of the sort which might reasonably be described as disinhibited; (2) there are societies whose members' drunken comportment has undergone marked transformation over historical time; and (3) there are societies whose members' drunken comportment is radically different from one set of socially ordered situations or circumstances to another. (p. 61)

In short, there is not the invariant reaction to alcohol that the pharmacologist's kind of formulation suggests. To account for the immense cultural and historical diversity in responses to alcohol, MacAndrew and Edgerton have suggested that drunken comportment is learned, and they hypothesize:

> Over the course of socialization, people learn about drunkenness what their society "knows" about drunkenness; and, accepting and acting upon the understandings thus imparted to them, they become the living confirmation of their society's teachings. (p. 88)

The next step in this sequence belongs to the biologists, who without explicitly phrasing the question have, in effect, begun to ask, "Why, biologically, do different societies learn such different things about alcohol?" To understand why this sort of question was even asked, it will be necessary first to describe the anthropologists' picture of the Chinese—who, as a group, appear classically to illustrate the anthropologists' point that alcohol need not lead to disinhibition. Though the Chinese drink freely, they appear to have virtually no problem with alcoholism and appear generally to react to alcohol with good humor and some silliness, perhaps, but with virtually no manifestation of violence or the release of any of the coarser emotions. This characterization is based on La Barre's (1946) observations on drinking in the region of Kunming, on Lin's (1953) data on alcoholism in three Formosan villages, and on Barnett's (1955) study of drinking behavior and alcoholism among the Cantonese of New York City's Chinatown. The three studies present a very similar picture, and rather than attempting to paraphrase, I shall quote directly Barnett's summary of these observations and of his interpretation of these facts:

Drinking of alcoholic beverages is widespread in New York's Chinatown. Drunkenness is, however, not prevalent because the attitude of the family as well as of the community discourages its occurrence. The incidence of chronic alcoholism is low and alcoholism as a social problem is relatively unimportant.

The role of alcohol can be understood from a study of the social environment. On the whole the fundamental expectations and obligations of Kwangtung culture persist in Chinatown. Within the home, and at social gatherings, drinking represents an important social function. At meals and banquets heavy eating is accompanied by considerable alcohol consumption. When intoxicated the Chinese drinker is usually quiet, and public drunkenness is uncommon and strongly disapproved. There may be a release of aggression which is rarely manifested in violence, but usually in expansive behavior and speech.

In the cultural setting of Chinatown, drinking by women is restricted and an intoxicated woman is treated more severely than a man. There is a permissive attitude to drinking by boys and they soon learn a set of attitudes which sanctions drinking socially but disapproves of intoxication.

The second generation exhibits considerable acculturation and there is a general loosening of the traditional controls in the Chinese family. In this setting one might expect the younger Chinese to show a trend toward heavy drinking—especially in view of the psychological strains of their position between American and Chinese ways of life. Thus far, however, the social controls seem to have proven more effective than the forces of disorganization and the younger generation show few cases of alcoholism. (p. 225–26)

It appears, then, that drinking is widespread among the Chinese, that the Chinese under alcohol are generally quiet and amiable, that alcoholism is virtually nonexistent,[1] and that the Chinese attitude to drinking persists among second generation Chinese-Americans despite the strain of acculturation. These are the apparent facts, and the anthropologist interprets these facts in terms of "social sanctions against intemperate drinking." However, just why these hypothesized sanctions should be so very strong and so remarkably effective among the Chinese as compared with most Caucasian groups is unclear. For one possible explanation, let us turn to some rather odd physiological facts about alcohol and the Chinese.

The Oriental flush

One of the more curious observations that the Chinese, and Orientals in general, make about themselves is that alcohol makes them turn red—an observation that was checked by the physician Wolff (1972), who, by means of optical densitometry of the earlobe, compared groups of Caucasians and Orientals (Taiwanese, Koreans, and Japanese). The observation is unquestionably correct, for overwhelmingly the Orientals responded to beer with a visible flush and a marked increase in optical density, whereas beer had virtually no effect on the skin coloration of Caucasians. Wolff next compared newborn babies by adding a few drops of port to a 5 percent glucose solution. Oriental babies responded to the port with a marked flush while Occidental babies were unaffected, a finding which suggests that these effects are not due to different diet or previous experience with alcohol. Comparing adult subjects on subjective reports after drinking beer, Oriental subjects tend to report palpitations, tachycardia, muscle weakness, dizziness, sleepiness, and "hot stomach," while Caucasian subjects report almost none of these effects.

These findings were replicated by Ewing, Rouse, and Pellizzari (1974), who administered small amounts of synthetic ethanol to groups of Occidental and Oriental (chiefly Chinese and Japanese) subjects. They found identical results on flushing and similar reports of dysphoric subjective symptoms. They also measured blood pressure and heart rate. In order to convey the magnitude of these effects, Table 6.1 reproduces their data on heart rate. It is obvious that alcohol has a dramatic impact on the heart

1. According to Barnett (1955), between 1933 and 1949 there were 17,515 arrests of Chinese recorded in the local police precinct in New York's Chinatown. In not one of these arrests was drunkenness specifically charged.

Table 6.1. Mean heart rates of Oriental and Occidental subjects before and after ingesting small amounts of alcohol

Period	Beats per minute in:		Significance level
	Oriental group (N = 24)	Occidental group (N = 24)	
Before ingestion	79.0	78.8	n.s.
30 min after ingestion	89.1	75.8	p < .001
60 min after ingestion	85.8	76.4	p < .02

Source: From Ewing, Rouse, and Pellizzari, 1974.

rate of Oriental subjects and little effect on Occidental subjects. Since their subjects all lived in the United States and most were eating a Western diet, Ewing et al., like Wolff, doubt that these differences can be explained by diet. There is also further independent evidence (Fenna, Mix, Schaefer, and Gilbert, 1971; Wolff, 1973) that these effects cannot be explained by differential experience with alcohol, for Orientals familiar with alcohol are still considerably more sensitive than are equally experienced Occidentals.

Obviously, there are major differences between Orientals and Occidentals in the physiological effects of alcohol. Quantities of alcohol that have virtually no measurable effects on Occidentals will produce a series of marked dysphoric physiological consequences in Orientals. These differences exist from the day of birth, and they do not appear to be explainable either by diet or by differential experience with alcohol.

Given this series of facts, it may be unnecessary to invoke the elaborate concepts of social science in order to comprehend the drinking behavior of the Chinese. It may be that the Chinese are temperate drinkers because excessive drinking makes them sick. They may be nonviolent drinkers because alcohol puts them to sleep before they can get violent. There may be few alcoholics among the Chinese because they can't drink enough to become alcoholic, and so on. One could, with little difficulty, compose a largely biological schema from which, without benefit of anthropology or sociology, it would probably be possible to deduce most of the known facts about Chinese drinking behavior. Unfortunately, however, such a reductionistic exercise would, as yet, be premature because of two Asiatic derived groups who confound an otherwise elegant schema. These are the North American Indians and the Eskimos, groups for which alcoholism and alcohol-induced violence have been notorious social problems.

Since North American Indians are commonly classified as "members of the Mongoloid major mating population," Wolff (1973) repeated on Indians the experiment on flushing that he had conducted on Orientals. He compared members of one American Indian tribe (the Eastern Cree of the Algonquin family) to Americans of pure Chinese or Japanese origin and to a group of American Caucasians. In this experiment, Wolff replicated his earlier finding: Alcohol induces a flush in the Oriental and not in the Caucasian group. As for the American Indians, their reaction was precisely the same as the Oriental group: Alcohol induces a flush. In addition to his densitometry measures in this study, Wolff also measured pulse pressure and cheek temperature. On both measures, the Indian and the Oriental groups were similar to one another and considerably more reactive than the Caucasian group.

We have, then, two Asiatic groups both demonstrating similar vasomotor sensitivity to alcohol. For one group alcohol is a major social problem and for the other no problem at all. To continue with the complications, Fenna, Mix, Schaefer, and Gilbert (1971) tested biochemical implications of the observation by Canadian police that drunken Indians and Eskimos thrown in jail take considerably longer to sober up than do drunken whites. They administered alcohol intravenously to groups of Eskimo, Indian, and white males and simply measured the rate of disappearance of ethanol from the blood during two hours after stopping infusion. The police observation appears to be correct, for the rate of decline of blood level alcohol and the rate of alcohol metabolism were markedly higher for whites than for either of the two native groups, which were almost identical in rate of metabolism and elimination. Fenna et al. also present evidence that these differences in metabolic rate are not due to dietary differences or, though there is some adaptation, to differential experience with alcohol.

There is no such study for Oriental groups, but Ewing et al., (1974) reported that after ingesting ethanol, overall acetaldehyde levels of Oriental subjects exceeded those of Occidental subjects—one more indication that the two groups differ biochemically in their reaction to alcohol.

We appear, then, to have racially related people, the Chinese and the American Indian–Eskimo groups, both similar to one another in their physiological and metabolic reactions to alcohol, both markedly different from the Caucasian group. Yet, the two Mongoloid groups are poles apart in the behavioral effects of alcohol. For the Chinese, alcohol appears to be far less of a social problem than it is for most American Caucasian groups, while for the Indians and Eskimos, it is considerably more of a social problem.[2] Just why this should be so is, of course, an absorbing puzzle, the solution of which seems once more to require the insights and the concepts of the social sciences. My own casual guess is that because for so many years it was illegal for Indians to drink or to have liquor, they may have developed a fairly unique drinking pattern. When they did obtain liquor (which, from all accounts, appears to have been no particular problem), they may well have drunk it as fast as possible in order to avoid interference by some overzealous law officer or missionary. If so, they got their liquor down before it could make them sick.

Whatever the resolution of this particular puzzle, the biologists will almost certainly continue to build on and perhaps replace the work of social scientists in this area. My suspicion is that a determination of the conditions that have led one Mongoloid group to temperance and another such group to excess may well lead to a major insight into the etiology of alcohol addiction.

Pharmacological explanations of cigarette smoking

As a final example of biological versus psychological approaches to a behavioral phenomenon, I shall describe my own work on cigarette smoking—a behavior that almost anyone would agree involves both psychological and biological components. On the one hand, the smoker is a junkie. He's hooked, addicted, and whatever those words mean physiologically, he's got it. Somewhere there is some set of cells that, when depleted, initiates signals to smoke.

On the other hand, almost any smoker can convince you and himself that there are major psychological components to smoking. They will convince you that smoking calms them; that they smoke more when they're anxious; that smoking helps them work; and so on. In short, smoking serves some psychological function; it does something positive for the smoker, and this is the reason he smokes. This emphasis on the functional properties of smoking is at the heart of virtually every serious psychological attempt to understand smoking. Presumably, nicotine or tar or some

2. Stewart (1964) reports that in the United States, alcohol is connected with Indian arrests thirteen times as frequently as it is with arrests of Chinese and Japanese. Indians have the highest rate of alcohol-related crime and Chinese and Japanese the lowest rate among all ethnically identified groups.

component of smoking is so gratifying that, despite the well-publicized dangers, the smoker is unwilling or unable to give up the habit. Undoubtedly, the ultimate eulogy of the act is Marcovitz's (1969) suggestion that

> as a psychological phenomenon, smoking is comparable to the ritual of the Eucharist. There the communicant incorporates bread and wine and in so doing symbolically introjects the Lord Jesus Christ. This is a conscious process, with the hope of identification, of attaining some of the attributes of Jesus. Similarly, the smoker incorporates the smoke, introjecting in an unconscious fantasy some object which will confer on him its magic powers. (p. 1082)

Among these magic powers, smoking serves to "delimit the body image in the quest for the sense of self," to "relieve the unconscious fear of suffocation," and to serve as "proof of immortality" (pp. 1082, 1083). Though no one has matched Marcovitz's panegyric, almost all attempts to account for the habit have assumed that it does something positive for the smoker. And this is an assumption that is shared by the smoker himself, for questionnaire studies (e.g., Coan, 1973; McKennell, 1973; Tomkins, 1968) indicate that heavy smokers report that cigarettes relax them or stimulate them, put them at ease, give them something to do with their hands, and so on. In short, for both the psychologist and the smoker, the act of smoking is functional; it does something for the smoker, and this is the reason he smokes. In my work, I have concentrated on one of the presumed motivations for smoking. Smokers widely report that they smoke more when they are tense, anxious, or upset, and they also report that smoking calms them. Smoking, then, serves a respectable psychological function, and this presumably is one of the motivations for and explanations of smoking under stress.

Before worrying about interpretations of these facts, let us make sure that they are facts. First, does smoking increase with stress? The available evidence indicates that it does. In two almost identical experiments, Schachter, Silverstein, and Perlick (1977) manipulated stress within the context of experiments presumably designed to measure tactile sensitivity. In high stress conditions, such sensitivity was measured by the administration, sporadically over an experimental hour, of a series of intense, painful shocks. In low stress conditions, the shocks were a barely perceptible tingle. Between the testing intervals, the subjects, all smokers, were free to smoke or not to smoke, as they pleased. In both studies, the subjects smoked considerably more in high than in low stress conditions.

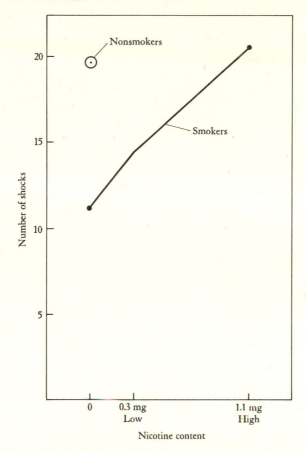

Figure 6.1. The effects of nicotine on tolerance of shock.

Turning to the effects of smoking on stress, we ask next if smoking reduces stress. The answer appears to be that it depends upon how you look at it. Silverstein (1976), in a modification of an experiment designed by Nesbitt (1973), attempted, within the context of a study of tactile perception, to answer the question by measuring how much electric shock a subject was willing to take. The procedure required that electrodes be attached to a subject's fingers, that he be exposed to a series of shocks of gradually increasing voltage, and that he report when he could first feel the shock, then when the shock first became painful, and finally when the shock became so painful that he could no longer bear it. Silverstein assumed that the more anxious and tense the subject, the less pain he would be willing to tolerate. There were four experimental groups—smokers who smoked high nicotine cigarettes during the experiment, those who smoked low nicotine cigarettes during the experiment, those who did not smoke at all during this time, and a group of nonsmokers who did not smoke.

The results of this experiment are presented in Figure 6.1. The ordinate plots the number of shocks the subjects endured before calling it quits. It is clear that smokers take more shocks when smoking high nicotine than when smoking low nicotine cigarettes, and they take the least number of shocks when not smoking. Given this pattern, one has a choice of interpretations: Either nicotine decreases anxiety, or lack of nicotine increases anxiety. The choice depends, of course, on the position of the group of nonsmokers—who, as can be seen in the figure, endured virtually the same number of shocks as smokers on high nicotine. It would appear, then, that smoking is not anxiety-reducing but, rather, that not smoking or insufficient nicotine is, for the heavy smoker, anxiety-increasing.

Precisely the same pattern of results emerged in an experimental study of irritability conducted by Perlick (1977). Within the context of a study of aircraft noise, subjects watching a television drama rated how loud and how annoying they found each of a series of simulated overflights. During the experimental session, heavy-smoking subjects were permitted to smoke at will high nicotine cigarettes in one condition, low nicotine cigarettes in another condition, and were prevented from smoking in a third condition. Finally, there was a control group of nonsmokers. The results are presented in Figure 6.2, where it can be seen that smokers on high nicotine cigarettes were markedly less irritated by this series of obnoxious noises than were smokers restricted to low nicotine cigarettes or prevented from smoking. However, these high nicotine smokers were neither less nor more irritated than the group of nonsmokers. Again, it would appear that smoking does not make the smoker less irritable or vulnerable to annoyance; it is nonsmoking or insufficient nicotine that makes him more irritable.

This same pattern appears to be characteristic of psychomotor as well as of emotional behavior. Heimstra, Bancroft, and DeKock (1967) examined the hypothesis that smoking facilitates driving performance by comparing ad-lib smokers with freedom to smoke at will, deprived smokers, and nonsmokers in a six-hour simulated driving test. On a variety of measures of tracking and vigilance, the ad-lib smokers did neither better nor worse than nonsmokers but did markedly better than deprived smokers.

Again and again, then, one finds the same pattern: Smoking does not

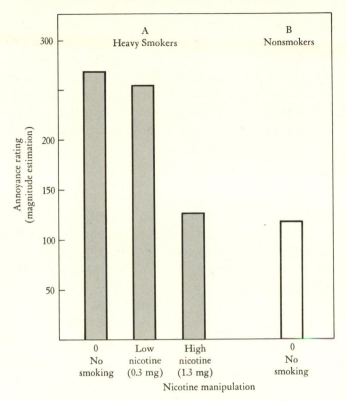

Figure 6.2. The effects of nicotine on irritability.

improve the mood or calm the smoker or improve his performance when compared with the nonsmoker. However, not smoking or insufficient nicotine make him considerably worse on all dimensions.[3] Given this persis-

3. There is, of course, one alternative interpretation of this consistent pattern. Rather than indicating withdrawal, it is conceivable that people who become smokers are by nature more frightened of shock, more irritated by noise, and worse drivers than people who never become smokers and that for such people smoking is indeed calming and does improve psychomotor performance. Though nothing short of a longitudinal study could unequivocally settle the matter, it should be noted that there have been a formidable number of studies that compared smokers and nonsmokers on virtually every personality dimension imaginable. Smith (1970), in his review of this extensive literature, concludes that the only variables that with reasonable consistency discriminate between smokers and nonsmokers are extroversion and antisocial tendencies. And even on these variables the differences are all quite small. To this writer, it seems particularly unlikely that selection, rather than withdrawal, can account for the numerous painful consequences of not smoking or inadequate nicotine,

tent fact, how, then, to account for the fact that the smoker smokes more when he is stressed? One can, obviously, account for the generally debilitating effects of no or low nicotine by assuming that the deprived smoker is in withdrawal, but this assumption alone cannot account for the effects of stress on smoking rate unless one assumes that stress in some way depletes the available supply of nicotine. And this hypothesis, of course, can account for this pattern of data only if the smoker, an addict, is smoking to keep nicotine at a constant level.

Nicotine as addiction

On the assumption that one manifestation of addiction is the regulation of nicotine intake, studies of the matter have either preloaded subjects with varying amounts of nicotine or have manipulated the nicotine content of the available cigarettes. Although the results of the many studies in this area are not wholly consistent (see Schachter [1977] for a review of the literature), the majority of studies do indicate that smokers will regulate nicotine, particularly if they are long-time, heavy smokers. A description of one study of such subjects will convey the magnitude of the effect. Schachter (1977) enlisted the cooperation of a group of subjects, all of whom had smoked a pack or more a day for at least nineteen years. For the course of the experiment, these subjects agreed to smoke only the experimenter's cigarettes, and on alternating weeks, each subject was presented with cartons of specially prepared and packaged cigarettes that contained either 1.3 mg of nicotine per cigarette or .3 mg of nicotine per cigarette. At bedtime the subjects noted the number of cigarettes smoked.

The effects of the nicotine manipulation are presented in Table 6.2. Obviously, the manipulation had a consistent effect on these long-time, heavy smokers; each of them smoked more low than high nicotine cigarettes. On the average, there was a 25 percent increase ($p < .01$) in smoking accompanying the manipulation of nicotine content.

It does appear, then, that heavy, long-time smokers do regulate nicotine. Given that the manipulation involved a fourfold difference in nicotine content, whereas smoking increased only 25 percent, it would appear to be at best a crude and imprecise regulation. There is, however, reason to be-

---

for to accept this interpretation requires that he concede that he was a thoroughly rotten, miserable human being before taking up smoking and would become so again were he to give up the habit.

Table 6.2. The effects of nicotine content on smoking

Subject characteristics					Smoking behavior (cigarettes per day)		
Subject	Age	Sex	Years as a serious smoker	Number of cigarettes per day (self-report)	Low nicotine (.3 mg)	High nicotine (1.3 mg)	Increase (%) (high to low)
J.A.	52	F	30	30	31.25	21.50	+45.3
S.S.	37	F	22	40	55.00	40.50	+35.8
R.R.	38	F	19	40	42.50	30.75	+38.2
R.S.	43	F	27	20	22.75	20.00	+13.8
D.R.	47	F	29	40–45	70.75	58.75	+20.4
R.A.	50	M	40	30	30.25	26.25	+15.2
J.E.	52	M	33	33	48.00	44.25	+ 8.5
Mean	45.6		28.6	33.6	42.93	34.57	+25.3

lieve that nicotine regulation is considerably more precise than these data suggest. First, several studies (Ashton and Watson, 1970; Herman, 1974; Schachter, Silverstein, and Perlick, 1977) report that smokers puff more at low than at high nicotine cigarettes—clearly a mechanism for increasing nicotine intake. Second, given the range of nicotine content in this study, precise regulation was virtually impossible. For example, a subject who normally smoked two packs a day of 1.3 mg nicotine cigarettes would have to smoke almost nine packs a day of our low nicotine cigarettes to get his customary dose of nicotine. Under these circumstances, virtually any theory of addiction would predict withdrawal for the subject on low nicotine cigarettes. Though unfortunately no systematic provision was made in this study to measure withdrawal, there is dramatic anecdotal evidence that the subjects who were the worst regulators in this study were in states of marked irritability and explosive emotionality while on the low nicotine cigarettes. Supporting this observation, Perlick (1977) and Silverstein (1976) have both demonstrated experimentally that heavy smokers on low nicotine cigarettes are markedly more anxious and irritable than such smokers on high nicotine cigarettes.

It does appear, then, that heavy smokers do adjust their smoking rate so as to keep nicotine at a roughly constant level. To account for this fact, one may suppose that there is an internal machine of sorts, one that detects the level of nicotine and regulates smoking accordingly. To begin consideration of the nature of such regulation, let us review some of the basic facts about the metabolic fate and excretion of nicotine. As summarized by Goodman and Gilman (1958):

> Nicotine is readily absorbed . . . from the oral and gastrointestinal mucosa and from the respiratory tract . . . nicotine is chemically altered in the body, mainly in the liver but also in the kidney and lung. The fraction of nicotine which escapes detoxication is completely eliminated as such in the urine along with the chemically altered forms. The rate of excretion of the alkaloid is rapid and increases linearly with the dose. . . . When the urine is alkaline, only one fourth as much nicotine is excreted as when the urine is acid; this is explained by the fact that nicotine base is reabsorbed from an alkaline urine. (p. 622)

The effect of the acidity, or pH, of the urine on the rate of excretion of unchanged nicotine suggests, given that smokers appear to regulate nicotine, that the pH of the urine may affect the rate of smoking. Whether an effect of any consequence is to be anticipated, however, depends on the proportion of unchanged nicotine that is excreted. One can make reasonably accurate estimates from the work of Beckett and his associates. Beckett, Rowland, and Triggs (1965) have shown that subjects who smoke twenty cigarettes a day excrete an average of 1.0 μg nicotine per minute under normal conditions, 5.0 μg nicotine per minute when the urine is made acidic by the oral administration of ammonium chloride, and 0.1 μg after oral administration of the alkalizer sodium bicarbonate. In another study, Beckett and Triggs (1967) have demonstrated that smokers whose urine has been maintained acidic excrete in unchanged form about 35 percent of known quantities of nicotine that have been administered either by intravenous injection, inhalation of nicotine vapor, or smoking. Putting these facts together, it appears reasonable to estimate that the proportion of nicotine that will be excreted in unchanged form will vary with the manipulated acidity of the urine, as follows: If the urine is acid, 35 percent of the nicotine will be excreted; if normal, 7 percent; and if alkaline, less than 1 percent.

Obviously, the exact proportions will vary with the precise pH of the urine. However, one thing seems clear: Given the quite low proportion of unchanged nicotine excreted under normal or placebo conditions, increasing the alkalinity of the urine can at best have trivial effects on plasma level nicotine, whereas increasing the acidity of the urine can have potentially substantial effects on plasma level nicotine. If, then, one assumes, first, that changes in urinary pH are reflected in circulating nicotine and, second, that the amounts smoked vary with changes in plasma level nicotine, it should be expected that experimentally increasing the acidity of the urine will increase the amounts smoked.

To test this guess, Schachter, Kozlowski, and Silverstein (1977) manipulated urinary pH in alternate weeks by administering to a group of thirteen smokers substantial daily doses of placebo or of the acidifying agents vitamin C (ascorbic acid) and acidulin (glutamic acid hydrochloride). The subjects were given cartons of their favorite cigarettes and kept count of the amount they had smoked each day of the study. The effects of these manipulations on smoking are presented in Table 6.3, where it can be seen that acidification is accompanied by increased smoking. During the period they were taking either of two different acidifying agents, subjects smoked 20 percent more cigarettes than during the time they were taking a corn starch placebo.

It should be specifically noted that, in keeping with the magnitude of the pharmacological effects (Beckett, Rowland, and Triggs, 1965; Beckett and Triggs, 1967; Haag and Larson, 1942), this 20 percent increase is not a particularly large effect. Judging from the work of Beckett and his colleagues on nicotine excretion, one would expect, at best, roughly a 30 percent increase in smoking with even a strongly effective acidifying manipulation, which ours was not. It seems clear that, of the body's two chief mechanisms for disposing of nicotine—enzymatic breakdown and urinary excretion of unchanged nicotine—urinary excretion plays by far the lesser role in the confirmed smoker. Nevertheless, acidification does affect smoking behavior, and this finding does at least raise the possibility that it may be useful to invoke this bit of pharmacological machinery in order to un-

Table 6.3. The effects of vitamin C, acidulin, and placebo on cigarette smoking

Condition	Cigarettes smoked per day	Mean percentage change from placebo
Vitamin C	26.7	+19.8
Placebo	23.1	—
Acidulin	28.1	+20.9

Comparison	Significance	
Vitamin C versus placebo	$p < .05$	$p < .05$
Acidulin versus placebo	$p < .01$	$p < .01$

derstand some of the presumed psychological and situational determinants of smoking rate. Conceivably, events that stimulate smoking may do so via their action on urinary pH.

In order to learn if this guess had any merit as a possible explanation of the stress-smoking relationship, Schachter, Silverstein, Kozlowski, Herman, and Liebling (1977) examined the effects of a variety of academic stressors on pH. In one study, subjects urinated immediately before an obviously stressful event, such as delivering a colloquium lecture or taking Ph.D. oral or comprehensive examinations. And for control purposes, these same subjects urinated at precisely the same time on routine, non-stressful days. The results are presented in Table 6.4, where it can be seen that for nine of ten subjects the urine is considerably more acidic on stressful than on control days.

Precisely the same pattern is manifest in another study of the effects of stress (Schachter, Silverstein, and Perlick, 1977). Nine of the twenty members of an undergraduate seminar were assigned to read highly technical material and prepare ten- to fifteen-minute oral reports for class. The remaining students were simply expected to listen to the reports. All of the students urinated shortly before class. For the reporters, pH averaged 6.01 and for the listeners 6.67 ($p < 0.05$). Before a control class, pH was

Table 6.4. The effects of academic stress on urinary pH

Subject	Stress day	Control day	Stress-control
A. Colloquium talk			
E.G.	5.50	6.35	− .85
H.T.	5.70	5.95	− .25
M.C.	6.70	6.90	− .20
H.K.	5.50	6.20	− .70
S.S.	5.40	6.45	−1.05
B. Ph.D. oral defense			
E.D.	5.40	7.10	−1.70
A.L.	6.00	6.20	− .20
C. Ph.D. comprehensive examination			
B.S.	5.85	5.80	+ .05
I.S.	5.20	5.70	− .50
D.P.	5.40	5.70	− .30
All subjects (mean)	5.67	6.24	− .57

identical for the two groups of students. It does appear that stress, at least of the sort endemic to academic life, acidifies the urine, a finding that at least encourages the exploration of a pharmacological interpretation of smoking behavior.

To review the line of argument so far: It has been widely reported that smoking increases with stress and that smoking is calming—observations that appear to go hand in hand and to support the assertion that nicotine or tar or some component of the act of smoking is anxiety-reducing. The experimental facts are peculiarly at variance with this interpretation. Smoking does indeed increase with stress, but smoking smokers are neither more nor less calm than a control group of nonsmokers. They are, however, considerably calmer than groups of smokers who are either prevented from smoking or permitted to smoke only low nicotine cigarettes. This fact can be interpreted not as indicating that smoking is anxiety-reducing but as showing that not smoking or insufficient nicotine is anxiety-increasing. In effect, the smoker smokes more during stress because of budding withdrawal symptoms and not because of any psychological property of nicotine or of the act of smoking. Such an interpretation is plausible if one assumes that the smoker smokes in order to keep nicotine at some constant level and that there is something about the state of stress that depletes the body's supply of nicotine. A variety of studies have been described that, via the effects of urinary pH on the rate of nicotine excretion, suggest a biochemical mechanism that could account for this set of facts.

Although this elegant juxtaposition of facts makes almost irresistible the conclusion that the smoker's mind is in the bladder, obviously we are hardly yet in a position to rule out psychological explanations of smoking. Though "anxiety reduction" seems, by now, a particularly unsatisfactory explanation of the stress-smoking relationship, innumerable other purely psychological explanations are still conceivable. Ferster (1970), for example, has attempted to explain the relationship in these terms:

> With the increase in emotional symptoms there is frequently a major cessation in most of the ongoing repertoire the person might engage in. With such a temporary decrease in the frequency in most of the items in a person's repertoire, the relative importance of even the minor reinforcers increases enormously. Thus, the relative position of smoking in the entire repertoire is increased considerably when other major items of the repertoire are depressed. Smoking becomes something to do when no other behavior is appropriate. (p. 99)

In short, although the effect of pH on nicotine elimination is a well-established pharmacological fact, it may have little if anything to do with the effects of stress on smoking, for it is certainly conceivable that stress, with or without accompanying pH changes, will affect smoking rate. In order to learn if pH changes are a necessary and sufficient explanation of the stress-smoking relationship, it is clear that we must experimentally pit the mind against the bladder. This Schachter, Silverstein, and Perlick (1977) attempted to do in an experiment that independently manipulated stress and the pH of the urine. If it is correct that pH changes are a necessary part of the machinery, we should expect more smoking in high than in low stress conditions when pH is uncontrolled and no difference between the two conditions when pH is experimentally stabilized. If, on the other hand, pH changes are irrelevant to the smoking-stress relationship, there should be more smoking in high than in low stress conditions no matter what the state of the urine.

In this study, too, stress was manipulated by use of electric shock. In fact, the experiment already described on the relationship of stress to smoking (Schachter, Silverstein et al., 1977) was replicated with one major modification. In one pair of conditions, the high or low stress manipulation began fifty minutes after subjects took a placebo; in the other conditions, fifty minutes after subjects had taken 3 grams of bicarbonate of soda—an agent virtually guaranteed to quickly elevate urinary pH and to stabilize it for a time at highly alkaline levels. Checking first on the effectiveness of the manipulations, I note that in the two placebo conditions, pH decreased in the high stress condition and remained the same in the low stress condition. In the two bicarbonate conditions, in sharp contrast, pH increased markedly from the beginning to the end of the experiment, and the stress manipulation had absolutely no effect on pH.

Next, I note that, on a variety of self-report measures, the manipulation of stress was highly successful in both the placebo and the bicarbonate conditions. Obviously, then, the conditions necessary to pit the psychological against the pharmacological explanation of the effects of stress on smoking have been established. Subjects in high stress conditions are considerably more tense than are subjects in low stress conditions, whether they have taken a placebo or bicarbonate. In the placebo conditions in which pH is uncontrolled, however, stress acidifies, whereas in the bicarbonate conditions, it does not.

The effects of these manipulations on smoking are presented in Figure 6.3, which plots the mean number of puffs taken by subjects in each

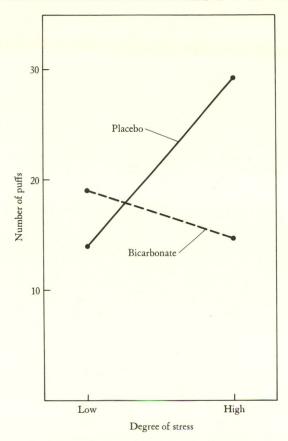

Figure 6.3. The effects of sodium bicarbonate
and placebo on smoking under stress.

condition once the stress manipulation had begun. It is clear that with the placebo there is considerably more smoking in high than in low stress conditions, whereas with bicarbonate, stress has no effect on smoking (interaction $p < .01$). It does appear, then, that smoking under stress has little to do with psychological, sensory, or manipulative needs that are presumably activated by the state of stress, but is explained by the effects of stress on the rate of excretion of nicotine. The smoker under stress smokes to replenish nicotine supply, not to relieve anxiety.

Given the facts in Figure 6.3, one is faced with a formidable question that, reduced to essentials, is this: So where is psychology? What's with the oral dependency needs or the habit strength or the misattribution if, as seems to be the case for stress, it all depends on the hydrogen ion concentration in the urine? Obviously, this has been an openly reductionist attempt to explain some of the effects of psychological variables without making use of the conceptual equipment of psychology. I believe that in the case of stress the attempt has been successful, for, given the facts outlined, attempts to formulate the stress-smoking relationship in terms of oral dependency needs (Marcovitz, 1969) or of attribution theory (Nesbitt, 1973; Schachter, 1973) or of learning theory (Ferster, 1970; Hunt, 1970) seem unnecessary, ad hoc constructions. Smoking increases under stress because that is the way the biological machine is built, and it makes as much sense to ask psychodynamically, cognitively, or situationally why smoking increases under stress as it would to ask why psychologically the car speeds up when I press on the accelerator.

Reprise

I have presented in some detail three case studies which have compared biological and social science approaches to a particular behavior or pattern of behavior. These behaviors obviously differ in the specificity and certainty with which one can identify biological causation, but they share a common history. They are all instances of the persistent tendency in the social sciences to interpret, psychologically and functionally, behaviors and maladies which appear to be more efficiently understood in purely biological, even mechanical terms. This tendency is by now an old story in medical psychology. It is a history that, I suspect, will be repeated in social and personality psychology. Even now, it doesn't seem too farfetched to suggest that much of what we consider interpersonal relations—the hatreds, passions, loves, aggressions, and anxieties—may in time be better understood in biochemical than psychological terms. Who hasn't observed a friend slip into or out of a depression? Who hasn't watched in surprise as he himself exploded in anger or euphoria without suspecting that there was something more "glandular" than situationally induced in these reactions? And, indeed, there are medical oddities such as the Lesch-Nyhan syndrome—a condition in which extreme interpersonal hostility as well as self-mutilation is apparently caused by the absence of a single enzyme, hypoxanthine-quanine phosphoribosyl transferase. As yet, no one claims the slightest insight into the relationship between the absence of transferase and this bizarre behavior, but there appears to be no question that the two are associated. I should note this is much the same level of ignorance we are faced with in our understanding of Tourette syndrome. Just why an excess of dopamine should lead to compulsive cursing or to an echoing tic is a complete mystery.

The fact that, despite our ability to implicate a guilty biochemical, we have barely scratched at an understanding of these maladies makes it clear that we're a long way from the encyclopedic utopia that a reductionistic approach to behavior demands before it becomes considerably more than a statement of scientific faith. Nevertheless, even in these early stages of comprehension, the simple assignment of a phenomenon to biological or psychological causation of itself can have profound consequences. In the case of Tourette syndrome, it is evident that the attribution to psychological causation led to decades of painfully ineffective psychotherapy. As for smoking, it may well be that the attribution to psychological causation is responsible for increasing the health hazards of the habit. The gist of the antismoking campaign is simply "Quit, and if you can't or won't quit, switch to a low-nicotine, low-tar cigarette." With the backing of the American Cancer Society, the Royal College of Physicians, and the Public Health Service, this message pervades the mass media and appears to be responsible for the tedious competition among tobacco companies for the safest cigarette, the search for an acceptable tobacco-free cigarette stimulated by the British government, and taxation policies such as that of New York City, which at one time taxed cigarettes by nicotine and tar content in an apparent effort to use economic muscle in order to help the smoker help himself. It's a fair guess that, in good part, the low-nicotine and tar campaign is based on the notion that cigarette smoking stems from a variety of psychological, sensory, and manipulative needs, which can probably be as well satisfied with a low as with a high nicotine cigarette.

As we have seen, however, there is evidence that nicotine is addicting and that the smoker, an addict, is probably smoking to keep nicotine or one of its active metabolites at some optimal level. If, then, the heavy smoker does switch to low nicotine brands, he may very well end up smoking more cigarettes and taking more puffs of each. He will, in the process of regulating nicotine, probably get the same amounts of nicotine and tar, and depending on cigarette construction, probably get more of gases such as carbon monoxide, which appears to be at least as much of a medical villain as tar or nicotine in that it is implicated in the increased risk to smokers of arteriosclerosis, ischaemic heart disease, fetal damage, and so on (Surgeon General's Report, 1972; Larson, Haag, and Silvette, 1961). If this shift in level of smoking is permanent, the net effect of switching to low nicotine cigarettes could well be to increase the dangers of smoking. From this point of view, the concerned smoker should smoke high, not low, nicotine cigarettes.

It is evident, then, that the attribution of a phenomenon to biological or psychological causation is of more than academic interest. It has major practical, as well as theoretical, consequences.

One final word. Since I assume that it is obvious that I am drawn to the possibilities of biological reductionism, I should emphasize that I am aware of the importance of psychological and situational factors; in fact, much of my work (Schachter, 1971) has been concerned with specifying the interaction of cognitive, social, and physiological determinants of emotional and appetitive behaviors of various sorts. I confess, however, that the results of my research on smoking have left me with an abiding fascination with the possibilities, even now, of a largely reductionistic approach to social and behavioral phenomena. There is something perversely satisfying about reducing a presumably complex behavior to the pH of the urine. Other than its titillation value, however, I suspect that the reductionistic approach has the potential, even now, of providing major insights into problems and areas that have seemed the exclusive province of social scientists and humanists—particularly, I anticipate, in one quite surprising direction: the understanding of aberrant mass phenomena. Since this is the area in which, to my mind, the efforts of social science have been almost totally unsatisfying (has there yet been a psychological, sociological, or historic analysis of Nazi Germany that made this period of human insanity comprehensible?), I have a cautious optimism about the possibilities of a biological approach to some mass phenomena. My optimism is based on the truism that we all breathe the same air, drink the same water, eat similar food, smoke similar cigarettes, and so on. If something biological changes or goes wrong, it can affect all or most of a population. When fluorine is added to a community's water, willy-nilly, everyone increases fluorine intake, and whatever the effects of this substance, they will be virtually universal within that community. When a large portion of an addicted population is attempting to quit smoking or switches to low nicotine brands, a very large number of people in that population will be in withdrawal. Given what we know of withdrawal, this means large numbers of people simultaneously in a state of irritability, irascibility, short temper, and so on. One could with reason anticipate high rates of divorce, assault, and general mayhem in such a population. This order of speculation is related just enough to such flaky speculative efforts as the impact of atmospheric ionization on mood or of lead poisoning on the demise of Rome to leave one somewhat uneasy, but perhaps the reader will agree that as yet sobriety has been the major virtue of more orthodox approaches to mass phenomena.

7

Social Comparison:
The Process of Self-evaluation

JEROME E. SINGER

How people form and develop attitudes, values, beliefs, and opinions is a genuinely interesting question. There are only a few possible general answers; most of the specifics are theme and variation upon them. One of the most popular answers involves innate mechanisms: Somehow, people are born with a self-contained capacity or template for judgments about their interactions with the larger world. When the fairy tale princess was unable to sleep, it was because it is part of the nature of princesses to be disturbed by provocations that those of us with mundane natures do not even notice.

In Western civilization up to the mid-nineteenth century, innate dispositions were often credited to a supernatural or religious origin—a divine spark or conscience. The rise of positivism and the social Darwinism of the late 1800s separated divine implantation from essential human nature, but found in the instinct a construct which could keep innate beliefs a feasible concept while not contravening the secularism of the newly developing social sciences. In his pioneering work on social psychology, McDougall (1908) founded his description of the entire field on the instinct concept, and his formulation was echoed by many others in a short time (cf. Allport, 1968).

But the concept of instinct had its critics as well as its proponents. Many scholars, of the tradition of the English and Scottish moral philosophers and even earlier, had depicted man as a creature akin to a *tabula rasa,* upon whom the environment works its will and creates the human cognitive superstructure. L. L. Bernard highlighted the untenability of simple instinct theory in his classic studies (1926, 1934), paving the way for the near-universal acceptance of environmental factors, social and physical, in molding human attitudes and beliefs.

But for a number of years, environmental explanations of belief formation proved as global and unsatisfyingly undetailed as the more complicated instinct theories had been. The mechanisms by which attitudes were formed were often murky and nonspecific. Even the developing stimulus-response theories initiated in the rising tide of behaviorism faced problems which seemed insurmountable. It was easy enough to demonstrate how social reinforcement could create attitudes in children which matched the attitudes of their parents or their play groups. It was difficult to account for so many instances in which people differed markedly or were totally deviant from the groups, family or otherwise, which presumably shaped their other beliefs.

The aims of this chapter are not global. It will not attempt to revise or resolve classic problems in nature versus nurture, nor will it extensively redescribe materials which are available in the primary literature. Rather, it will explore a selective history of one subproblem: By what processes do individuals evaluate their abilities and confirm the correctness of their new opinions? All of us have a large number of opinions, attitudes, beliefs, and values. Many of these are long-enduring and have roots that stretch back into childhood. Indeed, for most of us, it is impossible to remember when we didn't root for the White Sox or dislike cauliflower. Unfortunately, a cortex full of stable beliefs is not sufficient for an ever-changing world. We must choose what to believe in and value on a day-to-day basis. What neighborhood is desirable to live in? Who to blame for an oil shortage? Which rock group is worth listening to? All of these questions require, at least in part, a somewhat novel decision—a new set of beliefs.

Human belief systems have one striking characteristic. They are all true. They may be incorrect—my opinion that saccharine intake is unrelated to cancer of the bladder may be belied by the facts—but my beliefs are true for me at the time I hold them. I may hold some beliefs with more certainty than others, and may cease to believe some, but I never knowingly believe something which is false. If, then, I am about to make a judgment or voice an opinion about a novel event, person, or thing, how do I decide if my newly formed opinion (either *viva* or *sub voce*) is correct? How do I become certain? How do I change my mind and initial judgment? Similarly, how do I judge my own abilities? How do I decide how good a tennis player I am, or whether I'm repairing my car correctly? Much of the last four decades of social psychology has focused on answers to this question. We shall look at one of them, our best answer to date: the theory of social comparison.

This chapter is organized in rough chronological fashion, with a detour or two as needed. First, we will look at the temper of the late thirties, with several streams of research beginning to examine belief evaluation. From this we will proceed to the immediate background of social comparison in the pressures to uniformity studies. This will be followed by a brief look at social comparison itself, followed first by direct evidence for the theory—experiments directed at the propositions themselves—then by indirect evidence—studies in support of extensions and derivations from the theory. Finally, the chapter will conclude with a brief look at several nagging problems in the theory which raise issues for future research.

Early studies of social influence

In 1931, Gardner and Lois Murphy published *Experimental Social Psychology*. The book was a benchmark in reviewing the field up to that time. Yet its answers to the question of social influence do not seem at all appropriate to our current state of knowledge. In the section on the individual, there is a heavy emphasis on classical conditioning and suggestibility; in the section on groups, the theme of competition and cooperation is dominant. Systematic experimental studies of "social influence"—a term which in any of its synonyms does not appear in the Murphys' index—and their concomitant theories did not appear until the end of the decade.

There developed, at first, three lines of study of social influence: 1. Newcomb's investigation of the competing influences of family and college climates and its development into the mostly sociological study of reference groups; 2. Sherif's explorations of the development of norms around the autokinetic effect; and 3. the development of group dynamics and field theory by Kurt Lewin and his colleagues and its elaboration into social comparison theory.

Reference groups

Newcomb's Bennington study (1943) is rightly considered a classic in social psychology. Framed as a field study rather than as an experiment, it was addressed to a question of both theoretical interest and practical import: When people's social milieus possess differing values and opinions, how do they shape their own beliefs—with whom do they agree and differ? Newcomb explored this issue by following the college careers of the students at Bennington College. These girls, mostly from well-to-do, politically conservative homes, were living in a community where most of the faculty and older students were somewhat amaterialistic and politically liberal. A majority of the Bennington students became progressively more liberal over their careers, but some did not. Newcomb was able to relate the student's ultimate political orientation to the group she identified with—liberal, if she thought of herself as foremost a member of the campus community; conservative, if her primary identification was with her family. Newcomb's study of the dynamics of opinion stability and change under cross-pressures blossomed into and merged with the study of "reference groups"—a term later coined by Herbert Hyman (1942). The study of reference groups has, over the years, drifted into the sociological wing of social psychology. Although there have been occasional experimental studies of reference groups (cf. Siegel and Siegel [1957]) and some additional psychological development, such as Kelley's (1952) distinction between a reference group's normative and comparative functions, reference group theory and application have become primarily associated with symbolic interactionist theories of social development and explanations of survey research derived relationships. The study of how a group shapes an individual's opinion has gradually ceased to be a major research question in this tradition.

Norm development

In the mid-thirties, Muzafer Sherif (1935) ingeniously adapted the perceptual phenomenon of the autokinetic effect to the study of how norms develop—that is, how people come to form coherent, shared beliefs about novel events. It had long been known that a fixed point of light, when viewed under certain circumstances, appears to move spontaneously, i.e., perceived autokinesis. Sherif's innovation was to employ the effect to create a novel, anomalous stimulus in an otherwise routine world. When Sherif asked people, alone or in groups, to make judgments about the amount of light "movement," he could make controlled assessments of the ways in which social influence enables people to arrive at stable judgments about their world. Sherif's subjects, when tested in groups, coalesced in their judgments. They agreed on the amount of movement. This norm persisted even on subsequent individual testing. There were two major points of the studies. One was to establish that judgments and opinions which seem to be entirely our own are shaped, in part, by the judgments of others. The second was to demonstrate that interpersonal influence is not necessarily manipulative or pernicious but rather a natural and helpful part of the process by which we evaluate our environment. Sherif's studies provide an effective complement to Newcomb's investigations. Newcomb's studies were about important values and beliefs shaped among close friends and family on a continuing basis. Sherif sacrificed these real world linkages to obtain precise laboratory control of a variety of variables to examine how new beliefs are molded.

Field theory and the Lewinian group

At heart, the problems examined by Newcomb and Sherif were ones of intrapersonal dynamics. As a person is confronted with new situations, events, or issues, how does he or she find an anchor point? One line of theory and research which led to an examination of this question was that of Kurt Lewin and his colleagues. When Lewin came to this country in the 1930s, he brought with him a good, practical theory for studying motivated social behavior (1935, 1936). At Iowa, and later at M.I.T. and Michigan, the rather abstract notions of life-space, region, and tension were converted into concrete experimental studies of level of aspiration and group decision. Both of these areas can be considered precursors of the Lewinian-based exploration of the central problem: How do people evaluate their beliefs and abilities?

The Lewinian theories were conceived as models of the dynamics of an individual's learning, motivation, and personality. These topics were interwoven in the theories and not segmented into separate concerns, as is the fashion of introductory textbooks. The key features of the theories were an emphasis on the ways in which an individual represented the world in his own cognitive system. The individual's present status, beliefs, goals, desires, needs, and tasks were all among the elements denoted in the regions of his internal representation of life space. If, for a particular ability, the person's judgment of his current performance was in one region and the person's goal for a desired performance was in another, a tension between the two regions was established. One of the interests of Lewin and his associates was the exploration of how such tensions were relieved or resolved. One type of study particularly well suited to these theoretical issues was that of level of aspiration (e.g., Lewin, Dembo, Festinger, and Sears [1944]). By studying a specific belief—that of how well people thought they should perform on a specific, usually novel, task—the Lewinians started to examine several of the required evaluation processes—how people's performances are affected by their expectations, by other people's performances, and by other people's judgments of the subjects' performances.

During the Second World War, the Lewinian group entered into a phase of action research—studies to alleviate a social problem or issue, in this case the war effort. One of the problems they addressed was that of switching housewives' (and, perforce, through a gatekeeper mechanism, their families) food-buying preferences away from scarce foodstuffs to those more readily available. The series of studies on group decision explored the most effective ways to modify people's attitudes and behaviors—for example, to make them choose to buy, serve, and eat kidneys, liver, and sweetbreads instead of steaks, roasts, and chops. The theoretical Lewinian perspective focused on induced motivation, setting up tension systems which could be relieved by the person's decision to modify her own opinion and her behaviors concordantly. The mechanisms employed were those of group discussion, conjoint decisions to alter beliefs and behaviors, and public commitment to those decisions. Some later studies (e.g., Bennett [1955]) in this area attempted to identify the relative contributions of the several factors involved in the reevaluation and change of an attitude, whether it is the decision to eat sweetbreads and kidneys or the decision to volunteer for experiments. Among the issues made salient by the group decision studies were those involving the role of a group of similar people in shaping and inducing opinion formation and change in an individual. Both kinds of studies—level of aspiration and group decisions—derived from Lewin's general theories and raised, in nascent form, the problems to be directly studied in the self-evaluation theories to follow.

The background of social comparison

After the Research Center for Group Dynamics was established at M.I.T., some of its members conducted a study of a married student housing project at that university (Festinger, Schachter, and Back [1950]). The housing project, started shortly after the close of the Second World War, was populated by veterans and their families just returning to civilian life. The residents were relatively homogeneous with respect to age, educational background, and immediately previous experience. Festinger, Schachter, and Back observed, interviewed, and conducted field experiments among the residents of two parts of the housing project and analyzed how friendships grew and developed. The monograph reporting on their findings, *Social Pressures in Informal Groups: A Study in Human Factors in Housing,* deals extensively with architectual and spatial factors in friendship formation. However, as the title implies, the authors were concerned with a broader set of issues—in particular, the ways in which the members of an informal group acquire similar beliefs and opinions.

One part of the housing project, Westgate, was composed of residences arranged in a series of courts. The courts were ranked in terms of how cohesive or attractive to their members they were. The greater the proportion of friends the residents had within their own court, the more cohesive the court was deemed to be. During the school year, several minor crises occurred in Westgate, and a tenants' council was formed. The residents had a variety of opinions and participation rates in the organization. The modal evaluation in each court was ascertained, and the courts were ranked in terms of the percentage of deviant attitudes each contained. The finding which intrigued the investigators was a correlation of −0.74 between these two rank orders. That is, the more people relied on their court for their friendships, the more unanimity of opinion existed within that court. The friendships had been formed and measured before the issue of the tenant council arose, so that the authors concluded that something about friendship groups and social cohesiveness brought about this homogeneity of opinion. Although they did not then use the term, Festinger, Schachter, and Back developed a theory of "pressures to uniformity," which was elaborated in a coordinated series of follow-up studies which further framed the theory.

There are two basic classes of reasons why people are attracted to a group. One class is that of group goals, or more precisely, the goals the group mediates for the individual. Most of our activities, from sports to politics to work, require the presence or cooperation of other people. At least an informal group is needed to coordinate and make possible a tennis game or a PTA. The more a group facilitates a person's goals, the more the person will be attracted to the group. As issues arise that are relevant to the members' goals, there will be pressure on the individuals to agree. Partners have to agree on a morning or afternoon schedule before a tennis game can be arranged; parents must come to an agreement on educational objectives before they can pressure their school on "back to basics." The factors involved in moderating this source of pressures to uniformity are not too difficult to lay out: the importance of the group goal to the individual, the presence or absence of alternative groups, the relevance of the issue to the goal. All of these will affect the pressure on each group member to come to agreement with the others.

The other class of reasons producing pressures to uniformity of opinions was labeled "social reality" and was the immediate predecessor of social comparison. Festinger et al. (1950) argued that people who wish to validate a belief can get a direct test of it by subjecting that belief to physical reality. This is a strategy which will work for either opinions about the world or opinions about oneself. So, if I believe it is raining outside, I can test this by going out; if I believe I can play "The Flight of the Bumblebee" on the bagpipes, I can subject this to a physical test. There are some beliefs, however, for which there are no physical tests. These range from the belief that there is a God to any of a series of "Had I but known" opinions. Other beliefs may be subject to a physical test that I would be loath to undertake, such as my opinion that a particular mushroom is poisonous. In order to validate these latter type of beliefs, people have to employ social reality—validation by the consensus agreement of other people. Although there are some definitional ambiguities in establishing the exact margins of the physical and social reality concepts—is the encyclopedia a physical reality?—the basic difference between them is clear.

Given that people need social reality, from whom should they get it? In the concluding chapter of their monograph, Festinger, Schachter, and Back persuasively argue that members of a cohesive group—that is, one to which the members are attracted and to some degree bound—are precisely the ones on whom a person will rely for social reality. If all members of the group have beliefs on the same topic or issue, then all will come with the desire to have the others provide social reality, and the group's pressures to uniformity will be increased.

During the early fifties, a variety of studies on the pressures to uniformity were conducted. Some explored the question of how the pressures are resolved, how uniformity is achieved. If a person desires to obtain social reality for an opinion from a group composed of people with diverse opinions, he has only three options. He can persuade others to his view by communication; he can modify his view to match theirs; or he can psychologically reject those with widely diverse opinions by redefining the group and not considering it as appropriate for defining social reality. In simplified terms, the theory can be illustrated by a hydraulic model, as shown in Figure 7.1.

The contents of the cistern represent the pressures to uniformity. There are two sources of input, group goals and social reality. As the flow from either or both increases, the pressures increase. So, if a person's attraction to the group, for whatever reason, increases, that person should have a higher need to obtain social reality from the group, and raising the level of pressures to uniformity from that source should increase the total residual pressures. Correspondingly, if an issue being discussed should become more relevant to the group's goal or purpose, the flow from that source to pressures to uniformity should increase. There are three spigots for releasing the pressures, any one or combination of which may be effective. Once again, the members of a group can reach uniformity either by communicating to change other people's opinions, changing their own opinions, or rejecting divergent others as appropriate reference points. As uniformity is approached by any or all of these mechanisms, the pressures are reduced.

Schachter (1951) demonstrated the intersubstitutability of the three relief mechanisms. He also verified that if the belief being evaluated is made more relevant to the group goal, pressures to uniformity will be increased; and if the group is made more attractive, increasing the need for social reality, again pressures will be increased. Back (1951) showed that increasing the group's attractiveness increased pressures to uniformity, irrespective of whether the increased attraction was caused by interpersonal attraction, money, or fame. Festinger and Thibaut (1951) demonstrated that heterogeneous groups are more likely than homogeneous groups to utilize rejection as a method of achieving uniformity. They also confirmed that pressures to uniformity will increase to the extent to which an issue is not anchored in other beliefs outside the group's purview. And when pressures increase, all three ways of achieving uniformity—changing own opinion, communication, and rejection—also increase. Festinger, Gerard, Hymovitch, Kelley, and Raven (1952) predicted and found the intriguing result that in a group with a spread of opinions, extremely deviant members reject the group before the group rejects them. These brief mentions are not intended to be a thorough review of the pressures to uniformity literature but rather to indicate that the model is well studied and documented. Much of this evidence is summarized in review articles (Festinger, 1950) or in texts dealing with the topic (Jones and Gerard, 1967).

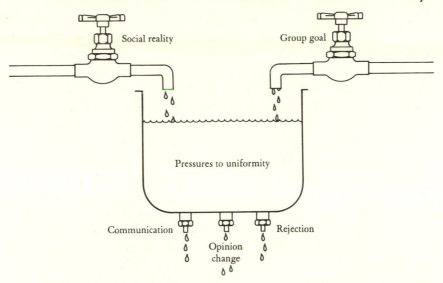

Figure 7.1. A hydraulic model of pressures to uniformity.

Social comparison

Despite the extent of confirmatory evidence for the pressures to uniformity theory, some aspects were more strongly supported than others. Most of the mediating variables in the model could be independently checked apart from the outcomes they produced. Cohesiveness, the net attraction to the group, is measurable. So, too, in principle, is the relevance of the issue to the group's task. In fact, it is possible to conceive of an empirical check on the status of almost any of the variables in the model except the desire or need for social reality. The experimenter can manipulate factors that can be reasonably expected to increase the desire for social reality, and he can then measure the consequences of the expected increase in pressures to uniformity. The evidence for the involvement of social reality is indirect and inferential.

In addition, the pressures to uniformity model is basically a group model. Certainly the group goal source of the pressures requires an issue of relevance to more than just one person seeking clarity about a particular opinion. We achieve social reality by getting the consensus of a group to which we are attracted. But even here the issue seems to depend on some sort of relevance. There is no clear reason to expect that my daily car pool to work, a very cohesive group, is necessarily the optimal, or even the appropriate one for providing social reality about my opinions of the qualifications of the various presidential candidates. Or another example: My family may be a highly cohesive group and an excellent source of social reality for my belief that Cape Cod is the best place for a summer vacation, but they can hardly validate my belief that increased newspaper advertising is the most effective way to increase my company's sales.

A more direct attack on the problem of self-evaluation appeared with the exposition of the theory of social comparison processes (Festinger, 1954). The theory explains the details of the motivations and mechanisms by which a person uses other people as clarifiers, evaluators, shapers, and modifiers of his opinions and abilities. The original article was written in the hypothetico-deductive style of exposition widely employed by psychological theorists in the early fifties; it consists of a series of nine hypotheses and an associated set of about a dozen corollaries and derivations. The heart of the theory is the first hypothesis, "There exists, in the human organism, a drive to evaluate his opinions and his abilities." The postulation of the drive differed from the antecedent use of social reality in three ways. It was clearer and more explicit, it encompassed abilities as well as opinions, and it shifted the focus of attention from the group to the individual.

Other postulates developed the theory along the same general lines as pressures to uniformity. A physical standard is the preferred basis of evaluation, but in its absence, comparison with others is used. In those cases where neither a physical nor a social standard is available, a person's self-evaluation will be unstable. When a person compares his opinions and abilities with others, he will choose and get the most stable evaluation from those whose opinions and abilities are close to his. People will be attracted to people and groups which agree with them, will feel less confident of their beliefs when the comparison groups disagree, and will seek to resolve divergencies.

One section of the social comparison article (Festinger, 1954) dealt with the distinctions between abilities and opinions and their implications. For most opinions, the spectrum of possible views has no "better" or "worse" side. For abilities, at least in our contemporary competitive culture, there is a clear better and worse, and Festinger postulated that there exists a unidirectional upward push for people to be better on any ability; they wish to be better than those with whom they compare. For an opinion, the only pressure is to be right, i.e., in as exact agreement as possible with comparison persons. In general, whether it is opinion or ability being evaluated, a person should proceed by a progression of gross and fine tuning. The gross tuning is the same for both cases: selecting comparison people who are roughly of the same general level as we are. Thus, we would evaluate our opinion of publicly funded abortions for rape victims with those who generally agree with us on abortion. We would evaluate our skill in tennis with those whose playing ability is roughly the same; it is not too simple for us to beat them or for them to beat us. Having chosen a comparison person or group and found that their opinions or abilities are in rough agreement with ours, how do we achieve that evaluative or validating consensus? Through the means developed by pressures to uniformity: communication, change of one's own position, or rejection.

The fine tuning of opinion comparison involves all three of these processes, but for abilities, the actual mechanics are somewhat altered by the fact that abilities are not as malleable. While it is possible to shift one's opinion to, say, the more liberal or more conservative end of the political spectrum, it is not possible either to improve one's abilities or to demand or persuade others to modify their skills. Of course, there is always the special case such as a child learning a game who, by playing an accommodating and indulgent adult, validates a spuriously high skill level. And of course, for whatever reason, a person can always lower his skill level to match a comparison group's. While there are no social comparison studies testing this point, there is an experiment deriving from cognitive dissonance which suggests that there are some occasions on which people do lower their abilities to match a norm (Aronson and Carlsmith, 1962). In general, then, although the processes of fine tuning opinions by social comparison are the same as for pressures to uniformity, the fine tuning of ability by social comparison should be somewhat different—only rejection functioning in a similar fashion for both cases. Twenty-five years later, there still has not been a direct experimental test of this difference.

Evidence for social comparison

Social comparison theory was supported in its initial presentation by two kinds of evidence: a reanalysis of studies conducted previously for other purposes and experimental tests deriving from the theory. The studies done previously are an interesting set. Not surprisingly, a good number of them are from the pressures to uniformity literature. Experiments by Hochbaum (1954), Festinger et al. (1952), Festinger, Schachter, and Back (1950), Back (1951), Festinger and Thibaut (1951), Gerard (1953), and Schachter (1951) were all cited and moderately reinterpreted in support of the theory. Other areas of social psychology were also presented as evidence. Early studies of competition, a wide variety of level of aspiration studies, and one of the autokinetic effect are listed in the theory's documentation. Shortly after, the development of reference group theory began to incorporate and consider social comparison within its own framework. These lines of convergence are presaged in early reference group works (Hyman, 1942; Merton and Kitt, 1950), and are more fully developed in recent writings on the topic (Hyman, 1968).

Direct evidence for social comparison

The presentation of the theory was accompanied by three experiments designed and executed specifically to test the theory. Since most of the opinion derivations could be buttressed by previous studies, the new studies addressed the issues of ability evaluation. A study by Dreyer (1954) tested a series of elementary school children on a task involving the sorting of playing cards. On a repeated number of trials, one group was led to believe that their performance was markedly superior to that of their classmates; another group was led to believe that they were of average ability; and a third group was led to believe that their performance was substantially inferior. By asking the children to evaluate their abilities, to rate their confidence in their evaluations, and to decide whether they wanted to continue for yet more trials, Dreyer was able to explore and verify several of the social comparison propositions. For instance, the average group had the most confidence in their ratings of their own abilities, and their ratings were the most stable. In addition, even though the experimental arrangement was similar to that employed in years past by the level of aspiration studies, some of the predicted and obtained social comparison outcomes were contrary to what level of aspiration would predict: The group of children much better than average—that is, the group getting little comparative information—was the first group to stop working on the task, although level of aspiration theory would have predicted that they would have persevered longest. Similar confirmations were obtained by Hoffman, Festinger, and Lawrence (1954). They conducted a study in which two subjects and a confederate of the experimenter engaged in a tripartite test of intelligence. The confederate, who always jumped out with a unique advantage, was presented in half the cases as someone incomparably superior to the subjects. In the other half, he was presented as someone comparable to the subjects. When he was comparable, the subjects coalesced against him in an effort to bring their scores up to his. When he had special qualifications, i.e., was not a source of comparison, the subjects ignored his advantage and competed with each other. A third study by Festinger, Torrey, and Willerman (1954) tested some of the derivations relating to social comparison in groups of differential attractiveness.

Once again, the aim here is not to review all the evidence for social comparison but rather to point out the wide variety of evidence, direct and reinterpreted, which accompanied the presentation of the theory. Surprisingly, in the next decade there was almost a dearth of additional social comparison studies. When a collection of such studies was published in a special issue of the *Journal of Experimental Social Psychology* (Latané, 1966) devoted to the topic, Radloff and Bard (1966) compiled a social comparison bibliography through the end of 1965. Not counting the studies discussed above, they identified thirty-five additional studies in which social comparison had "an important role in either the formulation of the study or the interpretation of its results." The assembly of a social comparison bibliography was not an easy task. For example, the term *social comparison* did not appear in the *Psychological Abstracts* in the interval between the original paper and the publication of the special issue. Even though thirty-five papers on the topic in eleven years would have been no great shakes, not even all of these were direct tests of the theory; many were about separate topics dependent on but spun off from social comparison. There were nine experimental articles in the journal issue, and only five of these were direct tests of the theory.

Articles on social comparison have appeared sporadically since 1966. And in 1977, after the lapse of another decade, a second collection of social comparison articles was published. Entitled *Social Comparison Processes: Theoretical and Empirical Perspectives* (Suls and Miller, 1977), the volume contains a review of the field since 1954, twelve original chapters, and a commentary on them. The combined chapter references provide an excellent bibliography of the field. And almost all of the chapters deal directly with social comparison—raising distinctions, discussing ambiguities, and weaving the theory in and out of a variety of other social processes, such as modeling, equity, and interpersonal attraction. The volume is too long and complex to be summarized, but the flavor of the book is much different than that of the 1966 collection. Social comparison is no longer on trial or even a hothouse flower. It is viewed as an established core of confirmed theory, one still needing a lot of work around the edges, but still with a lot of vitality. More experimental work has been done in basic social comparison two decades after its introduction than in the first decade.

Indirect evidence for social comparison

Perhaps the most dramatic impact of social comparison has come in the applications, some so well developed that they are independent theories in their own right. If, to use Arrowood's (1978) apt phrase, social comparison is everyone's "second favorite social psychological theory," the favorite is apt to be one with similar roots. These theories were not developed to test social comparison theory but rather took it as a given and applied it to a variety of settings and situations. As these theories are elaborated and confirmed, their success provides inferential support for social comparison, their ultimate base. For illustrative purposes, several cases will be considered.

Affiliation

In a coordinated series of experiments, Schachter (1959) examined the basis of informal affiliation—the desire of people to be with others. Schachter first demonstrated a link between anxiety and affiliation. Using what became a standard experimental procedure, Schachter threatened his subjects with an impending electric shock or a hypodermic injection. In some of his subjects, he induced high levels of anxiety; in others, low levels or none. He measured affiliation by determining his subjects' preferences in waiting for the shock, either alone or in the presence of others. When the results of the experiments confirmed that anxiety leads to affiliation, he speculated on the possible reasons and suggested five: escape, direct anxiety reduction, indirect anxiety reduction, cognitive clarity, and social comparison. A series of follow-up studies ruled out all but indirect anxiety reduction and social comparison. A companion study by Wrightsman (1960) showed that the predicted effects did in fact occur. A reduction of anxiety occurred and, in accord with social comparison predictions, when appropriate comparison persons were present, there was a greater consensus on self-ratings of anxiety by Wrightsman's subjects. The affiliation paradigm proved to be a rich source of studies for social psychologists, so much so that in many current texts it is treated as a topic separate from social comparison.

Cognitive and social components of emotion

In a development also related to social comparison, Schachter and Singer (1962) explored a long-standing problem in psychology—the question of how people identify their emotional states. They argued that similar physiological states underlie most emotions. The variety of states and emotions we experience are determined, in good part, by the labels we assign to the generalized arousal state. We arrive at a label by a cognitive appraisal of the circumstances of the environment we are in when the arousal occurs and by social comparison with other people in similar circumstances. In a complex study, Schachter and Singer surreptitiously gave subjects injections of adrenalin and placed them together with an experimental confederate posing as a second subject. In situations where the subjects needed an explanation for their arousal, they became angry in the presence of an angry confederate and euphoric in the presence of a euphoric one. The extension of social comparison to emotional labeling has woven the theory into a broad psychological framework.

Although when first propounded (Festinger, 1954) social comparison had a strong impact in social psychology, interest in it, even in that field, was soon eclipsed by various theories of cognitive consistency, and, in particular, by the more glamorous and exciting dissonance theory. Its revival, in its role as an underpinning for affiliation and emotional labeling, also changed the audience and the status of the theory. By its extension to such concerns as emotions and exploring its interactions with physiological arousal, the theory was brought to the attention of a larger group of psychologists than just those in the social area and was applied to a wider variety of problems than those of social influence. In return, social comparison became one of those formulations that is so taken for granted that, as with "learning theory" and "mechanisms of perception," it is sprinkled, in passing, over the problem the author really wishes to address.

Other extensions

There have been other attempts to apply social comparison to different formulations. Singer, Baum, Baum, and Thew (1979) applied the theory to the problem of mass psychogenic illness in an industrial setting (the phenomenon once called "hysterical contagion"). In a factory there may be several concurrent sources of unrest. Singer et al. argued that odors, inhalants, fatigue, odd shift hours, union-management disputes, and several other possible factors may leave workers in a general state of evaluative unease. They argued that the occurrence of an index case of a worker fainting or becoming sick provides the comparative stimulus necessary for other workers to label their state as illness or faintness and to produce an epidemic of symptoms. Singer et al. outlined the conditions necessary to make a case for social comparison—e.g., since the index case is a better comparison for friends than for other co-workers, the friends should be more likely to display the symptoms—and reviewed the mass psychogenic illness literature to show that the data fit the theory.

Berger (1977) commented on the relative neglect of a social comparison influence in the literature on modeling and imitation. He reviewed the circumstances under which similar and dissimilar models provide evaluative information and concentrated on the model success effect, the tendency of an observer to persevere longer on a task after viewing an unsuccessful model than after a successful one. He conducted an experiment, one of whose findings was that this task perseverance following observation of an unsuccessful model was greater when the model was similar rather than dissimilar to the subject. This result was interpreted to mean that social comparison processes were involved in modeling and social learning.

Austin (1977) considered the relationship of equity theory to social comparison. His essay notes that most of the equity theory formulations rely on one or another version of Adams' (1965) original formulation: Equity between two people exists when they have the same outcome-to-input ratio. Austin points out that comparison and evaluation are implicitly involved in equity, both in terms of adjudicating inputs and outcomes but also in assessing the degree of similarity between the people involved in the equity comparison. He suggests that although equity theory has been supported by an impressive amount of evidence, its major theoretical problems hinge on 1. knowing more about how comparisons of inputs, outcomes, situations, etc., are made and 2. knowing that social comparison speaks productively to those very issues.

In a provocative essay, Goethals and Darley (1977) have suggested that social comparison may be a redundant formulation; it can be subsumed as a special case of attribution theory. Relying heavily on Heider's (1958) original notions and on Kelley's systematic expositions (1967, 1973), they suggest that social comparison's drive for self-evaluation is functionally equivalent to attribution's postulate that people desire an understanding of the causal relationships in their environment. Further, the emphasis in social comparison on similarity as the appropriate dimension for accurate and stable evaluation is paralleled by Kelley's outlining of the consistencies and regularities that govern causal attributions. The authors' intent is not so much to replace propositions of social comparison with those of attribution but to use the parallels between the theories to apply attribution findings to ambiguities in social comparison. It is unclear whether the reverse process would also apply: Could some of the social comparison findings be useful in clearing up ambiguities in attribution theory? If this were the case, much of the attribution literature would be applicable in support of social comparison.

All of these ancillary applications of social comparison do more than provide support for the basic theory; they also demonstrate its robustness in a variety of problems, situations, and circumstances as well as its adaptability to complement other theories and perspectives.

Problems and prospects

Social comparison theory was phrased as a series of formal propositions: hypotheses, corollaries, and derivations (Festinger, 1954). If anything, the exposition traded graceful writing for clarity and rigor of presentation. Despite this, a number of ambiguities have developed. That is, people have interpreted aspects of the theory in contrary ways. Let us consider some issues directly related to the theory.

1. The notion of a unidirectional upward push has been interpreted to mean at times that people want to be better than those with whom they are compared, and at other times that they wish to be a little worse. For example, if you play tennis with a group of people, general social comparison suggests that you would get the most stable evaluation of your talent and find the people in the group most attractive when you are close in ability. The unidirectional upward push suggests that you would find things just a little bit better if you were slightly superior to all the others. If comparison is playing with people and having the matches end 6–4, 7–5, 8–6, etc., then happiness is playing those same matches but always being on the 6, 7, or 8 end of the score. Yet other commentators offer the example of having a net worth of one million dollars and a choice of two country clubs available to join. The members of one club all have a net worth of 1 million dollars; the members of the other club are all worth 1.25 million. They argue that you would want to join the second group because that represents an upward move.

Granting the assumption that net worth is comparable to athletic ability, the discrepancy is probably more semantic than real; it hinges on an interpretation of "better." Social comparison requires you to want to be competitively better than your comparees. It also suggests a difference between classic reference group theory, which predicts that you would join the 1.25 million group to further your upward mobility, and social comparison, which predicts that you would choose the million dollar club precisely to avoid being the one poor millionaire in the 1.25 million club. If you had 1.25 million, you could join the 1.25 million club for an exquisitely precise comparison group, but you would probably choose the plain millionaires; it is close enough for comparison, and it gives you a nice feeling to be just a little richer (more able) than anyone else.

2. There is a good deal of confusion over the meaning of similarity in choosing a reference group or person. A number of commentators have, in essence, asked the question: Do you want to compare with someone close to you in the opinion being evaluated but dissimilar in other ways, or do you want to compare with someone like you in most respects but of a discrepant opinion? The correct answer, of course, is neither. You want to compare with people similar to you and holding an opinion in the same general range as yours. Since you can't always get what you want, you have to compromise—sometimes for less general similarity than you would like, sometimes for a more discrepant opinion. Which compromise you make will depend upon a variety of situational factors—the importance of the opinion, the value of the group to you, and whether you have outside anchors for the opinion. It is unlikely that there is any simple, or meaningful, answer to the question—other than that it is better to be rich and healthy than to be poor and sick.

3. Several investigators have raised the possibility of two kinds of comparison which, for want of better terms, are sometimes called *validation* and *evaluation*. For example, if a person learns to play a musical instrument, one kind of comparison, evaluation, answers the question of how good an accordian player he is; the other comparison, validation, answers the question of how important it is to be able to play "Lady of Spain" faultlessly. That the problem is a vexing one can be seen from the number of times the issue has been discussed. Singer (1966), Suls (1977), and Thorton and Arrowood (1966) are among those raising it; Suls also believes the distinction is similar to one described by Jones and Gerard (1967) as information dependence and effect dependence. On reflection, it is not clear but that the distinction is brought about by a poor choice of

examples, and that it really does not pose a problem for social comparison. The major difficulty lies in the fact that two questions are asked of the same ability. If, instead, a person asks if he can jog as far as his friends and also asks how important it is to play the accordian, most of the difficulty disappears. For we can see that an ability or opinion is usually multidimensional and can raise several independent evaluative questions and spawn several additional opinions to be evaluated. If people must evaluate both the level of an ability and an opinion about the ability at the same time, and if they are given only one group from which to choose a comparison person, it is no wonder if the results are somewhat inconsistent and puzzling from study to study as the nature of their comparison alternatives is varied.

4. Social comparison is intimately bound up with interpersonal attraction, the cohesiveness of groups, level of aspiration, and a host of other motives, drives, and pressures. As one or another experimental situation is created, or real life example chosen for study, it is inevitable that a need for comparison will be pitted against one or another of these forces. There is nothing inconsistent about Hakmiller (1966) or Friend and Gilbert (1973) concluding that their subjects wanted self-enhancement as well as comparison and that their choice of comparison groups reflected the operation of both of these motives. Arrowood and Friend's (1969) suggestion that people want a "positive instance" of an unclear trait, as well as an evaluation of their level of it, is simply another instance of social comparison operating in conjunction with other processes. What is needed are more ingenious experimental situations so that purer tests of each of these motives can be made.

5. In 1954, there was little, if any, cognitive psychology as we know it today. Learning theory, in one or another of its S-R forms, was the dominant perspective in American psychology. Thinking was subvocal speech, and verbal behavior was pretty much word association norms. Social comparison was a cognitive theory depending on thoughts and judgments of the people involved. Times have obviously changed. Studies of how people combine information and make judgments are a routine part of research programs in experimental psychology. It would now be both useful and appropriate to integrate social comparison with that other body of findings. For example, it is reasonable to ask, how does social comparison differ from other kinds of comparison? Is the way in which I decide how good a mathematician I am fundamentally different from the way in which I choose a car? Do I evaluate the machines in my office in a differ-

ent fashion from the people in my office? Perhaps self-involvement affects social comparison. Is it a reasonable first approximation to suggest that opinions about self are more important than opinions about other things, with opinions about my wife, my children, my house, or my possessions somewhere in between? In any case, these are testable questions now, and ones which make sense not just for social comparison but for other areas of psychology, such as social cognition, information processing, and the like.

Recapitulation and summary

Let us look back at what we have covered. Forty years ago, the problem of self-evaluation was no further along than it had been one hundred or two hundred years previously. There was a general feeling that beliefs were formed by other people, but the how and why were not known and the best existing texts had no specific suggestions. Yet it was about that time that the first real explorations of the question were made. Sherif's study of norm formation (1935), Newcomb's Bennington study (1943), Stouffer and his associates' study of *The American Soldier* (1949), and Lewin and his group's field theoretical studies of group decision such as Lewin (1947), and level of aspiration, e.g., Lewin, Dembo, Festinger, and Sears (1944), all contributed. These latter sets of studies led into *Social Pressures in Informal Groups* (Festinger, Schachter, and Back, 1950), a work which paved the way for the flurry of activity in the late 1940s and early 1950s that marked the development of pressures to uniformity. This was a theory that united self-evaluation, group formation, and interpersonal attraction in coherent, ordered, systematic, counter-intuitive, and sensible theory. It was far from perfect, but it was better than anything previous.

Pressures to uniformity was not the last word on the topic. Three years after he published a summary of the work (1950), Festinger reopened the same issues with the introduction of social comparison theory (1954). This theory, though more developed and thorough than its predecessors, produced a disappointingly small volume of direct research through 1966. It did, however, provide the impetus for affiliation (Schachter, 1959) and emotional labeling (Schachter and Singer, 1962). Since 1966, interest in social comparison has been revived, and has been refined and improved, though fortunately not yet completed. With a burst of experiments and theoretical essays (Suls and Miller, 1977), social comparison has the health and vigor of a still vital conception.

In four decades, we have gone from vagueness to specificity in responding to one of psychology's fundamental questions, and the answer has been supported by direct evidence and productive extensions. Even if the theory were proven to be incorrect in many of its details, the accomplishment is still not inconsiderable.

8

Cognition and Social Cognition:
A Historical Perspective

ROBERT B. ZAJONC

In his history of social psychology, Allport (1954) observed that "social psychologists regard their discipline as *an attempt to understand and explain how thought, feeling, and behavior of individuals are influenced by the actual, imagined, or implied presence of other human beings*" (p. 5). Few of us would find cause to disagree with this definition. The classes of phenomena which Allport regarded as significant for social psychologists, and the emphasis that he gave to these phenomena, are worth noting. According to this definition of social psychology, we wish to understand and explain *thought, feeling,* and *behavior*—in that order—with *thought* at the top of the list. And it is certainly still the case today that in the vast majority of instances our data are about thoughts. They come in the form of judgments, beliefs, opinions, preferences, expectations, guesses, or attitudes.

And according to Allport's definition, what are we to understand about thought, feeling, and behavior? We are to understand and explain *how they are influenced by the actual, imagined, or implied presence of others!* There are few social psychological experiments in which the effects of the *actual* presence of others have been studied. Rather, the bulk of our work has to do with the effects of the *implied* or *imagined* presence of others on thought, feeling, and behavior. Thus, according to All-

Portions of this chapter were presented as part of a symposium on Social Cognition and Affect at the meeting of the American Psychological Association, September 1979, New York. Preparation of this chapter was supported by a fellowship from the John Simon Guggenheim Memorial Foundation.

port's definition of social psychology, we are cognitive on the side of the independent variables and on the side of the dependent variables as well.

In fact, however, social psychology is even more cognitive than Allport's definition would imply. Cognition pervades social psychology at various levels: It enters at the level at which the problem is formulated; it provides significant components of our methods and designs; it participates at the assumptive level in theories and hypothesis building; and finally, one aspect of cognition—social cognition—represents a field of interest in its own right.

Examples of the heavily cognitive emphasis in these aspects of social psychology are easily found. Any random issue of one of the journals in the field will reveal this emphasis. I have selected the last two issues of the *Journal of Personality and Social Psychology* that arrived as this chapter was being written: No. 10 and 11 of Vol. 36 (1978), and I shall draw upon them to illustrate my point.

Cognitive elements in formulating social psychological research problems

Below are specimens of problem statements from four typical articles in that issue:

(a) The present research was undertaken to test the notion that feedback of one's own autonomic activity acts as a self-awareness inducing stimulus. (Fenigstein and Carver, 1978, p. 1242)

(b) Our theory predicts that the learning interference components of experimental helplessness can be remedied by simply informing subjects that feedback was noncontingent in the past but will be contingent in the future. (Koller & Kaplan, 1978, p. 1179)

(c) What strategies do individuals actually formulate to test the hypotheses about other individuals with whom they interact? Do individuals systematically adopt confirmatory strategies and preferentially search for evidence that would confirm their beliefs? Or, do individuals systematically adopt disconfirmatory strategies and preferentially search for evidence that would disconfirm their beliefs? Or, do individuals adopt equal opportunity strategies and search for confirming and disconfirming behavioral evidence with equal diligence? We have sought answers to these questions in our empirical investigations of hypothesis-testing processes. (Snyder and Swann, 1978, p. 1203)

(d) The extent to which 4-year old children behave in ways expected of them on the basis of their gender will be related to the nature of the situations or areas in which they play. (Lott, 1978, p. 1088)

In all these examples, information processing plays a critical role. In the first experiment, self-awareness (i.e., information about the self) is related to information about the individual's psychological activity. In the second study, learning performance (i.e., the acquisition and retention of information) is related to information about feedback contingency. In the third, subjects manipulate information and make complex inferences. And in the fourth experiment, the subjects' behavior is related to the way they view their play situation (i.e., the meaning of the environmental setting).

Cognitive elements in social psychological research methods

Social psychologists define their dependent and independent variables (when they are not manipulated), manipulate their independent variables, and create the appropriate experimental context primarily in cognitive terms and through cognitive methods.

Defining dependent variables

Much if not most of social psychological research relies on the verbal response. For the most part, these verbal responses are given in answer to attitude questions, or they are judgments, predictions, expectations, choices, descriptions, or recognitions. Thus, for example, in the study of conformity, subjects are asked to make judgments of lines, quality of poems, populations of cities, and others. In the study of the level of aspiration, subjects are asked to make predictions of their performance and report their confidence in these judgments. In research on the risky shift phenomenon, individuals accept or reject a hypothetical level of risk in an imaginary choice situation. In the study of group performance, measures of time to solve problems, quality of the solution, and the strategy of approach are measured. Also observed is the intermember influence process, which, of course, relies on communication which, in turn, is the product of the members' cognitions. In the study of competition and cooperation, the seemingly simple Prisoner's Dilemma paradigm requires considerable prior knowledge on the part of the subjects, and a very complex cognitive process is involved in understanding a simple 2 × 2 payoff matrix. It requires subjects to make guesses about their partners' (or opponents') preferences, utilities, and estimates of probabilities and to entertain guesses about how their partners will estimate and predict their own behavior.

In the four articles from the randomly selected issues of the *Journal of Personality and Social Psychology,* the involvement of cognitive factors in the measures of the dependent variables is quite clear. In the Fenigstein-Carver paper, subjects are presented with hypothetical situations that have good or bad outcomes. They are asked to assign responsibility for these outcomes, and the final measure consists of the extent of self-attribution of responsibility. In the Koller-Kaplan article, subjects must turn off a tone by discovering a correct sequence in which to press six buttons. Measures are percent correct, latency, and errors. In the Snyder-Swann experiments, subjects are told that the experiment is concerned with the way people come to understand each other. They are provided with a list of questions and from them select those to which they would like to have answers. Their selections become the measures of the dependent variable and are used to determine whether a confirming, disconfirming, or equal-opportunity strategy is employed by the subjects in testing *their* hypotheses about the person. In the Lott study, observations are taken of children's sex role behavior. Also obtained are questionnaires on sex typing as well as ratings of children's behavior made by teachers and parents.

Even when the variables are behavioral, most often they are interpreted as indicators of some underlying cognitive processes, states, or antecedents. Thus, the level of shock which a subject administers to a learner is taken as a measure of obedience to experimental instructions (Milgram, 1963); helping a person in distress is taken as a measure of the degree to which responsibility is diffused (Darley & Latané, 1968); giving blood is taken as a measure of attitude change (Powell, 1965); contributing money for a gift to a departing secretary is taken as a measure of conformity (Blake, Rosenbaum, and Duryea, 1955); and changes in star-tracing performance are taken as a measure of evaluation apprehension (Innes and Young, 1975). All these measures, it should be noted, involve very powerful assumptions about the *connection* between the behavior measured and the cognitive state that is believed to control it. Thus, for example, in the bystander intervention research, it is assumed that the reluctance of an individual to help a victim having an epileptic fit includes complex cognitive elements that entail his or her overview of the number of other people present, the likelihood that others might help, that there might be someone else who knows more about epilepsy than the subject, and so on. And it is implicitly assumed that engaging in helping behavior is directly under the control of these complex cognitive factors.

Manipulating independent variables

It is typical in social psychological experiments to induce the subject to engage in considerable cognitive activity in order to produce in him a desired psychological state. This state might be a belief, an expectation, an attitude, a decision, or the like.

Often complex scenarios are composed to produce these states which represent different values of the independent variable. Thus, for example, in the Fenigstein-Carver study, subjects in the experimental group are told that the study is concerned with the effects of cognitive activity on physiological processes and that the specific interest of the experimenter is in these effects on heart rate. They are given to believe that they will engage in some cognitive activity and their heartbeats will be monitored. Explanations are furnished about the workings of a plethysmograph, changes in blood volume, photocells, and other technical matters, including the fact that the impulses in the photocells are transduced into clicks that represent the heartbeat. Thus, the subjects are told that they will be hearing their own heartbeats. Of course, the heartbeats are preprogramed.

Note that it is virtually taken for granted that the experimental manipulations will induce a cognitive activity in the subjects. This activity will produce in them a psychological state that corresponds to the experimenter's conception of the independent variables and of the latent factors which these variables are presumed to measure. For the most part, these psychological states—attitudes, expectations, inferences, attributions, preferences, etc.—are covert and not directly accessible to observation. And frequently, we know very little about the cognitive processes that might be implicated in these measures. Many experimental procedures, especially those found in complex scenarios, precede formal knowledge by years or decades. For example, in 1951 Kurt Back published a paper on the effects of cohesiveness on social influence. In one group of subjects, he manipulated cohesiveness within pairs of subjects by telling them that on the basis of a test they had previously taken, they were very similar to each other (for high cohesiveness) or very different (low cohesiveness). In turn, cohesiveness was defined in terms of mutual attraction. Thus Back assumed that perceived similarity would produce mutual attraction. At the time of his experiment, however, very little was known about this relationship, and Byrne (1961) did not publish his work on similarity and attraction until ten years later. One should not view these procedures too critically. On the contrary. They testify to the ingenuity and foresight of the author and suggest, at the same time, that the field had reached a stage of development and sophistication that allow many of its conjectures soon to turn into proven theorems.

Creating an experimental context

Sometimes extensive instructions are given in order to create a particular experimental context for the subjects. These instructions, of course, must be processed by the subjects, and they must produce a psychological state that we wish to create. For example, subjects are told that the experiment is concerned with psychophysical judgments of length and that accuracy is of some importance. In fact, however, judgments are given in groups and the experiment deals with conformity. Or we tell the subjects, as in the Fenigstein-Carver study, that the experiment is concerned with the effects of cognitive activity on physiological processes, expecting that they will interpret the behavior of the experimenter, the purpose of the apparatus, and the sequence of experimental procedures in just those terms. Sometimes we create a context which requires the subject to strive for accuracy, sometimes for speed of response, or a context which makes them vulnerable to the influence of others. All of these manipulations may at times require knowledge that is not available and, worse, knowledge that is sought in the experimental program. Yet, this sort of bootstrapping is common and necessary at the forefront of experimental work in new areas.

Cognition and experimental artifacts

Even the critique of social psychological experiments invokes cognitive psychology and is stated in cognitive terms. Experimenter effects are stated in terms of the expectations of the experimenter and their effects on the behavior that is involved in experimental procedures, measures, and observations. Demand characteristics, on the other hand, involve assumptions about the subjects' expectations. It is assumed that the experimental context leads subjects to process the available information in such a way that certain inferences about the purpose of the study become inescapable and that their behavior will be constrained by these demands.

Cognitive elements in the explanations of
social psychological phenomena

Many, perhaps most, social psychological phenomena are explained by invoking various forms of cognitive mediation. Thus, for example, the self-concept is assumed to develop as a result of processing information that is supplied by the behavior and expectations of others. Some explanations of social facilitation assume that the presence of others is itself a stimulus that arouses in the subjects concerns over being evaluated. And such areas as risky shift, bystander intervention, equity, cooperation-competition, and in fact, almost all others, contain cognitive mediators in their explanations.

Cognitive and perceptual processes as social psychological
problems in their own right

A glance at the index of any text in social psychology will immediately reveal a large number of problems that are basically problems in information processing. Some deal with encoding of social information, others with retaining or combining it, and still others deal with more complex processes that involve cognitive conflict or inference. The list will naturally include attitudes and beliefs, stereotypes, communication, rumor transmission, perceptual selectivity, self-schemas, person perception, impression formation, balance, cognitive dissonance, attribution, social inference, the sleeper effect, implicit personality theory, implicit social behavior theory, and others.

Of course, similar cognitive variables and cognitive methods are also employed in other social sciences, such as sociology, political science, or anthropology. However, it is only in social psychology that *all* the above features and aspects are so heavily dominated by cognition, and it is perhaps unique in social psychology that social cognition represents a *major* field of interest in its own right (although similar interests are now also true to a lesser extent of cognitive anthropology).

Why does cognition dominate social psychology?

Social psychology has been cognitive for a very long time. It was cognitive long before the cognitive revolution in experimental psychology—

which dates, I suppose, to Neisser's book of 1967, when experimental psychologists began slowly to suspect that the intensive study of the learning of word lists might not reveal all secrets of the mind. It is instructive to look at the popular postwar text in social psychology published by Krech and Crutchfield in 1948—roughly thirty years ago. In it one finds that there was a deep concern with the nature of cognitive representations, with the way they are organized, and with the principles that could draw upon the nature of this organization in order for us to infer the likelihood and the form of change of cognitive structures. Attitude change was, above all, cognitive change. Here is a typical quote: "How we perceive the world is a product of memory, imagination, hearsay, and fantasy as well as what we are actually 'perceiving' through our senses. If we are to understand social behavior, we must know how all perceptions, memories, fantasies are combined or integrated or organized into present *cognitive structures"* (p. 77). This was at a time when words like "cognition," "consciousness," or "mind" were purged from the vocabulary of experimental psychologists. As late as 1957, Verplanck in his *Glossary of Psychological Terms* defined "cognition" as a term which *pretends to theoretical status but which is not reducible to empirical terms and is equivalent in meaning to intuitive, literary, and conversational terms.*

And still today, Skinner (1977) holds fast to an anticognitive approach, insisting that the critical variables that control behavior are not in the head but in the environment. The associations among words or meanings is not located in the head but in the usage—out there. According to his position, children do not change their "identities"—they do not form new concepts of themselves. Children change only because the people around them change their way of behaving toward them.

There is no doubt that in a milder form this proposition is entirely defensible, and there is no arguing with Skinner that *some* portion of variance in behavior can well be explained by an appeal to environmental contingencies. We can argue with Skinner about the proportion of variance in behavior that is so controlled, but we cannot deny that *some* proportion of variance is so controlled. Whatever remains is, therefore, controlled through internal mediation—through cognitions. This proportion of unexplained variance was probably much more apparent and important to social psychologists than to experimental psychologists.

What are some of the historical reasons which promoted the preoccupation with cognitive variables among social psychologists?

Social behavior is complex

One of the popular reasons often given for the cognitive approach is that social behavior is complex. The social environment is terribly rich and complex, social stimuli are complex, and so are social responses. Somehow, the idea has emerged that reflexive behavior—behavior that is under the control of external stimuli and reinforcement schedules—must be necessarily fairly simple. Complex behavior requires more complex contingencies, and these are hard to fix by means of reinforcements and reflexes. So if it is complex, social behavior must be mediated by thought. This argument is not terribly solid because there are all sorts of complex behavior that are not controlled by thought. Take bicycle riding. Bicycle riding cannot be taught by verbal instructions alone. Verbal instructions might not even contribute a great deal to the speed of learning, which depends mainly on getting onto the bicycle and riding it.

Emphasis on attitudes

Social psychologists' early concern with attitudes must have played a most important role in turning social psychology to cognition. This interest was immense, and three-quarters of the text *Experimental Social Psychology,* published by Murphy, Murphy, and Newcomb in 1937, was about attitudes. Of the 559 pages of the Newcomb-Turner-Converse (1965) text *Social Psychology: The Study of Human Interaction,* 201 contain references to attitudes. Attitudes were always regarded as cognitive and affective organizations that were presumed to influence behavior.

World War II

Very significant in the heavy emphasis on cognition among social psychologists must have been the war experience. The Second World War was viewed by the Allies as a war of democracy and liberalism against the forces of fascism and authoritarianism. Opposed above all was an ideology which was racist, and which extolled the virtues of "purity" of race on biological and genetic grounds. It promoted biological solutions to social and economic problems—the extermination of entire populations. At the same time, the fascist ideology was proclaiming that its ends required social control to be maintained through discipline and obedience—unquestioning blind obedience.

The American social psychologists—Jack Atkinson, Jerry Bruner, Angus Campbell, Doc Cartwright, Al Hastorf, Nate Maccoby, Helen Peak, Sid Rosen, Ezra Stotland, and hundreds of others who took part in that war—had values that were quite opposite to the totalitarian doctrines of Nazi Germany. They believed that the perfectibility of man is not to be found in biological or genetic solutions, but in reason, in education, and in self-imposed standards of conduct and morality. Their values are clearly seen in Lewin's *Resolving Social Conflicts* (1948), Alfred Marrow's (1967) biography of Lewin, Adorno et al.'s *The Authoritarian Personality* (1950), Asch's (1952) *Social Psychology,* and many other volumes published by social psychologists during the late forties and early fifties. The American social psychologists were all immersed in the powerful ideological trend that engulfed the Allied countries as the war's end became imminent—a trend that pervaded all branches of life, that found its embodiment in the arts, literature, and the sciences, and that was ultimately reified in the formation of the United Nations Scientific, Educational, and Cultural Organization, whose pointed motto reads: "Since wars begin in the minds of men, it is in the minds of men that the defenses of peace must be constructed."

Like other intellectuals, the American social psychologists asked themselves how it was possible for a nation like Germany, with one of the richest literary, artistic, scientific, and philosophical traditions, to change so rapidly and so dramatically, to tolerate the murder of millions and the obliteration of humanist, humanitarian, and intellectual values. They were impressed, at the same time, with the powerful Nazi propaganda machine and believed that it was propaganda which succeeded in delivering the German population to Hitler and which made that population blind to unheard of atrocities. Germany was viewed as the product of a massive attitude change—a massive *cognitive* change—which was achieved by means of extremely effective propaganda.

If political, economic, and social changes of unequaled scope can take place by virtue of persuasion, through the induction of attitudes controlled by a relatively small group of people, the role of cognitive processes in social life must be exceedingly important. How then could social psychology be anything but cognitive? Add to it the fact that among those who escaped to the United States from Nazi Germany were people like Lewin, Heider, Koehler, and Wertheimer—all not only ardently humanist and liberal but at the same time deeply committed to Gestalt psychology, whose concern was mainly with the nature of perceptual and cognitive organization and representation—and it becomes inevitable for cognition to dominate social psychology.

The heavy emphasis on cognitive functions that characterized social psychology eventually had some impact on *experimental* psychology. There were other developments in experimental psychology which laid the ground for the cognitive approach—for example, the concern with probability learning and choice behavior. The inability of explaining in purely S-R associationistic terms several memory phenomena, such as differences between recall and recognition, made experimental psychology vulnerable to new approaches. Work on human factors and decision theory also contributed to the rising trend, and the word "cognitive" finally became acceptable among experimental psychologists in 1967. Today, one even hears the words "mind" and "consciousness."

The developments in experimental cognitive psychology have been substantial, accompanied by great methodological and theoretical sophistication. What we are witnessing today in social psychology is, therefore, somewhat surprising, for we are witnessing an attempt to import the methods and concepts of cognitive psychology into social psychology—a psychology that was cognitive all along! Many social psychologists today delight in borrowing from cognitive psychology and often indiscriminately apply their ideas, concepts, and methods to the problems of cognition.

No doubt, a great deal may be gained by building upon cognitive psychology, for substantial advances have been achieved in that field. At the same time, however, it is worth asking why is it that they—the experimental cognitive psychologists—and not we, are now pursuing problems that were natural for social psychologists of the early fifties, sixties, and seventies to pursue. Why was their present work not done by us earlier? The typical experiment in cognitive psychology today can be hardly distinguished from an early experiment in social psychology. After all, the title of Bartlett's 1932 book was *Remembering: A Study in Experimental and Social Psychology.*

There is one possible reason. Social psychologists have not dedicated more effort to developing concepts and methods for the more precise study of cognitive structures, cognitive processes, and cognitive representations—as Krech and Crutchfield (1948) admonished us to do—because they encountered difficulties by which experimental psychologists were *not* burdened. Had social psychologists been satisfied with what is done today by experimental psychologists in the area of memory and cognitive representation, this work would have been done by them ten or fifteen years ago.

The very fact that social psychologists have not engaged in the precise study of cognitive processes is a hint that social perception and social cognition are not just straightforward applications of the principles of perception and cognition to social stimuli.

Social cognition has several features, unique to its own problems, which make it a very special case. These features make social cognition qualitatively so different that the lock-stock-and-barrel application of the principles and methods of modern experimental cognitive psychology may be misleading.

Special features of social perception and social cognition

Lack of stimulus constancy

Social information processing is an integral component of social reality. Social information processing has real effects. That is, the results of social perception often have an influence on the objects perceived. When I perceive a prospective candidate for our graduate program as being likely to succeed, this will have a completely different effect on that person than when I perceive the candidate as likely to fail. The results of nonsocial perception (if such perception exists), too, have consequences on the objects perceived. If I perceive a branch blocking my driveway, I might want to cut it down; my perception of the branch will surely affect it. But there is an obvious and important difference: The branch can do very little to defend itself against the consequences of my perception, or for that matter, to *prepare* itself for this perception. People, however, do prepare themselves for such perceptions. They are able to display desirable aspects, conceal undesirable ones, and embellish others. This observation is so obvious that it hardly needs stating. And there is, of course, a great deal of social psychological literature that deals with just that aspect of social perception. The ingratiation phenomenon (Jones, 1964) and self-handicapping (Jones and Berglas, 1978), self-monitoring (Snyder, 1974), objective self-awareness (Wicklund and Duval, 1971), evaluation apprehension (Rosenberg, 1965), and many other related phenomena have been studied by social psychologists for decades, and a great deal is known about these phenomena. At the same time, it is less obvious, but certainly more troublesome, that these phenomena and our knowledge about them *have not been systematically integrated into a theory of social perception.*

More generally, the lack of stimulus constancy in social perception means that *ordinary* psychophysics does not apply, and that its methods cannot be imported without modifications. In ordinary psychophysics we must assume that stimuli do not change upon judgment. A 1000 Hz tone or a patch of monochromatic light of a given wavelength cannot do much about the fact that they are misjudged. If a subject judges a 500 Hz tone to be higher in pitch than an 800 Hz tone, neither have any recourse in the matter. Both stimuli will simply have to suffer the indignity. Nor can they prepare themselves for a future misrepresentation on the part of the same subject or on the part of a different one. People can.

I am sure that it is this feature of social perception that has prevented social psychologists from pursuing psychophysics, in spite of Stevens' (1966; 1972) admonition. The problem is, admittedly, a difficult one but certainly not insoluble. There are at least two solutions to the problem of stimulus inconstancy. One "solution" avoids the problem altogether, substituting words for their social referents. One substitutes adjectives for actual personality features of a live person. Or one supplants "live" social stimuli by pictures, films, or stories. These studies are in fact impervious to the confounding described above. An adjective is not influenced by our perception, and it cannot adjust itself so that a future perception of it would be more favorable. Of course, a great deal can be and has been learned about social perception from just such studies, and in many cases the perception of referents of words may not differ from the perception of the words themselves. But because we cannot assume a one-to-one correspondence between language and reality, we may not take it for granted that the same principles of social perception will be generated by studying words as by studying the actual social objects for which these words stand.

The second solution is to use actual social stimuli but different psychophysics—an approach that might be called "recursive psychophysics." In this form of psychophysics, several measures are obtained in succession. Thus, for instance, a measure of the *state* of the social stimulus at time $t(n)$ is taken both prior to the *judgment* of the stimulus taken at $t(n + 1)$ and following such *judgment* taken at $t(n - 1)$. The influence of the stimulus on the judgment—that is, the typical relationship observed in psychophysical functions—is obtained by the family of curves with stimuli measured at $t(n)$ and judgments at $t(n + 1)$. The influence of the judgment on the stimulus will be obtained from the family of functions relating the judgments taken at $t(n - 1)$ to the measures of the stimulus taken at $t(n)$. The families of these functions would describe both how perception of social stimuli varies with the nature of these stimuli and how these stimuli change as a result of perception.

Independence of stimulus measures

There is another problem in social perception that is similar and related to the lack of stimulus constancy. Psychophysics requires not only that the stimulus be constant under judgment but that it be measured *independently* of the judgment. This often proves to be quite difficult in social perception. In typical psychophysics of sensory dimensions, the stimuli are measured in physical measurement units, their equivalents, or other countable units. There are various social phenomena that can be so measured, or that can be measured objectively and independently of judgments. Sex, age, height, weight, and other characteristics of persons and groups, and such properties of social behavior as duration and repetition, may be described objectively. And the same could be done with estimates of intelligence, such that we could write a reasonable psychophysical function relating estimates of people's intelligence to their measured IQ or SAT scores.

But when we deal with the perception of such characteristics as likability, generosity, altruism, or honesty, the meaning of the corresponding psychophysical functions becomes ambiguous because there are no objective and independent measures of these attributes. Generally, they are described on the basis of a consensus of judgments very much like those that we seek to quantify in our psychophysical research. Hence, the measures of the stimuli are not entirely independent of the judgments of these stimuli. Since psychophysics yields as one of its products information about perceptual accuracy, a serious problem exists. How can we determine whether a subject's estimate of people's honesty is accurate if there are no independent measures of these people's honesty?

Again, we are not completely helpless here. A solution to this problem can be obtained—a solution which might be called "psychophysical triangulation." This solution entails some bootstrapping, made possible by the various techniques of path analysis and structural equations. For example, we wish to know something about the psychophysical function of honesty, and we wish to gain this knowledge in the absence of information about the validity of measures of honesty. We will require judgments of honesty and judgments of other social attributes which 1. are related to honesty and 2. can be measured objectively. Thus, for example, we may obtain judgments of income and intelligence. Both of these variables have fairly reliable and valid measures. The solution would be based on six variables: the *measures* of honesty, income, and intelligence, and the *judgments* of honesty, income, and intelligence. Required are the fifteen correlation coefficients among these six variables and a model that relates the underlying constructs to each other. The models estimated in structural equation analyses distinguish between latent variables (i.e., underlying constructs) and the measures of these constructs. The solution obtained by means of simultaneous equations describes the pattern of relations among the latent variables. A reasonable model for our example might be, for example, that the latent factor of intelligence measured by IQ has an influence on the latent factor of affluence (measured by income in dollars) and the latent factor of honesty (measured by some index or test whose true validity is not known but whose test reliability can be estimated). By means of a program (such as LISREL IV; Jöreskog and Sörbom, 1978), we can estimate the coefficient relating actual honesty to the judgments of honesty. Figure 8.1 shows both the model and a fictitious correlation matrix from which it was estimated by means of LISREL IV. This coefficient of .49 represents a linear relationship, whereas many psychophysical functions are of more complex forms. In order to discover the form of these functions, one could use a variety of transformations which seem reasonable and which keep the maximum residuals at their lowest values.

Once we have established an estimate of the psychophysical function for honesty in the context of its relationships to affluence and intelligence, we can get further confirmation of that psychophysical function and possibly better approximations by placing honesty in another context—with the variables of age and family size, for example. As we learn more and more about the psychophysics of honesty, the measures of honesty can be refined, and eventually honesty can be used to find psychophysical functions for other subjectively measured attributes, such as generosity or likability. Andrews (1979) and Andrews and Crandall (1976) have employed structural equation models on survey research data in investigations of the construct validity of social indicators. Note that the problem of psychophysics for dimensions for which there is no objective measure is essentially the problem of construct validity, except that in psychophysical triangulation we are not satisfied with linear correlation coefficients but seek to establish the nature of the psychophysical functions (which are commonly power functions) more precisely.

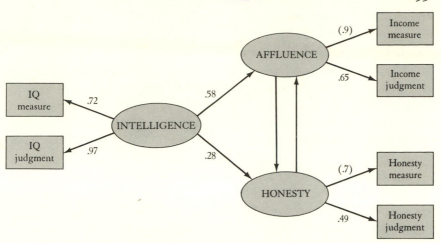

Figure 8.1 Bootstrapping of the psychophysics of honesty.
(Coefficients computed by Mary Grace Moore).

Affect and cognitions

While the lack of stimulus constancy and independence are features of social cognition that derive from the particular nature of the social *stimulus,* social cognition also differs from ordinary experimental cognition in the realm of *responses.* The psychophysical judgments of a subject comparing weights or hues are for the most part dispassionate, and can be viewed as comprising primarily, or even exclusively, perceptual and cognitive elements and processes. But social perception is rarely so immaculate. In the case of social perception, responses—be they judgments or ratings— are seldom emotionally neutral. There are few social perceptions and cognitions that do not implicate affect in some significant way. The role of affect in social perception constituted one of the major concerns of the pioneer social psychologists such as McDougall and Ross. Thus, for example, McDougall (1908) gave special prominence to the *sympathetic induction of emotion* as one of the basic problems of social psychology. And the widespread concern of social psychologists with attitudes that persist unabated further testifies to the importance of affective phenomena in social psychological research.

To some extent, affect is implicated in *all* perception (Zajonc, 1979). It is difficult, for example, to look at patches of hue without experiencing some emotional reactions, and a 1000 Hz pure tone might be music to some ears. Social perception contains affective elements because it is, above all, highly *evaluative*. There is hardly any social phenomenon—person, behavior, group, the product of some individual's work—which we perceive without at the same time having some form of reaction which can be described best on the good-bad, pleasant-unpleasant, safe-unsafe, likable-dislikable, and other such scales. To judge people as intelligent or stupid is not only to assign them to locations on the dimension of intelligence but also to make value judgments that may have profound consequences for them.

I have argued recently (Zajonc, 1979) that the affective reaction often, if not always, precedes the cognitive process. If it in fact precedes that process, affect can have extensive effects on the entire cognitive process. Affect might give it direction by diverting attention to some stimuli or some aspects of the stimuli to the exclusion of others. Affect can act selectively on the encoding of information. Thus, for example, Bower, Monteiro, and Gilligan (1979) hypnotized subjects to be in good or bad moods and found that the mood present during the learning of word lists had a distinct effect on retrieval.

Social psychologists are well aware of the detrimental effects of affect on social cognition. Stereotyping and prejudice are clearly affective phenomena which reduce the accuracy of social perception, to the clear detriment of the persons and groups so perceived. There is substantial literature on stereotyping and prejudice, and we know a great deal about the conditions under which they occur and how hard it is to eradicate them. But we know very little in this respect about the ways in which the affective components in these phenomena interact with the cognitive components to yield predispositions that are so robust.

Psychoanalytic theory also regards affect as a troublemaker. Affect pushes thoughts and impulses into the unconscious, prevents us from confronting reality, which it tends to distort, and gives us phobias and compulsions. As such, one would consider it primarily an important source of interference to efficient information processing.

But affect can also have facilitating effects on cognition. Above all, affectively charged stimuli can be discriminated at lower levels of stimulus energy than neutral stimuli, a finding which was once controversial but which is rapidly becoming much less so (Dixon, 1971; Erdelyi, 1974). For instance, when the words "happy" or "sad" are shown subliminally in association with a picture of a face, they influence the subject's perception of that face (Smith et al., 1959), a finding which was replicated recently with words presented through the auditory channel and also subliminally (Henley, 1975).

Affective discriminations and cognitive discriminations

Attitudes, stereotypes, prejudice, phobias, fixations, and related phenomena are structures combining affect and cognition. They are products of complex interactions between affective and cognitive processes. Thus, affect participates heavily in the processing of social information. The precise nature of this participation is not yet altogether clear, but that affect *is* deeply implicated in social information processing can hardly be questioned today.

The earlier writers, such as Shand (1896), McDougall (1908), and Bartlett (1932), attributed to affect an independent source of effects. Wundt (1907), too, treated affect as primary in consciousness and conjectured that it *precedes* ideational elements in both perception and retrieval. During the forties and fifties, however, affect had been treated more as a "quality" of the perceptual experience than as an independent process. Thus, for example, the work of Asch (1946) on impression formation or of Heider (1958) on the representation of affect in interpersonal relationships absorbed affect into cognitive processes. In the context of these approaches, the attractiveness of certain traits of people, the value of their actions and intentions, the appeal of certain properties of products not regarded as being particularly distinct from such attributes as, for instance, height in the case of people, speed in the case of actions, or weight in the case of products. Yet it is becoming increasingly clear that affect may not be treated as residing in stimuli, for affect is above all a reaction of the organism. Affective reactions to stimuli may readily change without any changes in these stimuli. With time we become attached to some objects and bored with others, and previously neutral stimuli can be conditioned to approach or avoidance reactions by means of simple conditioning procedures.

Thus, the early versions of affect may not have been far off the mark. Recent evidence indeed suggests that affective phenomena may represent a process that is partly independent and separate from cognition (Zajonc, 1979). As such, it can interfere with cognitive processes under some conditions or make information processing more efficient under others. The independent and primary role of affect in information processing has been shown especially clearly in the context of exposure effects. These effects consist of increased preference for stimuli which is generated solely as a function of repeated exposures. It has been conventionally thought, since the work of Titchener (1910), that the increased preference which is associated with familiarization through exposure occurs because of the subjective feelings of recognition. Yet a number of studies (Matlin, 1971; Moreland and Zajonc, 1977; 1979) have shown that with recognition memory held constant, the effects of repeated exposure are still quite pronounced. In an ingenious experiment, Wilson (1975; 1979) controlled for recognition experimentally. He used the dichotic listening procedure, whereby random melodies were presented several times to one ear while the subject shadowed a story read to the other ear. Under these conditions, the melodies were seldom heard, and a subsequent recognition memory test revealed that the subjects could not recognize these melodies at better than the chance level. Yet under these conditions, stimuli exposed frequently were liked significantly better than stimuli not previously encountered even though the subjects could not distinguish the former from the latter. These results were replicated in the visual mode by Kunst-Wilson and Zajonc (1980), who exposed polygons for brief intervals and later checked for recognition memory and liking. In this study, 67 percent of subjects liked objectively old stimuli better than objectively new stimuli, but only 21 percent were able to distinguish between them as being old or new at a level better than chance. Moreover, 71 percent of the subjects manifested better discrimination between the old and new stimuli using liking as their response than using "old-new" as their response. In addition, their liking responses were more reliable, and were made with greater confidence and greater speed.

Affect can also enhance memory. For example, Kleinsmith and Kaplan (1963; 1964) found that emotional words are remembered less well on immediate recall tests but show strong reminiscence effects on recall tests administered as much as one week later. Of these words only 10 percent were recalled correctly two hours after learning, but over 40 percent in one experiment and over 30 percent in another were remembered when tests were given one week later. On the other hand, low arousal words show the typical decay function, starting with 45 percent recall two hours after learning and declining to less than 10 percent after one week. Sadella and Loftness (1972) asked subjects to form pleasant and unpleasant images in association to some words. For other words they asked them to make associations that were emotionally neutral. The recall of these words was much better when they were accompanied by emotional imagery (good *or* bad) than when they were accompanied by neutral imagery.

Recall and recognition of words and of photographs of faces is considerably enhanced when, prior to tests, subjects are given these stimuli to view under conditions that require some affective involvement. Thus, for example, if words are judged for pleasantness, they are recalled better than when they are judged for the number of letters (Hyde and Jenkins, 1969). When photographs of faces are judged for likability or honesty, they too are remembered better than when they are judged for sex (Bower and Karlin, 1974) or other physical attributes, such as distance between the eyes or thickness of lips (Patterson and Baddeley, 1977).

Involvement of the self

There are few nontrivial phenomena in social cognition that do not involve the self in one way or another. Already at the turn of the century, the self was the center of social psychological inquiry and analysis. In the writings of McDougall (1908), the self-regarding sentiment was conceived of as the summit of the hierarchical organization of attitudes, and the self was equally prominent in the social psychological concepts developed by Cooley (1902) and Mead (1934). The most extensive analysis of the role of the self in social perception, however, was not undertaken until the late forties, when Combs and Snygg (1949) published their work, which regarded the self as an essential component of all perceptual and cognitive processes. Various areas of social psychological research implicated the self in many ways. For example, the research on social judgments (Sherif and Hovland, 1961) has shown powerful influences of the individual's position on attitudinal judgments, and it is customary today to attribute to the self an essential role in the experience of dissonance (Abelson et al., 1968).

Above all, social perception is highly *evaluative*. As such, it must invoke standards and comparisons. These standards and comparisons are derived from cognitive structures that comprise the self; in turn, the self is vulnerable to the individual's perception of others and others' behavior. Thus, by imposing our standards on these judgments, we necessarily implicate ourselves in the judgments. The judgments are influenced by the cognitive components comprising the self, and once made, they feed back into those components.

In general, preferences necessarily implicate the self. When stimuli are judged for such properties as weight, pitch, or brightness, the subjects' psychophysical function orders the stimuli on what Coombs (1964) calls the I-scale. I-scales are scaled stimuli ordered with respect to some property of theirs. However, when subjects judge stimuli with respect to preferences, the scale that emerges is the so-called J-scale—a scale on which are ordered stimuli jointly with the individual's ideal point on that dimension.

When such judgments are made with respect to social attributes, the implication of the self takes on added significance. Consider judgments of intelligence or honesty, for example. When one judges the intelligence of a person, one invokes a set of values. The decision that the person is intelligent carries very different evaluative components than the judgment that the person is unintelligent. And to judge someone on the dimension of intelligence is simultaneously not only to evaluate that person but to judge and *evaluate oneself* as well. Judgments of other people on socially significant dimensions often involve some degree of invidious comparison. When a subject judges the intelligence or honesty of a group or category of persons, he or she must consider the distribution of this attribute in the population, and with this subjective impression of the distribution will also come the individual's own location on that dimension. If the cues are such as to reveal the judged persons to be of substantial intelligence, the prior impression of the distribution of intelligence may have to be revised and one's own position on it displaced. One may discover that one is less intelligent relative to the population than previously thought. Or more intelligent. The early theorizing about the risky shift phenomenon involved just such an assumption about the distribution of risk preferences and the individual's position on the dimension of risk (Brown, 1965).

Because the self is highly charged with affect, because it resists derogation and, more generally, information that may require extensive changes,[1] the judgments of others may be powerfully influenced in a variety of ways. Markus and Smith (1980) have recently reviewed the pervasive effects of self-schemas on the perception of others, revealing various categories of influence.

In the above examples, the participation of the self in perception acts mainly to the detriment of accuracy and efficiency. But this need not be so in all instances. Like affect, the involvement of the self can also have beneficial effects on the processing of social information. Thus, for ex-

1. A. G. Greenwald. The totalitarian ego: Fabrication and revision of personal history. In press. *American Psychologist.*

ample, when adjectives are rated for self-reference—that is, when the subject is asked whether the adjective applies to him or to her—rather than whether it has the same meaning as some other word, for example, and recognition memory tests are administered later on these adjectives shown with an equal number of distractor adjectives, recall is much better when the prior task requires self-reference than when it requires comparison of meanings. Rogers, Kuiper, and Kirker (1977) found that more than twice as many self-reference items were recalled than meaning-comparison items under these conditions. Keenan and Bailett (1979), using recognition measures rather than recall, replicated the Rogers-Kuiper-Kirker results, adding the finding that not only are self-reference items easier to recognize on later tests but that the recognition judgments are made much faster for these items than for others.

Social perception recruits explanation as a slave process

There is an overpowering tendency to view social behavior and social phenomena as having *origins* and *causes,* and to view actors as having *intentions.* An action is not seen simply as a sequence of muscle twitches and motor movements: It is perceived as being goal directed and having its origins in some state of the individual, such as motive, intention, or habit. When perceived, all social behavior begs for explanation. When we see a man sitting quietly on a park bench, we ask ourselves, why is it that he sits so quietly? When we see a man fidgeting on a park bench, we ask ourselves with equal curiosity, why is it that he is fidgeting? Of course, we stop and pay special attention to the causes of behavior that appear strange, bizarre, or deviant. But we do not ignore the cause of *modal* behavior. Modal behavior, too, is perceived as being determined, as having underlying causes, purposes, or intentions, and these antecedents are perceived as integral parts of the actions on which we focus. People walking in the streets at 8 A.M. are not just seen walking—they are seen going to their jobs. And the same people seen walking at 5 P.M. are seen going home. Their intentions, feelings, anticipations, and purposes are seen in an entirely different light. When I see a man run, I am simultaneously aware of the direction of his progress, I am imagining his destination, and I have some awareness of where he must have come from. From the speed, manner, attire, and context, I perceive immediately and directly not just someone running, but I see a jogger, a thief escaping the police, or someone trying to catch a bus.

There is, of course, some tendency to seek explanations for nonsocial events, too. But this tendency is much more pronounced in social cognition because the demands of everyday life make it much more important for us to know the causes of the behavior of other humans than to know the causes of the physical aspects of our environment. We can easily survive without knowing the causes of rainbows and southerly winds. But it is more difficult if we are not familiar with the causes of people's anger and rage, or with the sources of their affection.

Seeking to explain social behavior has consequences for processing social information—consequences that reveal how important this aspect of social behavior might be. In a recent study, Bower and Masling[2] gave subjects some bizarre correlations to study. Examples of these correlations are: "As the number of hockey games increases, the amount of electricity increases," or "As the number of fire hydrants in an area decreases, the crime rate increases." In one group, the subjects simply had to study these statements of correlations. In another, they were supplied with explanations of why these relationships held. And in a third group, the subjects had to discover explanations by themselves. Following this initial task, they were tested in a paired-associates manner, such that the independent variable was supplied and the subject had to recall the dependent variable and the direction of the relationship. Subjects who generated explanations by themselves were able to recall 73 percent of the statements. But the study group remembered only 39 percent of the statements, while the group that was supplied with explanations did not perform much better: they remembered 45 percent of the correlations.

Even more interesting was the fact that correlations which the subjects succeeded in explaining in the time allowed (15 sec) were remembered considerably better than those which they tried to explain but were unable to do so: 81 versus 57 percent. So, it would appear that if we wish our students to learn psychological laws, we should allow them to prove these laws by themselves.

Conclusion

Upon closer examination, social perception and social cognition reveal features that make them quite distinct from their counterparts that are studied by experimental psychologists. Social perception and social cogni-

2. G. H. Bower and M. Masling. Causal explanations as mediators for remembering correlations. Unpublished manuscript, Stanford University, 1979.

tion create a social reality by affecting both the perceiver and the objects perceived. And even though not all of social reality is a function of social perception, a great deal of it is profoundly influenced by the way individuals view each other and the social world in which they live. Thus, I have argued, social perception requires equal attention on both sides: on the side of the observer or perceiver and on the side of the objects perceived. The ubiquity of affect as a companion, antecedent, and product of social cognition makes the study of social information processing as a dispassionate, computerlike activity less than an accurate representation of what is actually going on. Had these properties of social cognition been present only occasionally, it would have been most efficient simply to apply to social perception the methods and principles of cognitive psychology as they have been developed in experimental approaches, treating social perception as a special case. But the absence of object-observer interaction, the absence of affect and of the involvement of the self, are rather exceptional in social perception and cognition. It is thus more appropriate to view these phenomena as the general case and those studied by experimental psychologists as special cases in which these crucial factors and parameters have been arbitrarily set equal to zero.

The current interest among experimental cognitive psychologists in story grammars, scripts or schemas, mood effects, comprehension, artificial intelligence, and generally in the more complex forms of information processing indicates that the verbal learning tradition may have spawned oversimplified cognitive models. The perception and cognition of everyday nonsocial objects often acquire human and social qualities. The anthropomorphic metaphor is the most common one. We speak of vicious storms, fussy car engines, friendly fires, gloomy days, unruly hair, deceptive currents, and lazy rivers. David Rapaport has reminded us that "all sciences are anthropomorphic at the beginning, and all of them attempt to get away from this feature. . . . This is how the concept of 'forces' came about: on the basis of [man's] own experience, he knows that something can be made to happen by him if he uses force" (Gill, 1967, p. 179). Abstract line figures made into animated film sequences are seen as having intentions, goals, and conflicts (Heider and Simmel, 1944). Thus, the theoretical and empirical contradictions which appear with increasing frequency in the cognitive psychology that emerged from the verbal learning tradition are being generated, perhaps, because some critical features of information processing that cognition shares with social cognition have been ignored. The conclusion that forces itself upon us is that social perception and social cognition are *not* special cases of perception and cognition. And it will simply not do, therefore, for social psychologists to apply—simply and blindly—the principles, methods, and empirical findings of experimental cognitive psychology to the problems of social perception. For social perception is not the special case. It is experimental cognition which is the special case—a case, as I said, in which the critical variables and parameters have been arranged to have zero values. It is social perception that represents the general case. Perhaps we will not understand perception fully *unless* we understand social perception.

In this respect, Simon's recent (1976) observation is interesting. He said that cognitive social psychology is simply a special case of cognitive psychology, whereas I have thought of it here the other way around. He argued his position on the grounds that "it is not plausible that the processes of the human brain that handle social situations are quite distinct from the processes that handle other situations" (p. 258). While Simon's faith in a common set of processes is entirely shared in this chapter, it must be noted at the same time that the experimental paradigms and the theoretical constructs of traditional cognitive psychology have thus far *not accommodated* the special needs and features of social cognition such as I described here. Those paradigms and constructs apply to a rather limited domain of information processing within which only some fairly restricted problems in social information processing can be studied. And thus Simon acknowledged that cognitive psychology requires some social psychological knowledge, too, although the social psychological knowledge that he sought for cognitive psychology was that of individual differences. The special dynamic features of social information processing—particularly the dependence of the objects of perception on the perceiver and their capacity to alter themselves—suggest that a general cognitive psychology requires considerably more from social psychology than information about individual differences.

9

The Origins and Consequences of Group Goals

ALVIN ZANDER

The nature of the goal members choose for their group is influenced by conditions in the environment, in the group, and in the members. The chosen goal, in turn, determines what events occur within the group: its level of performance, the pride of members in their organization, their personal self-regard, the aims they develop for their own jobs, the attitudes and beliefs they invent about their organization, even the survival of the group itself. Group leaders and members commonly develop concepts for use in thinking about these issues and create their own explanations about why things happen as they do. There has been, however, little scientific understanding of such matters.

Prior to World War II, most of the published comments on processes in organizations were prepared by businessmen who wrote for colleagues about their own experiences in controlling a work force, paying workers, planning for the future, or increasing the productivity of individual employees on motor tasks. Dozens of such volumes were written during dozens of years, and many of these are well summarized by George (1968) in his account of management thought.

Behavior in groups: Some early assumptions

Forty years ago writers were beginning to make assumptions about the nature of purposive behavior in groups, and they expressed these ideas as incidental parts of their writings on managerial skills. Although the commentators provide nothing like a body of knowledge about purposes in groups, it is useful to consider examples of their wisdom because these illustrate what scholars thought were important at that time. Research directly concerned with group goals was not to begin for another ten or twenty years.

1. In order for an organization to be effective, members must cooperate with one another (Balderston, 1930; Barnard, 1938; Mooney and Reilly, 1931). Cooperation among participants can develop, however, only if the organization has a purpose because a purpose helps workers judge which actions of colleagues are for the good of the group and in what ways each member depends on the others.

2. Several useful consequences occur for a group when it has a purpose. A purpose provides members with a reason for the existence of their unit and an indication of what it is supposed to accomplish. It also affects the structure of the organization as jobs, procedures, and the relations among these are created so that they will best assure attainment of that end. The continued existence of an organization depends on fulfillment of its purpose. A unit cannot survive if it does not achieve its objective, yet neither can it survive after it reaches its objective, unless a new goal is soon named.

3. Barnard (1938) suggested that organizational purpose stimulates freedom (and perhaps vigor) of action among members. He supported his case by assuming, first, that our society ordinarily grants a citizen freedom of choice. When one is in an organization, however, one's power to make individual choices is necessarily limited; a member cannot be allowed to go his own way if he is to cooperate with others. Hence, specific limits are placed on the conditions of choice for participants. Given these guidelines, a member can have freedom, but he must operate inside the specified constraints. The restricting of certain behaviors and the encouraging of others is called by Barnard "making or arriving at an organization's purpose."

4. In 1930, Balderston conducted a study of group incentive plans. He collected written descriptions of such plans from a number of companies. In each instance, the pay of all members alike depended on the achievement of the group as a whole. He found that introduction of this method of work doubled the efficiency of the workers, increased their pay by about 25 percent, and reduced their costs a good amount, compared to the flat rate previously paid to each individual. The users of group incentives said that their plans were valuable because they increased cooperation and team

spirit among members, reduced monotony on the job, and caused workers to focus on a common goal.

5. The nature of a group's purpose is affected by the values of those persons who initially organize the unit. These values, called a "doctrine" by Mooney and Reilly (1931), are the basic principles members intend to support in their collaborative actions. The doctrine of a religious group is its expression of faith, stated in its creed. The doctrine of a governing body is put forth in its constitution. A business firm expresses a doctrine when it says it wants to do more than make a profit. Gantt (1910), as a case in point, pressed the idea of social responsibility by asserting that a firm can stand only by having *service* as its ultimate goal. The doctrine for an athletic team calls for teamwork, fair play, and trying hard, even when facing defeat.

Because a group's purpose is the product of a deliberate choice, it is easy to see why a doctrine influences what a group proposes to do and not do. Mooney and Reilly held that wherever there is a purpose, there must be a doctrine. These authors also contended that an enduring and strict doctrine, called a "dogma" if members did not want it to be altered, requires that the group's officers be granted considerable autonomy so that they can protect these basic principles against change. There has been no research on how the doctrine preferred by members affects their choice of purposes for their group.

Two early research themes

During the 1940s and 1950s, social psychologists and other social scientists began to be interested in groups as a field of study and introduced rigorous methods of research into their investigations (Zander, 1979). Although the goals of groups were a minor interest of investigators during those years, two themes in research are pertinent and have had a continuing influence on studies today.

The first is that members may become more concerned about the fate of colleagues (or about their group as a unit) than about their own personal fate. Barnard had earlier suggested that accomplishment of an organization's purpose depends to some degree on members' *willingness to contribute* to their organization. He remarked that there can be large variations among members in the intensity of this willingness and that only a small fraction of participants will be ready to aid the group in attaining its goals. He held that this willingness is not constant in degree but is intermittent and fluctuating, diminished by fatigue or discomfort. Thus, the number of individuals willing to serve the group, but near the neutral point in their zeal, is always fluctuating, and the aggregate willingness of potential contributors to any cooperative task is unstable.

In 1944, while investigating the role of the ego in work, Helen Lewis discussed the limitations of person-oriented motives in helping one to understand joint endeavors. She held that theories which make use of personal needs as exclusive causal factors cannot account for the causal dynamics in the social environment except in a vague and categorical way. Motivation in work need not necessarily be egotistical; on the contrary, the person is frequently motivated directly by the demands of the objective situation, including the requirements of another person. "On still other occasions, man enters upon and pursues tasks in order to help others or to help achieve an ideal. In such cases, the person's aims are not restricted by his own self-demands, which are often pushed aside" (p. 115). The results of her research supported her beliefs. These were new ideas thirty-five years ago; they still are today.

Following the work of Lewis, Horwitz (1954) sought answers to two questions: Can an individual develop a tension system coordinated to a group's attaining a goal? Can movement by the group toward its goal reduce this tension? Horwitz assumed that no participant can singly achieve a group's goal; therefore, he measured the tensions that arise in all members for completion of their group's task. He showed that his subjects became more involved in the progress of their group than in their own personal progress as the experiment proceeded. In a related study, Emmy Pepitone (1952) investigated the origin of the responsibility members develop toward their group. She did not permit any direct influence from one member to another and assumed that a member's perception of what his group requires is in itself a motivating condition. The strength of this requirement was based, in her view, on the perceived importance of a task in ensuring the group's success. Such a perception by a member of the group gives rise to a force, she assumed, the strength of which corresponds to its degree of importance. In a laboratory experiment, each subject in a group was engaged in exactly the same activity while out of sight of the remaining members. Each subject believed that teammates were performing tasks different from his own. In one condition, members were told that their work was necessary for achievement of the group's goal; in another condition, that their job was not important; and in a third condition, that all assignments were equally important. Pepitone observed that participants felt more responsibility toward the group and showed this by working harder when performing the more important role than when performing either of the other two. The studies by Horwitz and Pepitone indicate that members become motivated to have their group achieve its goal and are satisfied when it does so. The success of the group, rather than personal gain, is the major source of this satisfaction.

In 1949, Deutsch reported that when members are aware that each of them will get exactly the same reward if their group completes a joint task, the members perceive themselves to depend upon one another in their efforts toward that end. They are, in short, in a cooperative relationship, and they support each others' efforts.

A second theme in the 1940s and 1950s was that the environment of a group affected the nature of its goals. Thompson and McEwen (1958) proposed that environment and group interact through competition with other agencies, bargaining for resources, absorbing new elements into the group's leadership, or joining forces with other organizations for a common purpose. Dent (1959) reported that managers of 145 business establishments were fully aware of external pressures on the goals of their organizations.

It is interesting to note that speculation about the relation between a group and its environment is compatible with an explanation of individual behavior offered by Lewin (1935). The work of Lewin was guided by the belief that behavior is the result of interaction between a person and his surroundings, as they exist for him at that time. Lewin also held that any description of behavior requires the concept of direction, moving from one activity to another as in progress toward a goal. To attain a goal, an individual (or a group) must move along a path through a sequence of regions in his (or its) psychological environment.

In his research on individual goals, Lewin investigated the goals a person chooses, whether he selects ones that are difficult to accomplish or easy to reach. The goal, called a "level of aspiration" (Lewin et al., 1944), was defined as "the level of future performance in a familiar task which an individual, knowing his past performance in that task, explicitly undertakes to reach" (Frank, 1935, p. 119). Research on level of aspiration explained why a person develops feelings of failure or success, and why he changes his goal. The early work on personal levels of aspiration was a useful guide for later research on group aspirations (Zander, 1968).

Most of the ideas about organizational objectives mentioned thus far are accepted today, or are not openly rejected, perhaps because they have not been thoroughly tested. A number of issues were not given attention in earlier years even though they were close to ones being considered. These include: the relations between a group's doctrine, purpose, programs, and goals; how a group's purpose influences the choice of its goal; the effect of a group's goal and of no goal; interaction between the desires of members and a group's goals; conditions that make a group's goal acceptable to members; the properties of goals; and the effects of multiple goals. Some of these topics have been taken up during the 1960s and 1970s. We turn now to work during those years.

The purposes of groups

A "group" is a collection of individuals who have relations with one another that make them interdependent to some significant degree. We assume that every group has a purpose, a reason for existing and for doing what it does. It cannot exist unless its purpose is comprehended by some of the members. In order that we may better understand group goals, we must first consider the purpose of a group because its purpose influences its goal.

One of the prime decisions members make describes the purpose of their activities together. They may in fact give more attention to the purpose than to other properties of their nascent group. Such an emphasis was apparent in an informal study I made of the descriptions of brand new social entities. In that investigation I collected seventy-eight stories, each published in the popular press over four years during the 1960s, announcing the birth of an organization. Examples of the purposes were to: plan efforts in behalf of disadvantaged persons; encourage public awareness of ecological problems; improve the physical environment; provide for protection of private property; encourage research in social problems; and press for changes in a university's curriculum. The announcements of these new units elaborated on their purposes but said little about such matters as covering costs, persons who are eligible for membership, or the unit's activities. Presumably these latter processes were thought to be less worthy of public notice.

Because a group develops a purpose as part of its organizing efforts, it would help if we knew more about why groups choose the purposes they do. Consider that there are over 14,000 national associations in the United States and millions of corporations and smaller firms, along with an array of clubs, teams, and other kinds of groupings to do labor, make things, solve problems, generate social change, mediate between units, make laws, or improve the members in some way. In general, a group is formed when particular actions or states are sought and these can best be pursued through the collaboration of a number of persons. It is plain that problems and interests of the times influence what founders of a group wish to accomplish through joint action, but there are no data on what leads to the formation of a new unit or a decision not to form one.

A practical illustration of how members develop a purpose for their group has been provided by Christopher (1974). He believes that members of a firm must answer the questions: What are we? What do we intend to become? And in order to settle these issues, they must decide what the product of the group's activities will be, who will use the product, what competencies are wanted among those who make the product, and what facilities and resources are needed. A group should have a formally stated *identity*, Christopher believes, which describes the values of the members, the purposes of the organization, and the actions members must take to fulfill these purposes.

Because the purposes of an organization are usually stated by the officers in a unit's hierarchy, and because these officials have general interests that are removed from the daily routines of regular members, we can understand (as Barnard suggested in 1938) why purposes may be expressed in abstract and impractical terms. Nor is it surprising, as Etzioni (1960) alleges, that a group's purposes are not always salient to members of lower status, or even known by them.

The direction of members' efforts, whether they are turned inward toward the group itself or outward toward the group's environment, can influence a group's purpose. Mohr (1973) has distinguished between "transitive" and "reflexive" groups. A transitive group, he says, is concerned with conditions external to it; members take overt action on such situations instead of merely intending to do so; and the effect of their action is immediate and direct, not distant. A reflexive group, in contrast, induces contributions from members to help the group itself survive. National associations (Zander, 1972) have transitive objectives such as: arousing public acceptance of certain views, responding to federal regulations, or preserving reverence for certain historical events. Reflexive objectives are: improving procedures in units that belong to the association, developing common standards for production among members, or collecting information about the practices of units in the association. It is known that transitive associations put more weight on social values and on enlarging their membership than reflexive associations do. Transitive associations are also younger, larger, and more often engaged in social action. Kanter (1972) has described the sharp contrasts to be found in the purposes and programs of transitive and reflexive communes.

The most visible aspects of a group are its *activities*, and these are selected by members with a view toward implementing its purposes. There may be any number of programs conducted within a group. In a sample of 290 national associations, for example, 20 kinds of activities were noted, such as: newsletter, annual meeting, training program, exhibit, placement service, and publishing of books (Zander, 1972). Which programs are conducted in a group depends, we may guess, on two conditions: first, that the activity will help in pursuing the group's purposes; second, that there is sufficient talent, ability, energy, time, and resources within the group to ensure that the activity can be performed well. The stronger these two conditions are, and the more value members place on the group's purpose, the more members probably will be attracted to its projects. There has been no research, however, on these matters.

The activities in a group may not suit its purposes if the latter are so ambiguous that program planners cannot decide which activities will best fit the unit. Then, too, some actions may be introduced in a group (even though they have nothing to do with the purposes) because they are fashionable, attractive on other grounds, or assigned to the group by external agents whose intentions differ from those of the members. It seems clear that purposes can guide the selection of group activities but cannot limit or control them.

While participants are working toward fulfillment of the group's purposes, let us assume, they become interested in the quality of the group's performance. If the activity is repeated periodically, and if they think about it at all, they no doubt have difficulty at the outset in judging whether the group's performance has been superior, inferior, or average. After a few opportunities to see what scores the group attains, members are able to speak of their past record, their best performance, or their poorest showing, and are able to judge (roughly) what the chances are of getting a given amount of output from their joint efforts. This assumes there is no normative information on hand showing how well other groups have done in similar work and that the group has reasonably reliable feedback about its performance.

If, in contrast, the group's activity is performed only once, and this single trial continues for a long time, over a number of meetings, or never ends, the members may have difficulty in judging the quality of their group's performance because they have no comparative data—only a single product, if that. Before or during their work on the task, members nevertheless are inclined to predict how much their group will accomplish within a period of time. We assume that, for each of the programed activities conducted by a group, members become aware that the group is more likely to reach one degree of accomplishment than another. Participants are then ripe to decide if they want a group goal, and which one.

The goals of groups

Just as groups vary in the content of their purposes and activities, they vary in their goals. Joint objectives are stated in terms of quantity, as in dollars to be received, products to be made, pounds wasted, or points earned. Or the quantity may be an index based on the processing of several kinds of information, such as profit, cost, share of market, or return on investment. There are units whose goal describes the reactions of individuals, the number of complaints by customers, degree of satisfaction among workers, or extent of change in the views of certain persons. Still other groups provide help to people outside it, and the members accordingly choose goals describing the number of persons to be helped and dollars to be disbursed in doing so. Some goals require a certain amount of conformity to codes or of not failing to do so. Groups that try to change their members set goals for the improvements these persons should make on tests of achievement. McBurney (1963) and Dent (1959) have described the nature of the goals in a number of companies.

Those who write about group goals usually have a particular group in mind. Definitions of the abstract concept "goal" have reflected these special interests and fall under one of three types. One category describes the direction of a group's movement and takes no notice of the intentions or preferences of members. Perrow (1961), for instance, remarks that the daily decisions and the operational policies in a group reveal what it is trying to do, regardless of what its goals happen to be. A goal is an aim or a guide for intermediate decisions, according to Granger (1964), while Thompson (1967) defines a group goal as some imagined state of affairs which can be approached or attained at some future time.

A different method of defining a goal emphasizes gains for individual members. To illustrate, Gross (1965) remarks that a group objective is that which has the widest acceptance among members. Shaw (1976) thinks of a group goal as some composite of individual goals, or an end state desired by a majority of those in the group. Ryan (1973) conceives of a goal as a collection of words or symbols describing general interests of participants.

A third class of definitions emphasizes benefits for the group as a whole. Deniston and others (Deniston, Rosenstock, and Getting, 1968; Deniston, Rosenstock, Welch, and Getting, 1968) propose that an objective is the desired end result of the activities conducted as a part of a program (in a public health department). Etzioni (1960) observes that a goal is a valued state of affairs which the organization attempts to realize. Zander (1971) defines a group goal as an outcome desired by members for the group as a unit.

We will define a goal as in the last sentence above because this definition is based on the output of the whole, not merely of individual members, and it allows us to assume that selection of a goal is influenced by the motives of participants. The decisions and actions in a group are due, of course, to the behaviors of individuals, even when the decisions are joint agreements among many persons and lead to active teamwork among them. In order that we not mix levels of discourse between group and individual goals, it is useful to recognize that any of four different types of goal may be at work within a unit and that a circular-causal relationship exists among these four. 1. *The member's goal for the group* is the state, score, or outcome that each member privately would like to see the group attain. 2. *The group's goal* is the result of an overt agreement among members on what they jointly expect the group to accomplish; it is the group's goal for the group. 3. *The group's goal for the member* is the level of output the group expects each participant to achieve. 4. *The member's goal for the self* is the personal goal an individual brings to the group as modified by special demands of the group. It is plausible to believe that different matters determine the character of each of these four types. A full understanding of the origin and effects of group goals must accommodate the distinctive nature of these different variables.

Many writers believe a goal provides benefits for a group. A group's efficiency is improved when it has a goal because it: 1. helps members decide what needs to be done (Ansoff, 1965); 2. encourages a division of labor among members; 3. stimulates coordination among participants (Ansoff, 1965); 4. ensures that each of the steps in accomplishing a series of objectives is taken in its turn (Miller, 1978); 5. requires that planning be realistic; and 6. guarantees the productivity of members (McBurney, 1963). A group goal makes certain actions legitimate and others not so (Etzioni, 1960). It signals when efforts in a given direction may be ceased. It makes possible an appraisal of the group's efficiency and effectiveness (Ansoff, 1965; Etzioni, 1960; Zander, 1971) by comparing the level of actual performance with that initially desired. Such consequences of a goal are probably used by decision makers to justify having a goal in their group. It does not seem likely, however, that a goal would be established solely in order to attain such outcomes since many of them can be attained without a goal at all. Later, we shall examine empirical data on the effects of having a goal in a group.

Not everyone thinks a group goal is useful. There are critics, in fact, who assert that a goal is never necessary or that it is an imaginary notion with no basis in reality (Georgiou, 1973). One reason for this cynicism is that goals are often stated in such vague terms that they could not possibly be effective guides for the actions of members. Another reason is that many members, when asked, cannot accurately describe the goals of their group, and thus the objectives can have no impact on these persons. Goals, in certain cases, are not determiners of members' efforts because they do not come close to describing what is being done there. When appraisals of progress are made, moreover, groups have fallen short of their goals, more often than not, according to Etzioni (1960), which suggests that the goals are not being closely followed. Yuchtman and Seashore (1967) assert that organizations do not try to accomplish anything; they just exist or use up resources. And although no critics have stressed the point, they might complain that goals too often are said to be desirable states members *should* try to achieve. Yet, many goals mention matters to be avoided. It is plain that goals can be stated imprecisely or may not be acceptable to members, but these facts in themselves provide little support for the allegation that the concept of "group goal" is invalid. They merely suggest that goals must be stated with care.

In many groups, members probably do not find it necessary to publish explicit goals. An informal unit where no work is done perhaps needs no goal. Nor do groups want a precise goal if they place much value on flexible activities, new ideas, or new approaches, or if their members work on quite separate tasks. Among business firms, McBurney (1963) observed, goals are less likely to be set when sales are less predictable and when the transaction in making a sale is larger and more complex. Schools usually forgo the selection of institutional goals because progress toward them is difficult to measure. Cameron (1978) suggests that, in place of goals, educational agencies ought to use "measures of effectiveness" such as satisfaction of students' plans for their careers or openness of the educational system. Finally, in some groups it is enough that members show good faith in trying to fulfill the purposes of their unit without engaging in planned activities or intending to gain a given goal. Although a group may have no goal, it must have a purpose. Where the purpose is excessively vague, there is little to be gained by setting a goal.

Why a particular goal is chosen

After some experience with a given activity, we noted earlier, members develop an estimate about what their group will accomplish. I believe that this estimate, along with other considerations, helps members choose what goal they want for their group, if any. Let us call this judgment the members' "subjective probability of success by the group (Pgs)" and assume it is placed at a point on a scale of accomplishment that extends from no chance at all to absolute certainty that the group will successfully reach a particular degree of achievement. This perceived probability, it is likely, will be larger for an easier level of accomplishment than for a more difficult level. Thus, for each possible degree of achievement in a group's activity a member can, in principle, develop an estimated probability of attaining it. A member's "subjective probability of failure by the group (Pgf)" is his judgment of the probability that the group will fail to attain a given degree of achievement. This probability will be smaller for an easier level than for a more difficult level. For each potential level of achievement a member can also develop an estimated probability of failure. The subjective probability of failure is the inverse of the probability of success; that is, perceived probability of failure decreases as perceived probability of success increases, and the sum of the two probabilities equals unity.

When these comparative estimates of potential achievement are on hand, it is noteworthy, members begin to react to evidence about their unit's attainments in a way that is no longer simply cognitive. Their expectations about the group's future performance can now stimulate affect-laden responses to the group's output: satisfaction if the group does well and dissatisfaction if it does poorly. The "incentive value of group success (Igs)" is the amount of satisfaction a member develops in the group following its accomplishment of a given level. The "incentive value of failure (Igf)" is the amount of dissatisfaction a member develops in the group following its failure to reach a given level. Any attainment by the group, in short, now serves as a source of more or less satisfaction, or more or less dissatisfaction.

We assume next that a member's satisfaction in his group is greater after it attains a more difficult level than after it attains an easier one. That is, the satisfaction (Igs) is inversely related to the perceived probability of group success (Pgs). Also, a member's dissatisfaction is less after a failure to reach a harder level than an easier one. That is, dissatisfaction in a group's failure to attain a given attainment (Igf) is inversely related to the perceived probability of failure (Pgf) to attain that level.

Participants in a group, it is sensible to assume, prefer to be satisfied rather than dissatisfied, and this preference plays a part in helping members decide what they can anticipate from their joint efforts. We know that the level of achievement they expect of their group is the one that best resolves the attractiveness of success, the repulsiveness of failure, and the perceived probabilities of success and failure. Members' expectation of their group accomplishment accordingly is put at a level that will provide as much satisfaction as is reasonably probable if the group attains that level (Zander, 1971). An individual's goal for his group is the level of performance the person expects the unit to attain in the future. The group's goal for the group is a decision jointly reached by members concerning the level of performance they believe the group will attain. This decision can be influenced by agents outside the boundaries of the unit—an issue we will take up in a moment.

Now, let us assume that a member's goal for the group is placed at the level of accomplishment which assures the greatest probability of success (Pgs) as well as the greatest satisfaction from success (Igs) (that is, the product of Pgs × Igs) minus the level which assures the least probability of failure (Pgf) as well as the least dissatisfaction from failure (Igf) (that is, Pgf × Igf). We shall see that a number of conditions, such as the views and motives of members, the quality of the group's performance, or the pressures on and evaluations of the group, determine whether the term (Pgs × Igs) or (Pgf × Igf) is larger and has the greater part in influencing the joint goal set by members.

It has been found that a group's success strengthens a member's expectancy of future success; that is, Pgs becomes larger for more difficult levels of achievement. Also, a group's failure strengthens the expectancy of future failure; that is, Pgf becomes larger when failure is at easier levels (Zander, 1971). Because of the inverse relationship between incentive and probability, a group success increases the desirability of success for members and a group failure increases the repulsiveness of failure for them. Thus, the perceived potential attractiveness of success is greater and the potential repulsiveness of failure is less, the more difficult the task is perceived to be. Also, the perceived potential attractiveness of success is less and the potential repulsiveness of failure is greater, the easier the task is seen to be. A welcome success, in sum, heightens the attractiveness of success, and an unwanted failure the repulsiveness of failure.

There are groups that regularly repeat all or most of their activities and whose members routinely receive feedback about the group's product after each trial. This feedback helps members improve the performance of their unit because it allows them to identify errors and necessary changes in the group's procedures (Glaser and Klaus, 1966; Zajonc, 1962). In a repetitive group activity, members can set a goal for each new trial and, if they do so, placement of each new goal is influenced by the immediately prior performance of the group. It has often been observed that when a unit succeeds in attaining a goal that has been accepted by its members, the latter tend to raise the goal for the next trial; and when the group fails, they tend to lower the goal. The rule is then: succeed, raise; fail, lower. They raise the goal more consistently after a success than they lower it after a failure, and they raise it by a greater amount than they lower it. The net effect is that over a series of trials the average level of a group's goal tends to be above the average level of the group's performance. Thus, on a repetitive task, in the long run, groups fail more often than they succeed (Zander, 1971).

In a contrasting situation where the group's activity is not repeated but covers one long or unending trial (i.e., members are writing a report, solving a special problem, or planning an event), any feedback about the group's progress is likely to be unreliable because quantified scores are not available to members, as they would be at the completion of any trial. Generally speaking, when feedback is not provided, or is not trustworthy, members' interest in the task (Igs) is more important than Pgs in determining their effort, and they are inclined to believe that the performance of their group is good—as good as the beliefs among members whose units have succeeded repeatedly. Thus, members of groups with no feedback set goals similar to those set in groups that have regularly succeeded. No news is taken to be good news (Zander, 1971).

On a group activity that continues without repetition, it follows, there is not much chance that members will feel their group has failed, because they obtain little reliable feedback and ordinarily take this lack of news to be good news. But on a task with a number of trials, we have noted earlier, failures tend to occur more often than successes. Thus, members ought to like one-trial tasks more than tasks with several or many trials, but this deduction has never been tested. A group with an extended history of working toward a stated purpose (e.g., supervising the construction of a large building) has to proceed through a number of steps in turn. The definition of these steps, their assignment to particular persons, their performance, and their completion are analogous to fulfilling a number of smaller goals. As each step is finished, the members ought to obtain a typical sense of accomplishment.

External social pressures on a group's goals

Members of a group frequently receive information from external sources that can have, intended or otherwise, an impact on the goal they chose. There is no way of knowing how often such influences occur, but in some kinds of groups they are bound to happen frequently. There are writers who contend that most groups exist to serve or influence individuals outside their boundaries and that the members in these units may be exposed to pressures from those sources (Lawrence and Lorsch, 1967; Thompson, 1967; Thompson and McEwen, 1958). Persons in units that receive external pressures, we suspect, become especially sensitive to the stimuli arising in their social environments.

In a pilot study, I asked the supervisors of dozens of groups, all within the same company, to rate how they feel about parts of the world outside the firm, such as unions, customers, rival businesses, consumers' groups, and stockholders. It was evident in their responses that they give more attention to certain parts of the environment than to others and that the respondents see in these external agents what it is in their interest to see. Men in different parts of the company, for example, have different feelings about the significance of unions and stockholders. Sales supervisors are most aware of environmental conditions because they are more often on the periphery of the organization and more often exposed to environmental pressures (Zander, 1969).

We shall assume that social pressures acting on members of a group, originating in an external source, and directed toward either harder or easier degrees of achievement influence members to choose harder or easier goals, respectively, than they select in the absence of such pressures. Pressures on a group to work toward a particular goal may arise from at least four sources: 1. information about how well comparable groups have done; 2. comments made about the group by people who can see the group at work; 3. a request for help made by persons outside the group; and 4. a direct order from an agent who has the right to make such a demand. Let us consider these four.

When members have an opportunity to compare the performance of their team with the performance of comparable groups, they may observe that the product of the other groups is higher or lower than their own and be inspired by that observation to modify their collective's goals. The effects of such comparisons apparently are sought by the national association that establishes standards for United Funds because that body encourages each community to compare the results of its own financial campaigns with the results of campaigns in five or so other communities. The association provides a manual of procedures for each fund to follow when it is deciding which towns to use as models in making these comparisons. Although there are no data on the consequences of such efforts, we may guess, on the basis of earlier paragraphs, that the Funds prefer to compare their town with ones similar in size and economy and that, after making these comparisons, they select more difficult goals than the other Funds have reached.

An illustration of the effects of group comparisons can be seen in a laboratory study of teams working on a motor task. After each of fourteen trials, the groups were told the average score of all other groups taking the test. The reported averages were fixed so that a given team could see that it was either doing better than the other teams or worse. Regardless of the scores their group had actually earned, those who could see that their group was worse than the average set a higher goal for the future, and those who could see that their group was better than the average set a lower goal for the future. Thereafter, the higher goals (chosen by the below-average groups) remained unchanged, but the lower goals (chosen by the above-average units) were soon raised to match the average. Apparently doing worse than other groups (which pressed members to select more difficult goals) had a more extreme effect on the group's plans for the future (Zander and Medow, 1963).

The second kind of external pressure arises when comments about a group's performance are made by observers who do not belong to the group and who have no authority to put direct pressure on it. Because the observers have informed themselves about the quality of the group's work, and apparently have made appraisals of it, their remarks are of interest to members. In an experimental study, a group working on an activity that required close teamwork was watched by observers seated behind a glass screen. Before each trial, the observers discussed and decided what score they believed the team would be able to earn on its next trial, and this prediction was delivered to the group. When the observers expected the group to do well in its next attempt, the prediction had a stronger effect on the goals of the group (the goals were set higher) than when the observers predicted the group would do poorly (goals were kept the same—not changed). Thus, external expectations or harder goals again seemed to be more influential than ones looking toward easier goals (Zander, Medow, and Efron, 1965).

Now we come to the third kind of external pressure on a group: a request for help from persons who depend on it. A group's goal is not really a matter of choice if the group receives such a request. If a special manufacturing department receives unusual orders, the sales personnel (and the customers) get what they want from the department's workers even if fulfilling the orders involves considerable effort on their part. An exotic order has to be filled because it is a legitimate request, a part of the understanding between the sales force and the assembly unit: The sales people have the right to promise delivery of a new and different thing, and the assemblers' duty is to meet the schedule.

A fourth kind of external pressure on a group is a direct order. A familiar example of this occurs when a superior requires a group to reach a given level of attainment. A superior often wants an improved performance from a group. In a typical instance, in a slipper factory, managers set daily goals for each of twenty-eight assembly lines. These goals were not achieved on 80 percent of the days, yet the managers lowered the groups' goals on only 20 percent of the days. The managers believed that those on each line could do as well as they were being asked to do if they really tried (Zander and Armstrong, 1972).

In a laboratory experiment in which small groups repeatedly performed a collaborative task and learned their score after each trial, the members were requested by a "standards committee" to attain a particular level of performance at each attempt. The requested levels were consistently very difficult. In one treatment, in addition to the request, members were promised a reward if they did as well as they were asked and in another treatment were told of an unpleasant consequence if they did not. Measures were made of the degree to which the group's future goals exceeded immediately prior levels of performance. This amount was greater when members were offered a reward or a punishment than when they were requested to attempt a given level with no mention of a sanction (Zander, 1971). Board members of United Funds revealed, in their responses to a questionnaire, that they were exposed to strong pressures to set a particular goal for their campaign. Persons with more responsible roles on the board were more sensitive to these pressures than those with less responsible positions, and more so if the Fund had recently failed to reach its campaign goal than if it had recently succeeded (Zander, Forward, and Albert, 1969).

We have considered the impact of several kinds of stimuli that arise outside a group. Is one generally more effective than the other? There is no clear indication of this. In an experiment that compared the three forms of social pressure—the effect of meeting others' needs, social comparison, and overt demands on the group—each pressure had a wholly independent effect, about equal in size. The stronger each condition, the more impact it had on the group's goals. Thus, members appeared to have no inherent tendency to respond more readily to one form of social pressure than to another, all else being equal (Forward and Zander, 1971). It is noteworthy, however, that members are usually more influenced by external pressures than by their group's past performance when choosing a goal.

Because group members appear to have a predilection for harder goals, social pressure on a group to choose a difficult level is more effective than pressure on it to choose an easier level. But requests for better performance typically generate more failures than successes, yet the group's aspiration is not always lowered after the failure. And pressures toward a lower output generate more successes than failures, so that the goal is usually raised after a success. To some unknown degree, then, a charge given to a group to set a more difficult standard may be more influential (or appear to be so) in determining a group's goal because members ordinarily dislike lowering their aspiration after a failure, and a charge to set an easier goal may be less influential (or appear to be so) because members prefer raising their group's goal after a success. It seems probable that members' responses to their group's success or failure and their responses to external social pressures each affect the other in such a way that the contribution of one may be simply a product of the other. We need, therefore, to examine separately the effect of external pressures and the effect of success and failure; this was done in a laboratory experiment (Zander and Ulberg, 1971).

The study was so constructed that every group failed on some of the trials and succeeded on some of the trials in attaining goals set by the team members. Immediately after half of each of the failing trials, members were asked to raise their goal, and after the other half requested to lower it. After half of the successes, the members were likewise asked to raise their goal, and after the other half requested to lower it. It was expected that the request to set a harder goal would be more effective than the request to set an easier goal. That is what happened, but only because pressures directed toward an easier goal were rejected when the group had just been successful in attaining its goal and thus preferred raising its goal rather than lowering it. When adjustments were made (statistically) for the natural tendency of members to prefer harder goals, one could see that external pressure on a group to select a difficult goal was apparently no more influential than pressure on it to choose an easy goal. The pressure on the group, moreover, was more influential in determining the level of the group's goal when it was in the direction members already intended to move the goal—toward a higher level after a success and a lower level after a failure. When the pressure upon the group was in a direction that opposed their tendency to shift the goals, the members more readily listened to the views put forth by one or another of their colleagues and then set their group's goal based on their group's past performance rather than on the basis of demands from outsiders. It appears that what matters most is whether the direction of the external demand makes sense to members and is acceptable on those grounds; most often this direction is toward a more difficult goal.

Concern for group achievement

It is reasonable that the strength of the desire among members to experience pride in their group would affect their choice of a goal. They would be more likely to gain a sense of pride, for instance, if they chose a goal that allows their group to attain a favorable outcome. How may we conceive of a desire for group achievement? How does such a motivation influence members' choice of a goal?

People of affairs have no trouble in recognizing that under some conditions, individuals become as concerned about the fate of their group as about their own personal fate. Bennis (1966) has shown, for example, that ten different theories of management are alike in their emphasis on the reciprocity between members' needs and goals and the organization's goals and rights. Researchers have seldom studied group-oriented concerns of members. Instead, scholars usually view a group as a site for study of socially stimulated behavior of individuals, of interpersonal interactions, or of mutual influence. Occasionally, investigators *assume* that members' plans and energies are devoted to attaining their group's goal (not merely the members' personal objectives), but this assumption is rarely tested.

So that we may be somewhat precise about members' desires for group achievement, let us take it for granted that there can be two group-oriented dispositions. The "desire for group success (Dgs)" is the readiness of a participant to experience pride and satisfaction with his group if it successfully accomplishes a challenging group task. The "desire to avoid group failure (Dgaf)" is the readiness of a member to experience embarrassment or dissatisfaction with his group if it fails on a challenging task.

· We will assume that the experience of satisfaction in group success and dissatisfaction in group failure generate, respectively, the desires Dgs and Dgaf in the member. These desires generate tendencies to select particular kinds of goals for reasons given elsewhere in greater detail (Zander, 1971). Among persons in whom Dgs is stronger than Dgaf, the tendency is to prefer a group goal with a Pgs of .50 (a goal in the middle range of difficulty) since this is the level at which the favorable effects of success are most likely to occur for them. Among persons in whom Dgaf is stronger than Dgs, the tendency to avoid, given that they are required to engage in the activity, is greatest where Pgf is .50. Therefore, they will least prefer to choose a goal with that subjective probability and instead will favor one that is either very hard or very easy for them. They will probably choose the difficult goal if it is more important to experience little embarrassment than it is to fail on a hard level; they will choose the easy level if it is more important not to fail, even though an easy success is not a satisfying one. But these matters have not yet been investigated. A good guess, based on evidence we shall consider later, is that members more often wish to avoid embarrassment than to avoid mere failure.

Because group-oriented desires affect the difficulty of the goal chosen, it is important to note that certain conditions modify the strength of Dgs. (For the sake of simplicity, we will not take up ways of enhancing the desire to avoid group failure.) Qualities of a group that are understood, on the basis of research evidence, to generate greater desire for group success are: more unity in the group; greater strength of the group; rewards available to the group for success; frequent successes; and evidence that teammates are trying hard. Special characteristics of members as individuals also give them a stronger desire for group success: competence in the role assigned to the member; a central position in the group's activity; and a stronger motive for individual success (Zander, 1971).

John Forward (1969) has observed that "personal motives to achieve individual success (Ms)" and "to avoid individual failure (Maf)" are separable and independent from desires Dgs and Dgaf. This independence implies that person-oriented and group-oriented motives can supplement one another in an additive manner, increasing the strength of the members' total tendency to approach or to avoid, or that the person and group motives may act in contrasting direction, each weakening the effect of the other.

Consequences of group goals

We return now to a question posed earlier. Does it make a difference if a group has a goal? Does the presence of a goal cause behavior among members unlike those in a group with no goal?

It is plausible that pursuit of a goal will influence a group's achievement. In some groups this effect is easy to discern because the goal is expressed in countable units such as dollars, doughnuts, minutes, or miles. In other groups, accomplishment is harder to specify because the gains are described in abstract terms or cannot easily be measured. Deniston, Rosenstock, and Getting (1968) and Deniston, Rosenstock, Welch, and Getting (1968) have addressed the difficulty of assessing the effectiveness and efficiency of action programs. The authors remark that the most frequent causes of confusion in making such evaluations are the lack of a clear distinction between an activity (what is being done in the unit), the objective of that activity, and the extent to which achievement of the objective can be attributed unambiguously to the activity itself. As is often true in assessing other kinds of achievement, identifying goalward movement by a group involves problems of validity and reliability in measurement, as well as difficulty in making a distinction between means and ends.

Locke (1968) and his associates have conducted extensive research into the contrasting effects of having and not having a goal. Although he has usually studied individuals working on solo tasks, it is clear that he believes his ideas apply to groups as well as to individuals. The main premise behind investigations done by Locke and his associates is that an individual's conscious intentions regulate his actions. Thus, when a person has decided on particular plans, goals, or tasks to be performed, this commitment to self guides his behavior. Locke defines a goal or intention as what "the person is consciously trying to do," what he has decided to attempt. Locke ignores motives that are not directly and overtly evident to the actor. It seems clear that the members of a group, even more than solo persons, are aware of what they are up to in choosing a group goal or working toward it. Thus, Locke's theory is especially appropriate as a basis for thinking about the impact of a group's goal.

Locke's notions led him to the question: Does a group with an explicit goal produce more than one with no goal? To study this question, groups were given specific goals by the experimenter and their output was compared with that of groups merely asked to "do their best," without specifying what "best" is. Latham and Kinne (1974) used crews of loggers as subjects. The teams with goals did better than those asked to do their best. Ronan, Latham, and Kinne (1973), using similar subjects, noted that the performances of the crews with goals were better if the foreman stayed around to monitor their work than if he did not stay. This suggests that the goals may, in some degree, be perceived as demands by the boss, and that a more specific goal is a sharper demand. Latham and Yukl (1975b) reviewed the results of twenty-seven field studies and found general support for the hypothesis that individuals and groups do better if they have a stated goal than if they are only asked to do well.

When a group has a goal, members tend to use it as the criterion for evaluating how well the group has performed. Zander (1971) describes eleven investigations in which a group had a goal, members worked to achieve it, and then rated the quality of their group's performance. In most instances, as one would expect, they gave more favorable ratings if the group had attained its goal and less favorable ratings if it had failed to do so. Under some circumstances, however, members did not evaluate their group in that way. Reasons for this inaccuracy are worth noting, as they suggest why a group's goal may not be accepted by members.

Individuals were more inclined to misrecall the score of their group after it had failed than after it had succeeded. When board members of the United Funds were asked how much money their local Fund had raised in its most recent campaign, those in towns that had failed four times in a row recalled an amount that was significantly higher than the amount actually raised, whereas those in Funds that had succeeded four times in a row recalled their intakes correctly. Peripheral members of boards, whose jobs made them less responsible for the group's fate, more often misrecalled the group's score than did central members (Zander, Forward, and Albert, 1969). Dustin (1966) has reported similar results from a laboratory experiment.

When circumstances make it less important for members to have a reliable appraisal of the group's performance, they are less likely to use the group's goal as the criterion for evaluating that performance. To cite an example, appraisals by peripheral members of boards in United Funds were less in accord with the facts than were ratings by central members. Also, persons with a stronger need to avoid personal failure were less accurate than those with a stronger need to achieve personal success (Zander and Wulff, 1966). The group's goal was less often taken as the standard of excellence when achievement of that goal had little interest to persons outside the group (Zander, 1971). Also, a group's failure was taken to be less serious if the members tried hard, even though they were incompetent, than if they were competent and did not try (Zander, Fuller, and Armstrong, 1972). More board members in unsuccessful United Funds wanted to abolish campaign goals than in successful Funds. In sum, it appears that if members are less concerned to have their group perform well, they are less careful to identify the true relationship between the group's goal and its movement toward that objective; that is, the goal is not taken to be the criterion of excellence.

When a group has chosen a goal or has had one assigned to it, managers of the unit have a basis for deciding what duties are to be assigned to separate parts of the group. Barnard (1938) proposed that it is the responsibility of an executive to divide the organization's objective into fragments so that detailed goals and detailed actions follow in the correct sequence. In doing this, the executive states the general direction for the organization and asks heads of subunits to decide what this broad goal means in terms of actions within each of their departments and eventually for each member. Steers and Porter (1974) emphasize that the main point of a group's goal is that individuals can thereby be provided with targets to attain for their group.

When a group sets a goal for an individual to achieve in his own work, what determines whether that member accepts the goal? The congruence between a member's personal goal and the one the group asks him to attain increases as he becomes more aware that his actions are more instrumental for the group's achievement. In support of this general statement, Zander (1971) cites the results of several studies. A member chooses a personal goal that more closely resembles the one suggested by the group as: 1. the attractiveness of the group increases; 2. the proposed goal is perceived to be more important to groupmates; 3. the member's personal activity is more relevant to the work of the group; 4. colleagues express a stronger desire to have the member achieve a given level of performance; and 5. the proposed goal is a moderate challenge rather than an extremely difficult one.

The attributes of group goals

A group goal has particular properties, such as specificity, difficulty, or similarity to other goals. Such attributes modify the effects that a group's goal can have on behavior within the group.

Clarity in statement of the goal

As we have already noted, the description of a given goal may be either precise or imprecise, exact or uncertain. Sometimes a vague goal cannot be avoided. Other times, such a goal may be ambiguously defined if the decision makers in a group have had little experience in the activity for which the goal is to be set and therefore cannot anticipate very well what they ought to be able to accomplish. Some purposes are shapeless (to improve the well-being of members, to provide cultural opportunities in this town, to increase respect for the flag) and do not suggest activities that could have a precise goal. The executive bodies of national associations are concerned with broad purposes such as developing standards, changing attitudes, collecting knowledge, preserving values, or responding to regulations. Intentions like these seldom lead to precise goals (Zander, 1972). Descriptions of the difficulties in defining goals are put forth in several books by Mager (1962, 1972). In these volumes he provides step-by-step advice on what a teacher must do to delineate useful goals for a classroom.

In some situations there are advantages in choosing a goal that is loose enough to cover various activities. A group of persons each of whom is conducting separate pieces of research will derive little benefit from an exactly stated joint target. And if they attempt to specify one, the scientists may learn, as Gross (1965) suggests, that trying to choose a group goal causes more interpersonal conflict than the effort is worth. Korten (1962) has proposed that vague goals are sensible when it is important that sub-parts of an organization have freedom to function autonomously.

When a group's goal is vaguely expressed, we have already noted, it is difficult to assess the amount of progress toward that end. The consequence is that members obtain little feedback on the group's performance and have little opportunity to benefit from past experience. It follows that groups with imprecise goals often have poorly developed procedures and operating plans, and because a fuzzily defined objective provides uncertain guidance for actions of members, we expect more discoordination in the functioning of the group and less effectiveness in its work. Warner and Havens (1968) suspect that ambiguously stated objectives cause members to develop more interest in maintaining the group than in having it be productive toward ends that cannot clearly be seen. If goals are uncertain, moreover, members do not know how well their personal efforts contribute to the group's achievements, if at all. This was noted in a study of professional persons working in a business firm (Zander, 1971).

There is evidence suggesting that more precisely defined objectives lead to more favorable results. As we observed earlier, Locke, Latham, Yukl, and others report that a specific goal, in contrast to an admonition that members do their best, creates in them more interest and more productivity. When the group's goal as well as its path for attaining it are quite clear, members are more attracted to work for it, less bored in doing so, and more certain that they belong to the group, according to the results of an experiment by Raven and Rietsema (1957). Deans in colleges with clearer goals are more willing to listen to the ideas of faculty members and more willing to influence the professors by being a good model, rather than by attempting to persuade them (Wieland, 1969).

Difficulty of the group's goal

Everyone knows that changes in the difficulty of a group's goal cause changes in the behavior of its members. For instance, groupmates make more careful plans and use more effort when their goal is harder. The results of research support the hypothesis that more difficult goals generate better performances. There are different explanations for these results or separate aspects of them; we have already touched on parts of these explanations.

In one set of studies, stimulated by the work of Locke (1968), it was found that groups (logging crews) performed better if their goals were difficult than if they were easy (Latham and Saari, 1979; Latham and Yukl, 1975a, 1975b). These authors emphasize that a strong relationship exists between productivity of a team and difficulty of its goal only if workers accept that goal. Accepting the goal, they believe, is tantamount to establishing an intention to achieve it. Thus, tougher goals generate more productivity than easier ones simply because members commit themselves to do what is necessary.

The results of studies in a tradition different from Locke's also indicate that performance of a group improves as its goal becomes more difficult (for that unit). But the difficulty must not be too great. In one investigation, by Stedry and Kay (1964), work groups were assigned either of two kinds of goals. One kind was at a level similar to what the group had been achieving at least 50 percent of the time in the past six months. The other kind was at a level the group had achieved only 25 percent of the time. After some experience with these goals, the foreman of each crew was asked to rate the difficulty of his group's goal as either normal, a moderate challenge, or impossible. In the ensuing months, there was a 28 percent improvement if the goal was taken to be a challenge, a 16 percent improvement if it was normal, and a 35 percent *decrease* if the goal was impossible. Apparently, a goal is less motivating if it is too hard.

In another case, Zander and Newcomb (1967) observed the goals and levels of performance in a series of four financial campaigns conducted by each of 149 United Funds. The amount of change in goal was compared with the amount of improvement in performance. As the change in goal grew larger, (in an upward direction) the performance improved; harder goals generated better output. This relationship, however, was entirely due to the towns that had had more successes than failures in the past and that typically made moderate increases in their goals. Among towns with more failures than successes, which typically made large increases in future goals over past levels of performance, the correlation was near zero. Comparable results have been reported by Zander, Forward, and Albert (1969).

Apparently, then, a goal that is harder than the group has attained in the past will generate an improvement in output, but only if the discrepancy between future goal and most recent score is not greater than some optimal amount. The new goal ought to be moderately challenging, not impossible, closer to the .40 level of probability, say, than to the .20 level in the eyes of those who are working to reach it. A more difficult goal is preferred by members, we have earlier proposed, because the consequences of success on a difficult task are perceived to be more favorable, and the consequences of failure on such a task are perceived to be less repulsive. There can be pressures on a group from external agents, moreover, to try for harder goals and to avoid easier ones, which adds an increment toward choosing more difficult ends. The tendency to work hard, whether to achieve a success or to avoid a failure, ought to be stronger on a demanding level than on an easier one, and the performance of a unit should be better on a more difficult task than on an easier one, all else held constant.

If the criterion for achievement must not be too far removed from the past level of performance in order for it to arouse maximal effort, we can anticipate that gradual increases in the difficulty of the goal, each step a small one, will cause members to press themselves harder at each upward move. By the end of a series of trials, the group should be performing considerably better than it was at the outset. Zajonc (1962) has provided support for such ideas and has demonstrated, furthermore, that most of the improvement in the group's performance is due to improvement among the initially less competent members, who are responding to an awareness that the score of the group depends on a better output by them.

When a group does not reach its goal because that target is too difficult, we naturally expect that members would do whatever they could to improve their group's effectiveness. We may observe instead that they put major effort into overcoming embarrassment caused by the group's bad performance and do little toward improving the group. In planning ways of improving its effectiveness, members may lower their group's goals or may try to improve the group's procedures, equipment, tools, supplies, or skills. Attempting to reduce embarrassment, however, requires participants to take steps that help them duck the impact of a poor group score, change its meaning, distort its nature, or do other things to reduce the shame they feel. The following actions, identified in a number of studies, are described in Zander (1977).

After a series of failures by a group, we assume, members place more weight on reducing their embarrassment than on ensuring future success because there is a better chance (given the group's recent failures) of lowering embarrassment than of attaining success. Embarrassment-reducing responses concentrate on one or more of the following aspects of group life: 1. the group's goal, 2. the group's way of doing work, or 3. the member's responsibility to the group.

1. When the group's goal is the focus, members seek to convince themselves or others that the group is being improperly held to a given

standard of excellence. They may prefer an impossibly difficult goal so that their chagrin will be small if they fail and they will win approval for attempting to reach such a difficult objective. They may prefer not to set a goal at all, because if there is no goal there can be no failure (Zander, Forward, and Albert, 1969). They may perceive external demands on the group to be easier than they actually are or they may deny they are embarrassed by failure.

2. When the group's way of working is the focus, they may blame the ineptness of members and make derogatory remarks about how they collaborate. They may disapprove of how the group's output is measured, doubt that the group's score is correct, that the task is a true test of the group's ability (they can do better on other things), or that observers' ratings of the group are valid.

3. When the members seek to reduce their responsibility for the group's failure, they may misrecall the group's score or deny they were at fault.

The irony of efforts to reduce embarrassment is that these actions do little to ensure future success. Thus, a group that concentrates on lowering embarrassment will most likely fail again. This new failure once more generates efforts to reduce embarrassment, leading to another failure. Thus, a circular-causal system develops that is difficult to escape.

The power of a group's goal

Because a group's goal stimulates particular behaviors, it may be thought of as an inducing agent, a source of influence on the members. Goals with greater power generate stronger and more persistent efforts to fulfill them, while goals with less power are ignored. Thomas and Zander (1959) demonstrated that military personnel worked harder to reach a goal that had greater *instrumental value*. The size of this value was the resultant of their estimates about two matters: 1. the chances that attainment of the goal would ensure achievement of a more ultimate goal and 2. the amount of value they placed on that ultimate aim. Based on ideas considered earlier, we can guess that the power of the goal will be greater if it is a challenge but not too difficult; is precisely stated; the members accept it; they receive accurate feedback about their group's performance; external sources advocate attainment of that particular goal; the members have a stronger desire for group success; they are able to compare the performance of their group with units similar to their own; and they judge they are performing well in the duties assigned to them as individuals.

Thibaut and Kelley (1959) propose that a group goal is a special instance of a group standard, meaning that it is a decision made by members about how they should act in order to help the group accomplish its purposes or maintain its existence. With this type of approach in mind, we may assume, as has been assumed earlier in respect to group standards (Cartwright and Zander, 1968), that the power of the goal increases as the cohesiveness of the group is greater. We foresee, furthermore, that members will exert pressures on one another to conform to the requirements of the goal and that members who do not conform will be excluded from the group. It follows that changes in the group's goal might be more difficult to bring about as the cohesiveness of the group is stronger (Janis, 1972). There is merit, it appears, in more research on the origins of strength in a group's goal.

Multiple group goals

More commonly than not, a group may have a number of goals. This multiplicity can be valuable because several objectives may be additive in their impact on members. Also, different goals provide many criteria for appraising the group's work. As a result, a group will usually have some successes even though it has some failures, and an awareness of needs for improvement can be accompanied by satisfaction from successes. A group performs better, according to Zajonc (1962), if each member can simultaneously evaluate three separate aspects of its effort: the production of the group as a whole, the production of the member himself, and the production of each remaining member. As yet, there has been no research on how several group goals supplement one another.

Typically, writers devote most attention to the unfavorable effects when a group has several objectives. There may be a conflict between or among the goals of a group so that members' efforts toward one goal interfere with efforts toward a different goal. Or concentration on one activity prevents concentration on another. A firm cannot improve its product and also increase its dividends. It cannot press for more productivity yet decrease the size of its payroll (Seashore, 1965). Some conflicting goals probably interfere with the effectiveness of a group, but there are no studies on the point.

If there are several goals, different members may have different perceptions of these, according to Wallroth (1968), which leads to incongruence, inconsistency, and inconsonance among efforts to attain the goals. Because all goals cannot be satisfied simultaneously, managers of a group must choose among them at any given moment. The conflicts between goals are often resolved by assigning different objectives to different parts of the group—thus keeping separate the work being done toward separate goals (Cyert and March, 1963). Or the group's officers may take up unlike goals in a sequential manner, or allow subunits to go their separate ways.

Summary

Forty years ago there was little research on behavior in groups and no investigations of purposes or goals in groups. Some writers at the time, mostly businessmen recounting their personal experiences and beliefs, assumed that purposes were important for organizations because they fostered cooperative behavior, determined characteristics of the organizations, and stimulated action among members.

In the 1940s and 1950s, students of groups began to examine the notion that members could be as concerned about the fate of their group as about their own personal fate. The results of these studies, combined with findings of research on individual levels of aspiration, suggested that the goals of groups call forth the interest and effort of members. Thus, a group goal can be a source of motivation for persons in a group.

Today, we assume that every group has a purpose, a reason for existing and for doing what it does. Without a purpose it cannot initially be organized or survive. The activities and programs in a group are developed to fulfill the group's purpose. While participants work on these activities, they become interested in the quality of their group's performance. After some experience with the group's activities, members are able to speak of their past record, their best performance, or their poorest showing, and are able to judge what the chances are of reaching or failing each of several degrees of output in a given period. This judgment helps members choose what degree of accomplishment they desire from their group—that is, what goal they want their group to have, if any. Under some circumstances, it is not unusual for members to avoid the constraints created by the presence of a goal, and hence they choose none.

When estimates of potential achievement are on hand, members react to evidence about their unit's attainments in a way that is no longer simply cognitive. Their expectations about their group's performance stimulate affect-laden responses: satisfaction if the group does well and dissatisfaction if it does poorly. Satisfaction is greater as the success is earned on a more difficult task and dissatisfaction is greater as the failure is on an easier one. As a consequence, members prefer a goal that assures the greatest probability of success as well as the greatest satisfaction from success. They commonly expect more of their group than it can achieve, and thus it fails more often than it succeeds. If members are engaged in an activity that provides no score or other form of feedback about how much their group has accomplished, members are inclined to judge their unit as doing well, as well as those in a successful group.

Pressures on a group to work toward a particular goal arise from at least four sources: information about how comparable groups have done; comments made about the group; requests for help from persons who depend on the group; or a direct order from an agent who has the right to make such a demand. These pressures appear to have a stronger impact on the choice of a goal than does the group's own experience.

Under appropriate conditions, members develop a stronger or weaker desire for group success, a readiness to experience pride and satisfaction with their group if it successfully accomplishes a challenging task. And they develop a stronger or weaker desire to avoid group failure, a readiness to experience embarrassment or dissatisfaction with the group if it fails on a challenging task. Among persons in whom the desire for group success is stronger than the desire to avoid group failure, the tendency is to prefer a group goal in the middle range of difficulty.

A group with a goal performs better than one with no goal. The goal is used as the criterion for evaluating the group's quality of work, and these evaluations are made with greater care when members are in situations that make them more concerned to have their group perform well. Members appear to do better when the goal is more clearly stated and is a moderate challenge. If the task is difficult and generates many failures, members tend to devote more attention to activities that lower embarrassment because there is a better chance of lowering embarrassment than of attaining success. Such a choice causes further failures.

10

Looking Backward

LEON FESTINGER

This book does not, nor was it intended to, paint a comprehensive picture of the growth of social psychology. It was intended to be selective, reflecting primarily the personal interests and views of each individual author. And the various chapters in the book are just that—personal views and personal interpretations of where we were, where we are, how we got here, and where we ought to be going. Each of them has, to me, a delightfully different flavor that identifies the writer.

The original plan for this chapter was to present an integration of all the contributions to this book as a summary statement. My various lines of thought about how to summarize, organize, or interrelate these different personal statements, however, kept ending in blind alleys. After a number of approaches, I decided that there was only one way to avoid being pedantic, uninteresting, and trivial—namely, to write a personal statement of my own. So this chapter is, indeed, a personal view—actually, an extremely personal one—of some aspects of the history of the trend begun by the Research Center for Group Dynamics and its relationship to social psychology.

A few friends of mine who read and criticized an early draft of this chapter persuaded me that it should be read in conjunction with the Preface, where the genesis and purpose of the book are stated. They also persuaded me that very few persons read prefaces to books. So, for self-protection, I urge you to read the Preface before reading this concluding chapter. It won't take long; the Preface is very brief.

A small bit of personal history

In September 1939, some forty years ago, I arrived in Iowa City as a new graduate student at the University of Iowa. I had gone there to study with Kurt Lewin, whose writings I had read while an undergraduate. I worked and studied with, and learned from, Lewin until his death in 1947.

When I came to Iowa, I was not interested in social psychology. Indeed, I had never had a course in social psychology. My graduate education did nothing to cure that. I never had a course at Iowa in social psychology either. As an undergraduate, I had done a study on level of aspiration (Hertzman and Festinger, 1940) and had become interested in the concepts that Lewin had developed in connection with the work of his group in Berlin—tension systems and the remembering and completion of interrupted tasks; boundaries and psychological satiation; force fields and *Umweg* situations. There was creativity, newness, and a sense of importance in these ideas of Lewin. Also, the closeness between theory and data was particularly appealing to me. I arrived in Iowa with great enthusiasm.

Unfortunately for me, by the time I arrived, the things that fascinated me were no longer on center stage. True, we talked about life spaces and forces and regions and tension systems, but the main interest of Kurt Lewin was now in the area of social psychology; he wanted to understand the behavior of groups. The work of Ronald Lippitt and Ralph White (1943) on groups operating in "autocratic" and "democratic" atmospheres had been the beginning of this new direction. Kurt Lewin already spoke of his dream to create a new, independent Institute for Group Dynamics.

Undeterred, and enjoying the tolerance of the others, I did research on level of aspiration, on a mathematical model of decision making, on statistics, and even strayed to doing a study using laboratory rats. The looser methodology of the social psychology studies, and the vagueness of relation of the data to the Lewinian concepts and theories, all seemed unappealing to me in my youthful penchant for rigor.

In 1945 I joined Kurt Lewin, Ronald Lippitt, Dorwin Cartwright, and Marian Radke (now Yarrow) as an Assistant Professor at the Research Center for Group Dynamics at the Massachusetts Institute of Technology. It was a research center rather than an institute simply because one couldn't have an institute within an institute. At this time I became, by fiat, a social psychologist and immersed myself in the field with all its difficulties, vaguenesses, and challenges. Just as Elliot Aronson recalls his days at Stanford University as a time of excitement, the years at M.I.T.

seemed to us all to be momentous, ground breaking, the new beginning of something important.

The impact of Lewin on social psychology

Of course, social psychology had been developing for many years. It flourished long before Lewin became interested in it. People like Allport, both Gordon and Floyd, Sherif, Newcomb, Katz, and many others had done, and were doing, very significant work. This work has endured and is still important. For example, Richard Nisbett, in his chapter, goes back to Hartshorne and May (1928) and to Newcomb (1929) to find some of the best data about "trait consistency." Singer, in his chapter, properly points out that the beginnings of theory about interpersonal social influence and social comparison processes go back to Newcomb (1943) and to Sherif (1935).

But Kurt Lewin and his co-workers had changed something, had brought something new and original into the field. In retrospect, it is perhaps possible to specify what some of these new things were.

In part, the originality of Lewin's early contribution to social psychology lay in the choice of problems to investigate—in the judgment of what was, or was not, an interesting or important problem. I would like to be able to explain how such judgments are made and why some persons seem to do it so well. Unfortunately, the way in which one makes a priori judgments about "interesting" and "important" are, to me, still in the realm of unverbalizable art. But Kurt Lewin had a fine talent for it, and somehow that talent rubbed off a little on those around him. In his paper "Formalization and Progress in Psychology," Lewin (1940) describes how, from "three years of experimentation with hundreds of series of nonsense syllables and after thousands of measurements of reaction times," he decided that he had to discard the classic law of association. Convinced that it was necessary to distinguish between habits (associations) that did or did not involve needs or quasi-needs, he emerged with his ideas about the importance of "tension systems." This idea led to a long series of very fruitful experiments on goal-directed activities and the effects of interrupting them. From the classic law of association to Lewin's concept of tension system is quite a long leap, however, and how he got there remains mysterious.

Similarly, when Lewin turned to social psychology, together with all his other concepts, he emphasized the idea that the small face-to-face group was a powerful factor in people's lives and in the transmission of social forces. So group atmospheres, group decision, group cohesiveness, group goals, and the like became important problems to theorize about and to investigate.

Another aspect of "important," however, is more easily verbalizable. It was important if it made a difference with respect to actual problems in the world, real events and processes. It is no accident that so many of the chapters in this book, chapters by Kurt Back, Al Zander, Mort Deutsch and Stan Schachter, deal, in a major sense, with practical problems.

Out of such an orientation in which a priori "importance of problem" reigned supreme there emerged a methodological approach that was distinctive. It arose from the insistence on trying to create, in the laboratory, powerful social situations that made big differences. This seemed necessary in a field so new, where so many things were probably multiply determined. So experiments were done with all these things in mind, plus a large dose of bravura and enthusiasm. Who would have imagined doing a "scientific experiment" in which the independent variable to be manipulated was autocratic versus democratic atmospheres? Certainly no one can describe, with reasonable precision, all the facets that were experimentally varied in those studies. When one experimenter (group leader) seemed unable to run a group democratically, a third group atmosphere came into being—namely, laissez-faire. Who would have imagined doing experiments in real world situations—comparing lectures and group decisions for their effectiveness in getting women to buy glandular meats during World War II? I still have no clear conceptual understanding of what all the differences were between these procedures. I have always admired the fantastic skill of Alex Bavelas, a grand master in dealing with groups, that enabled him always to produce a unanimous group decision in the desired direction.

But big changes were produced, we did learn things from these studies, and the spirit of them had a lasting impact (Bavelas, 1942; Lewin, 1943; Lewin, Lippitt and White, 1939; Lippitt, 1940). We learned that one could, indeed one must, do studies both in the real world and in the laboratory. And when one was in the laboratory, it was vital not to lose sight of the substance in the quest for greater precision. Precision is highly desirable but only if one has retained the reality and essence of the question. Thus, a tradition grew of bringing very complicated problems into the laboratory. That tradition also included maintaining, always, a mixture of laboratory and field work. And how did one manipulate complicated variables in the laboratory? Well, that too is an art form. As Bob Zajonc points out in his chapter, Back's (1951) experiment employed a manipulation that was based solely on intuition. Not until ten years later was it shown to be valid. As Mort Deutsch so vividly describes in his chapter, it was wonderful to find a tool, such as the Prisoners Dilemma game, that enabled more precise control of important variables. But precision had to take its place in the context of the primary question.

As a small aside, I would like to quote some things that Kurt Lewin wrote on these issues in 1944 (Lewin, 1951). The reader may want to compare these statements with the chapter by Kurt Back and with his own impressions of social psychology today.

> The relation between scientific psychology and life shows a peculiar ambivalence. In its first steps as an experimental science, psychology was dominated by the desire of exactness. . . . Experimentation was devoted mainly to problems of sensory perception and memory, partly because they could be investigated through setups where the experimental control and precision could be secured with the accepted tools of the physical laboratory. (p. 168)

> The term "applied psychology" became—correctly or incorrectly— identified with a procedure that was scientifically blind even if it happened to be of practical value. As the result, "scientific" psychology that was interested in theory tried increasingly to stay away from a too close relation to life.

> It would be most unfortunate if the trend toward theoretical psychology were weakened by the necessity of dealing with natural groups when studying certain problems of social psychology . . . close cooperation between theoretical and applied psychology . . . can be accomplished . . . if the theorist does not look toward applied problems with highbrow aversion or with a fear of social problems. (p. 169)

What was the theoretical aspect of Lewin's contribution that was new and different? I have always felt that Kurt Lewin had an exquisite sense of the relation of theory to data. If you deal with highly formalized, specific theoretical statements, then perhaps you don't need this sense. You simply write down your statements in mathematical form, do your mathematical manipulations, a theorem falls out that is testable, and you then test it. But that was not, and is not, the situation in social psychology—nor do I think it is ever the situation at the forefront of knowledge in any science. When theory is not fully formulated, when much of the content of the theory is carried by the connotations of somewhat vague words, then the problem of the relation between theory and data is a difficult one.

Was there a relationship between the theoretical concepts that Lewin and his colleagues and students used and the empirical work they did? What did "life space," "region," "force field," "tension system," and the like have to do with group functioning, group decision, or social influence, for example? It is easy to say, and it is partly correct, that the whole Lewinian system served as a heuristic device. It provided a framework within which to think, and for some it was more useful, as such, than for others. To the extent that it served this function there was, of course, no clearly explainable relation between theory and data. The experiments and field studies did not test theoretical predictions in that strict sense.

There was more to it than that, however, and it is still difficult to verbalize precisely what it was. It is surprising to me that so many of the contributors to this book find that the roots of their topic go back to some aspect of Lewinian theory. Perhaps this should not be surprising in view of the basis for choosing the authors—namely, their close connection to the Research Center for Group Dynamics. But, nevertheless, it seems to stand in rather sharp contrast to the fact that for at least two decades the social psychology literature has been virtually devoid of mention of those old Lewinian concepts and terms.

From an historical viewpoint, however, we see Al Zander making connections between group goals and the early work on tension systems and on level of aspiration. We see Dick Nisbett resting some of his current conception of trait generality on Lewin's early conceptions of field theory and of behavior as an interactive function of the person and the environment. Hal Kelley traces the roots of attribution theory to the concept of force fields. Elliot Aronson sees dissonance theory as having emerged from views that were intrinsically inherent in the Lewinian approach. Jerry Singer finds the theories about social influence and comparison processes stemming from the concepts of life space, region, and tension. Even more explicit and direct influences from Lewin's concepts are spelled out by Mort Deutsch. The clarification of different kinds of conflict situations came directly from Lewin's analyses of force fields, driving forces, and restraining forces.

There is a kind of greatness that provides new ideas, new directions, and new frameworks for thinking. Just as Franz Boaz, who is rarely referred to today, transformed the face of anthropology, Kurt Lewin had a general but profound influence on social psychology. His ideas, their meanings and connotations, heavily directed the research and were taken over, modified, and embodied in the newer, somewhat more specific theoretical formulations.

The postwar surge in social psychology

The immediate post-World War II period was, in my view, the most seminal period in the history and development of social psychology. Four distinctly new influences were brought to bear on the field. All these influences had their roots in the war itself, either methodologically or ideologically:

1. During the war the techniques of surveying attitudes and opinions of persons, randomly sampled from specified populations, had developed markedly. It became a practical tool that was available to social psychology. It could be used, for example, to study such diverse matters as voting patterns (Lazarsfeld, Berelson, and Gaudet, 1944), reactions to real or imagined crises (Cantril, 1940), and political attitudes (Campbell, Eberhart, and Woodward, 1947). It made it more feasible to investigate many questions in social psychology outside the laboratory or the classroom. It has remained a powerful though expensive tool.

2. After the war, Carl Hovland started a research program at Yale University that stemmed from work he and others had done in the armed forces (Hovland, Lumsdaine, and Sheffield, 1949). Before the war, Hovland had worked in the area of human learning, and he brought his experimental psychology background with him to his new interest in social influence, social persuasion, and social communication. Together with his colleagues at Yale, particularly Irving Janis, Hovland did controlled experiments on communicator credibility, retention of effects of persuasion, primacy and recency effects in persuasion, and the like. In addition to the substantive contributions to the field, this group brought a different theoretical and methodological orientation to laboratory experiments in social psychology.

3. At the University of California, a group of people who had come to the United States to escape from the dangers of Nazi Germany brought a personality approach more strongly into social psychology. Adorno, Frenkel-Brunswik, and others were convinced that at least part of the explanation of what had happened in Europe lay in personality characteristics. Their book *The Authoritarian Personality* (1950) had a very large impact at the time.

4. At the Research Center for Group Dynamics, over and above what I have already described, there was new emphasis on what was called "action research." The phrase did not have an exact meaning. It somehow connoted research oriented toward social problems and social action, research together with social action, or research as a part of social action. One of the more direct outgrowths of this emphasis was the growth of workshops to train people in social sensitivity and in how to deal effectively with social groups (Lippitt, 1949). These activities eventually led to the formation of the National Training Laboratory, which ran annual workshops in Bethel, Maine.

Doing research in an action context was a difficult endeavor, but it was very seriously pursued. I remember very well the massive research effort that was undertaken at the first workshop in Bethel in the summer of 1947. Almost every graduate student from the Research Center for Group Dynamics, and many from the Social Relations Department at Harvard, were there to observe, record, and take notes on the processes of leadership, interaction, and change. The urgencies of social action, however, tended to take priority and seriously interfered with the perhaps too massive research effort. Subsequently Jack French worked hard for many years to get whatever he could out of the data. These workshops led gradually to a wide proliferation of training groups, sensitivity groups, and the like. But emphasis on research soon disappeared. The research that did go on for a while seems to me to have been little more than the gathering of testimonials.

Together with these new trends and new influences there also existed an active, more traditional center of social psychology at Harvard University, the newly formed Department of Social Relations. For historical reasons, and simple geographical proximity, there was considerable interaction between that department and the Research Center for Group Dynamics. In 1938, and again in 1939, Kurt Lewin had spent one semester at Harvard. Doc Cartwright, who came to Iowa in a postdoctoral position and later helped start the Research Center for Group Dynamics, was a graduate student at Harvard during those two years. Jack French, who joined the Research Center slightly later, was similarly attracted to Kurt Lewin during these two semesters at Harvard.

Thus, while we were at M.I.T. there was easy contact with Gordon Allport, Jerome Bruner, and others because of already existing personal relations. Also at that time (I don't know whether the arrangement still exists), students at either of these neighboring institutions could take courses at the other freely. It was in this way that we and Henry Riecken, who later worked with me and Stan Schachter at Minnesota, first came to know each other. That was also our first contact with Gardner Lindzey, who has never forgiven me for giving him a B in a seminar, thus spoiling an otherwise spotless transcript.

The Harvard Department of Social Relations added a healthy current to the field. Because of the inclusion of social psychology, sociology, and cultural anthropology in one department, the people there had a broader, and different, perspective. And our contacts with them helped keep us in touch with other points of view.

It seems clear to me in retrospect that the postwar surge had its roots deeply embedded in vital social problems. It also seems clear to me that these roots, together with daring to deal with difficult issues in novel and ingenious ways, gave a vitality to social psychology at that time.

The strands through the fifties

For many reasons there was considerable interaction among all of these centers of social psychology. When Kurt Lewin died in 1947, the young Research Center for Group Dynamics found itself without a secure home. The Research Center had, from its beginning, been quite peripheral to the activities, interests, and goals of M.I.T. Without the leadership, the persuasiveness, and the prestige of Kurt Lewin, that institution was not very receptive to the idea of the Research Center remaining there.

With the help of Rensis Likert, director of the Survey Research Center, and Donald Marquis, head of the Psychology Department, we moved the Research Center for Group Dynamics in 1948, faculty, students and all, to the University of Michigan, where we, together with the Survey Research Center, constituted a newly created Institute for Social Research. Thus, Michigan, which already had Theodore Newcomb and Daniel Katz on its faculty, became a huge institution with regard to social psychology. There ensued a natural interchange of ideas among all of these people. For example, the book *Research Methods in the Behavioral Sciences,* edited by myself and Katz (1953), was undertaken there as a truly cooperative venture involving all of us.

Hal Kelley, after completing his doctoral work, went to Yale to work with Carl Hovland and Irving Janis. Thus, there was mutual influence on ideas and methodology between Yale and Michigan. The book by Hovland, Janis, and Kelley (1953), in addition to its substantive value, shows,

I think, some of the beneficial effects of this mutual influence. The early death of Carl Hovland meant the end of that particular coordinated research program at Yale but did not end the interactions.

Social psychology was growing rapidly during this period, and movement of people among universities contributed much to maintaining active contact and interaction. In 1951, for example, I left the Research Center for Group Dynamics for the University of Minnesota, where Stan Schachter and Ben Willerman already worked. Later, Henry Riecken came there and we formed a very active research group. The new Ph.D.'s from the various centers added to the expansion and interaction. To give a few examples: Bob Cohen, from the Research Center for Group Dynamics, and Jack Brehm, who worked with me at Minnesota, were both on the faculty at Yale; William McGuire, who worked with Carl Hovland, did postdoctoral work at Minnesota; Elliot Aronson was, for a time, on the faculty at Harvard.

Perhaps the least active interaction took place with those who carried on the work stemming from the book *The Authoritarian Personality*. Although the Berkeley group stimulated a very large amount of research, it seems to have remained more separate from the rest of social psychology. This was not because of lack of contact, however. The field had not yet come to the point where almost every department of psychology had to have a program in social psychology. There were still relatively few active research workers in the area, and we all knew each other.

However, despite the active interaction and the easy contact, mutual influence among the various trends was slow to develop and remained incomplete. I think there were deep philosophical and methodological differences that could not be totally bridged because they were never fully and openly addressed. Let us examine a few of them.

There was in American psychology, and in social psychology also, a tradition of emphasis on individual differences, on the measurement of the characteristics of the person. Intelligence testing and testing for vocational guidance were well established. In social psychology, techniques were devised and scales constructed to measure social attitudes, social stereotypes, and relevant personality traits. Dick Nisbett presents, in his chapter, an excellent analysis of this tradition and where it went. The work on the authoritarian personality already mentioned, the work by McLelland et al. (1953) on need for achievement and need for affiliation, the developments stemming from the authoritarian personality work that led to measuring rigidity, tolerance for ambiguity, and the like were all in this tradition. On a conceptual level, Gordon Allport (1937) was, perhaps, the major proponent of such an approach. The idea that each individual is unique and that social psychology should focus on that uniqueness appealed to many. Recently, as Nisbett points out, Bem and Funder (1978) have revived this view as a way out of the problem of low generality across situations of measured traits. One can perhaps describe the bottom line of this approach as the study of individual differences about individual differences.

In contrast, it appears strange that those connected with, and influenced by, Kurt Lewin virtually ignored the entire question of individual differences. It seems strange because, if there was serious acceptance of the simple statement that behavior is a joint function of the person and the environment, how could one ignore measurement of the person? The philosophical ideas that explain this are easy to locate. They are perhaps best expressed in the paper by Lewin on Aristotelian and Gallilean conceptions of science (1935). Too much concern with individual differences could create a mask that hid the underlying dynamic processes. These underlying processes had to be discovered. The kind of analogy that existed in our minds was something like the following. It would be hopeless to have tried to discover the laws concerning free-falling objects by concentrating on measuring the different rates of descent of stones, feathers, pieces of paper, and the like. It is only after the basic dynamic laws are known that one can make sense of the individual differences.

The way I have always thought about it is that if the empirical world looks complicated, if people seem to react in bewilderingly different ways to similar forces, and if I cannot see the operation of universal underlying dynamics—then that is my fault. I have asked the wrong questions; I have, at the theoretical level, sliced the world up incorrectly. The underlying dynamics are there, and I have to find the theoretical apparatus that will enable me to reveal these uniformities.

We tend, too much, to ignore the impact of philosophical underpinnings on how scientists approach their task. These varying approaches to individual differences came from deep philosophical disagreements that, I think, were partly responsible for an incomplete meeting of minds and of less than optimal mutual influence among social psychologists.

The tradition of behaviorism that dominated much of American psychology also had its impact on social psychology. One consequence of this impact was avoidance of concern with "inner" experience, such as cognition and affect, and a taboo on theorizing about matters that were not directly measurable. When I was a young student, the phrase "dust bowl empiricism" was used by many in a self-congratulatory manner. Another far-reaching consequence of behaviorism was the specification of what things were legitimate for study. One could describe the characteristics of a physical stimulus and one could observe the behavioral response of the organism—that was all. Hence, the task of the science was to find the laws relating stimulus to response. Starting with Thorndike's (1927) work on the "law of effect," there was major emphasis on the variables of reward and punishment. Hull (1943) and Spence (1948) brought theoretical thinking along these lines to their peak.

The problems with which social psychology dealt were a bit too complex for the straightforward application of stimulus-response theorizing. Yet, at a more general level, this orientation affected the kinds of problems studied and how they were approached. The orientation of the group at Yale around Carl Hovland perhaps best illustrates the behaviorist approach in social psychology. The problem of social persuasion was seen as elucidating the relations between stimulus characteristics (e.g., stating the conclusion or not, order of material in the communication) and the response magnitude (degree of measured opinion change).

The orientation of Kurt Lewin and those around him was drastically at odds with behaviorism. The theoretical ideas were primarily about internal states. Many of the chapters in this book illustrate this: goals and aspirations that people and groups have (Zander); how people evaluate themselves (Singer); cognitions about others (Zajonc); processes of self-persuasion (Aronson). There was a basic incompatibility between such different orientations as behaviorism and the Lewinian approach. This can be seen in their impact on formulations of problems and theory in social psychology. Elliot Aronson, in his chapter, gives some good examples of difficulties produced by this incompatibility which interfered with mutual influence and a coherent approach to problems in social psychology.

In spite of these difficulties, or perhaps because of them, great progress was made in social psychology through the fifties and sixties. In addition to the small number of topics covered by the chapters of this book, there was research on social perception, leadership, the relation between personality and social behavior, group productivity and effectiveness, affiliation, and much more. The approaches to the field of social psychology were diverse and fruitful.

But the negative aspects of the philosophical divergences were there also. Much of the field seemed to me to be fragmented. Unfruitful disagreements and controversies arose all too easily. New work that appeared could be quite ignored by others. For example, Stan Schachter's early work on emotion and affiliation (1951, 1959) was ignored for much too long. I still remember my own reaction to the review in *Contemporary Psychology* of my book on dissonance theory (1957) by Professor Solomon Asch (1958). He summarized his view of the book by declaring: "This reviewer is compelled to return a verdict of *not proven*" (italics in the original, p. 195). And I said to myself, "What an interesting choice—the other two possible verdicts in Scottish law being 'guilty' and 'not guilty.'"

Too often the notion of originality lay in finding an alternative interpretation to someone's work. At one point there must have been at least three different models of opinion change, each supported by one carefully constructed study. Although this kind of thing did not dominate the field, it was in the atmosphere and somewhat of a hindrance. Too often the approach to data was such as to make apt a recent quip by a representative of the tobacco industry, commenting on a new report about the harms and evils of cigarette smoking. The authors of that report, he said, use data and statistics the way a drunk uses a lamppost—more for support than for illumination.

As I said, this is an extremely personal view of recent history and is undoubtedly distorted. It is not bad to have independent trends, disagreements, and controversies. It lends spirit and excitement. One would not desire a monolithic approach to a subject matter. Anyone who reads the chapters in this book will readily see the cumulative progress made in a number of areas in social psychology. And it must be emphasized again that these chapters do not, in any way, represent a total statement of that progress.

The "malaise" as seen from outside

I left the field of social psychology in 1964. This had nothing to do with the importance of the problems—they are very important—or with the vitality of the field—it was, and remains, vigorous. It had to do only with a conviction that had been growing in me at the time that I, personally, was in a rut and needed an injection of intellectual stimulation from new sources to continue to be productive. But the fact is that for the last fifteen years I have been pretty completely out of touch with social psychology. My friends kept telling me that social psychology was in the doldrums, was ill, was devoid of new developments. At least two of the chapters in this book, those by Zajonc and Nisbett, are in part related to understanding that period of real or imagined malaise.

Two things happened in the latter part of the sixties that had unfortunate consequences for social psychology. One of these was the particular direction that the general increase in concern with ethics took; the other was the impact of student activism and the general questioning of social values on an area of study which was substantively so close to those troubling issues.

No one would want to minimize the importance of ethical considerations. It is rather shocking to learn, for example, that persons were given large doses of a potentially dangerous substance like LSD, without their knowledge or consent, in order to explore possible military uses of such drugs. One need not even discuss such an example. But what about the well-publicized, and criticized, study on syphilis? A sample of persons who had syphilis, living in very poor rural areas with no medical attention, were randomly divided into two groups. One group was treated; the other was also followed in time but not treated. Was this an ethical violation? Is it "harming" someone, who would have had no medical attention anyway, to withhold an experimental treatment for the purpose of having a comparison group? I am not so sure about this. These persons were not harmed by the research in the sense that they were no worse off than if the research had not been done at all. But the judgment of society was that it did violate our ethics.

I don't want to dwell too long on such difficult problems, however. In social psychology the ethical issues were much simpler. Was it ethically justifiable to require students, as part of a course, to be subjects in experiments? (This used to be, perhaps still is, a widespread and easy way to get subjects.) Was it justifiable to deceive subjects, to lie to them, in order to create desired laboratory conditions, even if, following the experiment, all was explained and discussed? Was it all right to join a public group and pretend to be ordinary members in order to observe that group? This is the kind of question that arose.

These ethical issues never seemed extraordinarily difficult to me. Students should not be required or coerced to participate in experiments only to provide the investigator with an easy way to get subjects. The investigator can expend some energy to obtain subjects who are volunteers in a true sense. On the other hand, I do not see the harm in temporarily deceiving persons in order to study some important question. Clearly one cannot investigate something like the effect of threat on social interaction without creating a real, believable threat. That's hard enough to do in the laboratory, and one certainly cannot tell the volunteer, ahead of time, that he will be deceived and lied to. On the contrary, one wants to convince him that dreadful things will indeed happen. Of course, the dreadful things do not happen and the investigator has to take seriously the responsibility for explaining what was done, why it was important to do it, and for discussing it adequately.

But enough. In none of these issues do questions of harm to the subject arise in any real form. In many years of doing experiments involving elaborate deceptions, I have never encountered an instance in which a subject felt harmed or ill used. On the contrary, with good explanation and discussion, most subjects felt that they had learned something about how and why experiments are done. Others whom I know confirm this. There is also no real issue of invasion of privacy or maintaining confidentiality that cannot be adequately and easily dealt with.

It has frequently seemed to me that the continued concern of some individuals with these issues was really an attack on empirical work in social psychology in principle. Many researchers, however, were affected by it. Why involve oneself in such problems? Instead of creating powerful and real conditions in the laboratory, it is easier and safer to present hypothetical situations on questionnaires. I think the attack on ethical matters has had a long-run impact on the field. I think that the great emphasis today on cognitive information processing in social psychology is, in part, the result of these pressures on the field. One can stay far away from ethical questions and at the same time be quantitative and precise. But it seems to me that steering clear of these difficulties keeps the field away from problems that are important and distinctive to social psychology. The chapters by Bob Zajonc and Dick Nisbett are illuminating on this issue.

Let us move on to the other development that left its mark on social psychology—the social turmoils of the late sixties. The issues that produced these upheavals and the problems addressed by them were too close to the core of social psychology for that science to remain unscathed. In the United States it seemed that at the core of the trouble was the war in Vietnam, but this cannot have been the single or even the central issue. The unpopular war provided the substance by means of which deeper, more universal concerns were manifested. After all, the same turmoil, the same dissent, the same protest movements were prevalent at the same time, perhaps even earlier, in France, Germany, Japan, Holland, and many other countries which were not involved in the Vietnam war.

The deeper issues more likely centered on basic values concerning the individual in his social milieu. Why were some groups socially, educationally, and economically disadvantaged? Why were women treated differently from men? Whence came the dicta that alcohol was okay but other drugs were not, that short hair and ties were the proper attire for men, and the like?

The cry that research should be "relevant" could not be ignored totally by researchers in a field that presumably dealt with such questions. The cries for relevance were urgent, but they were ill defined. Was research on conflict, on social comparison processes, on social perception and causal attribution relevant to these large, major issues? Distantly, I am certain the answer is yes. But "distantly" was not satisfactory. Even research that dealt more directly with practical problems was not acceptably relevant in the mood of the time. That mood demanded instant solutions to the most difficult social problems.

There were two major ways in which researchers reacted to these pressures. If one were going to continue to "play around" in the laboratory, it was more comfortable to work on problems far away from these urgent social questions. If one moved far enough away, the issue of relevance was no more severe than it would be to a biochemist working in his laboratory. The other reaction was to plunge into the real world and deal with the real issues.

However, without a backlog of scientific knowledge, scientists are no better at solving social problems than anyone else. They are only more troubled because they do not know the "truth" as securely as do others who engage in social action. And research on such global questions often ends up with disappointingly few findings. Some excellent long-term effects did grow out of this research, however. New areas such as environmental psychology and community psychology were established and developed. They are productive but difficult areas and should be more closely intertwined with the rest of social psychology.

Other, less productive, trends also grew from the headlong dash into the relevant world, however. From my biased point of view, there was some confusion between "relevant" and "newsworthy." Certainly, if some finding was picked up by the mass media, that was clear evidence that it was relevant. One can improvise a jail and have subjects volunteer (with full, informed consent, of course) to be "prisoners." One can then report some interesting reactions of certain individuals. It's an important topic and clearly newsworthy. But it's not research, does not seriously attempt to look at relations among variables, and yields no new knowledge. It's just staging a "happening."

One could insert a questionnaire on an interesting topic such as "sex," "loneliness," "shyness," "happiness" or "preposterousness" in some nationally distributed magazine and ask readers to fill it out and return it. It turns out that one can get very large numbers of replies. The data can be analyzed and reported—usually in the magazine that carried the questionnaire. But who knows how seriously the questionnaires were answered or who chose to return them and who didn't? One doesn't even know the characteristics of the population from which the highly distorted sample was drawn. But I suppose it makes no difference anyway.

Also about this time, the field had to bear the assaults of Rosenthal (1966), who questioned the trustworthiness of the results of any experiments in social psychology. Rosenthal showed that, in various kinds of experiments, the hypotheses of the experimenter influenced the results. I've always wondered why, if these spurious experimenter effects were so strong, so many of my own experiments did not show the expected results. I've also wondered how Rosenthal protected his own experiments from these pernicious effects. But others didn't seem to have these worries. If the experimenter's expectations could affect the results, even in rat studies, then what must be the impact on much more complicated experiments in social psychology? For those social psychologists who chose to work on theoretical problems in the laboratory, the "experimenter bias" attack exerted additional pressure toward simpler problems that could be handled with doubly buffered precision.

But precision of measurement and precision of experimental control are means to an end—the discovery of new knowledge. Too much emphasis on precision can lead to research which is barren. There is, in my opinion, such a thing as "premature precision"—that is, insisting on precision at the empirical level while, at the theoretical level, concepts are still somewhat vague. It is crucial to accept the notion of vagueness in discovering new knowledge. How can one insist on empirical precision at the beginning of an idea that seems important and promising? If one does, the idea will be killed; it cannot at birth live up to such demands.

The results of such pressures on, and strains within, a scientific field can have serious consequences. The questions that are posed can become very narrow and technical; research can increasingly address itself to minor unclarities in prior research rather than to larger issues; people can lose sight of the basic problems because the field becomes defined by the ongoing research. I am reminded of a luncheon conversation I had recently with a colleague. He was questioning me, persistently, about why I was currently spending so much time reading books and articles in archeology and ancient history (which I am doing). After many attempts to answer, none of which satisfied him, I tried to summarize by saying: "Well, I guess I want to see what can be inferred from different vantage points, from different data realms, about the nature, the characteristics, of this species that we call human." Whereupon he asked his last question: "But is it going to have anything to do with psychology?"

Conclusions about social psychology today

In spite of the disturbances and pressures and the feelings of malaise, one can look at the period from a different perspective. In part, the later sixties and the seventies represented a period of consolidation of knowledge in social psychology, a necessary activity in any field of study. By now, controversy has receded and there is more general agreement about an established body of knowledge. I feel that in the last five years new formulations have begun to emerge as a result of the consolidation process. This is, I think, reflected in many chapters of this book, particularly the ones by Mort Deutsch and Hal Kelley. The malaise is probably over.

How does one assess the overall progress in a field as complicated as social psychology? There are, of course, some very clear examples of significant accumulation of new knowledge. We can see such instances in the chapters by Al Zander (a data base, albeit spotty, has replaced sheer "wisdom"); by Jerry Singer (the progression from "reference groups" to "social comparison processes"); by Elliot Aronson (better understanding of the durability of attitude and opinion changes); and, to some extent, in most of the other chapters. There are also, as mentioned above, some clear instances of the attainment of greater conceptual clarity.

Other kinds of developments are less clearly seen as progress—although they may be. The return to the examination of questions that had, for a period of time, been neglected (trait consistency, for example), or the questioning of the adequacy of some current approaches (as cognitive information processing) may not reflect much progress. On the other hand, however, the returns and the questioning are done with new perspectives and increased understanding of the problems involved.

The most difficult assessment of progress is the kind reflected in the chapter by Stan Schachter. Problems which once seemed appropriate to psychological inquiry turn out not to be. A long sequence of studies leads an investigator toward physiological variables and to the judgment that social psychological factors are much less important, for a given problem, than he had previously imagined. To me, this does represent progress of a very significant kind. Others may disagree, however.

How can I present my own overall evaluation of the progress of social psychology over this forty-year period and my own sense of this book? Perhaps the best way is by analogy and there is one, probably distorted by my own memory, that keeps intruding into my mind. It is a scene from the movie *The Horse's Mouth*. I have checked the book itself and that scene does not exist there, but I will describe my memory of the movie.

The main character, a rather self-willed and eccentric artist, has just finished painting a mural, unauthorized, on the wall of an apartment whose owners are away on vacation. In the process he has pawned furniture, fixtures—everything pawnable from the apartment—to pay for his oils, brushes, and models, scrupulously putting every pawn ticket in a jar. He is now about to leave. The apartment is a chaotic mess, but he has finished the mural. He opens the door to depart, looks back at the mural, which is later to be considered a masterpiece, and says: "It's not exactly what I had in mind."

References

Chapter 1

Aronson, E. Dissonance theory: Progress and problems. In R.P. Abelson, E. Aronson, W.J. McGuire, T.M. Newcomb, M.J. Rosenberg, & P.H. Tannenbaum (Eds.), *Theories of cognitive consistency: A sourcebook*. Chicago: Rand-McNally, 1968, pp. 5–27.

Aronson, E. The theory of cognitive dissonance: A current perspective. In L. Berkowitz (Ed.), *Advances in experimental social psychology,* (Vol. 4). New York: Academic, 1969, pp. 1–34.

Aronson, E. The theory of cognitive dissonance: A current perspective. In L. Berkowitz (Ed.), *Cognitive theories in social psychology*. New York: Academic, 1978, pp. 215–220.

Aronson, E. & Carlsmith, J.M. Effect of severity of threat on the valuation of forbidden behavior. *Journal of Abnormal and Social Psychology,* 1963, *66,* pp. 584–588.

Aronson, E., Chase, T., Helmreich, R., & Ruhnke, R. A two-factor theory of dissonance reduction: The effect of feeling stupid or feeling "awful" on opinion change. *International Journal of Communication Research,* 1974, *3,* 340–352.

Aronson, E. & Mills, J. The effects of severity of initiation on liking for a group. *Journal of Abnormal and Social Psychology,* 1959, *59,* 177–181.

Asch, S.E. Effects of group pressure upon the modification and distortion of judgments. In H. Guetzkow (Ed.), *Groups, leadership and men.* Pittsburgh: Carnegie Press, 1951, pp. 177–190.

Brehm, J.W. & Jones, R.A. The effect on dissonance of surprise consequences. *Journal of Experimental Social Psychology,* 1970, *6,* 420–431.

Carlsmith, J.M., Collins, B.E., & Helmreich, R.L. Studies in forced compliance: I. The effect of pressure for compliance on attitude change produced by face-to-face role playing and anonymous essay writing. *Journal of Personality and Social Psychology,* 1966, *4,* 1–13.

Chapanis, N.P. & Chapanis, A.C. Cognitive dissonance: Five years later. *Psychological Bulletin,* 1964, *61,* 1–22.

Cohen, A.R. An experiment on small rewards for discrepant compliance and attitude change. In J.W. Brehm & A.R. Cohen (Eds.), *Explorations in cognitive dissonance.* New York: Wiley, 1962, pp. 73–78.

Collins, B.E. & Hoyt, M.F. Personal responsibility-for-consequences: An integration and extension of the "forced compliance" literature. *Journal of Experimental Social Psychology*, 1972, *8*, 558–593.

Cooper, J., Zanna, M.P., & Taves, P.A. Arousal as a necessary condition for attitude change following induced compliance. Unpublished paper, 1977.

Deutsch, M. & Gerard, H. A study of normative and informational social influences on individual judgment. *Journal of Abnormal and Social Psychology*, 1955, *51*, 629–636.

Fazio, R.H., Zanna, M.P., & Cooper, J. Dissonance and self-perception: An integrative view of each theory's proper domain of application. *Journal of Experimental Social Psychology*, 1977, *13*, 464–479.

Festinger, L. *A theory of cognitive dissonance*. Stanford, Calif.: Stanford University Press, 1957.

Festinger, L. & Carlsmith, J.M. Cognitive consequences of forced compliance. *Journal of Abnormal and Social Psychology*, 1959, *58*, 203–210.

Freedman, J.L. Long-term behavioral effects of cognitive dissonance. *Journal of Experimental Social Psychology*, 1965, *1*, 145–155.

Freedman, J.L. & Fraser, S.C. Compliance without pressure: The foot-in-the-door technique. *Journal of Personality and Social Psychology*, 1966, *4*, 195–202.

Gerard, H.B. & Mathewson, G.C. The effects of severity of initiation on liking for a group: A replication. *Journal of Experimental Social Psychology*, 1966, *2*, 278–287.

Hovland, C.I. Reconciling conflicting results derived from experimental and survey studies of attitude change. *American Psychologist*, 1959, *14*, 8–17.

Hovland, C.I. & Weiss, W. The influence of source credibility on communication effectiveness. *Public Opinion Quarterly*, 1951, *15*, 635–650.

Jones, E.E. & Davis, K.E. From acts to dispositions: The attribution process in person perception. In L. Berkowitz (Ed.), *Advances in experimental social psychology*. New York: Academic, 1965.

Kelley, H.H. The processes of causal attribution. *American Psychologist*, 1973, *28*, 107–128.

Kiesler, C.A., Collins, B.E., & Miller, N. *Attitude change: A critical analysis of theoretical approaches*. New York: Wiley, 1969.

Lecky, P. *Self-consistency: A theory of personality* (2nd ed.). Hamden, Conn.: Shoe String Press, 1961 (rpt. of 1951 edition).

Lepper, M.R., Zanna, M.P., & Abelson, R.P. Cognitive irreversibility in a dissonance reduction situation. *Journal of Personality and Social Psychology*, 1970, *16*, 191–198.

Lewin, K. Group decision and social change. In T.H. Newcomb & E.L. Hartley (Eds.), *Readings in social psychology*. New York: Holt, 1947.

Lewin, K., Lippitt, R., & White, R. Patterns of aggressive behavior in experimentally created "social climates." *Journal of Social Psychology,* 1939, *10,* 271–299.

Linder, D.E., Cooper, J., & Jones, E.E. Decision freedom as a determinant of the role of incentive magnitude in attitude change. *Journal of Personality and Social Psychology,* 1967, *6,* 245–254.

Marrow, A.J. *The practical theorist: The life and work of Kurt Lewin.* New York: Basic Books, 1969.

Miller, N.E. & Dollard, J. *Social learning and imitation.* New Haven: Yale University Press, 1941.

Nel, E., Helmreich, R., & Aronson, E. Opinion change in the advocate as a function of the persuasibility of his audience: A clarification of the meaning of dissonance. *Journal of Personality and Social Psychology,* 1969, *12,* 117–124.

Olson, J.M. & Zanna, M.P. A new look at selective exposure. Paper presented at the Annual Meeting of the American Psychological Association, San Francisco, August, 1977.

Sears, D.O. & Abeles, R. Attitudes and opinions. In P.H. Mussen & M. Rosenzweig (Eds.), *Annual Review of Psychology,* 1969, *20,* 253–288.

Tolman, E.C. & Lewin, K. Obituary. *Psychological Review,* 1948, *55,* No. 1, 1–4.

Wicklund, R.A. & Brehm, J.W. *Perspectives on Cognitive Dissonance.* New York: Wiley, 1976.

Zanna, M.P. & Cooper, J. Dissonance and the pill: An attribution approach to studying the arousal properties of dissonance. *Journal of Personality and Social Psychology,* 1974, *29,* 703–709.

Chapter 2

Back, K.W. A model of family planning experiments: The lessons of the Puerto Rican and Jamaican fertility studies. *Marriage and Family Living,* 1962, *25,* 14–19.

Back, K.W. Small group research and the issues of micro vs. macro sociology. *Representative Research in Social Psychology,* 1973, *4,* 83–92.

Back, K.W. & Fawcett, J.T. (Eds.). Population policy and the person: Congruence or conflict. *Journal of Social Issues,* 1974, *30,* No. 4.

Back, K.W., Hill, R., & Stycos, J.M. The Puerto Rican experiment in population control. *Human Relations,* 1957, *10,* 315–334.

Back, K.W., Hill, R., & Stycos, J.M. Population control in Puerto Rico: The formal and informal framework. *Law and Contemporary Problems,* 1960, *25,* Summer, 558–576.

Back, K.W. & Winsborough, H.H. Population policy: Opinions and actions of governments. *Public Opinion Quarterly,* 1968, *32,* 634–643.

Beckman, L.J. Exchange theory and fertility-related decision making. *Journal of Social Psychology,* 1977, *103,* 265–276.

Beckman, L.J. Couples' decision-making processes regarding fertility. In *Social demography.* New York: Academic, 1978.

Blake, J. *Family structure in Jamaica.* Glencoe: Free Press, 1961.

Coale, A.J. & Hoover, E.M. *Population growth and economic development in low income countries.* Princeton: Princeton University Press, 1958.

East-West Center *The value of children.* Honolulu: The University Press of Hawaii, 1975–1979.

Fawcett, J.T. *Psychology and population.* New York: Population Council, 1970.

Fawcett, J.T. (Ed.) *Psychological perspectives on population.* New York: Basic Books, 1974.

Freedman, R. & Takeshita, J.Y. *Family planning in Taiwan: Tradition and change.* Princeton: Princeton University Press, 1969.

Freedman, R., Whelpton, P.K., & Campbell, A.A. *Family planning, fertility and population growth.* New York: McGraw-Hill, 1959.

Hass, P.H. Wanted and unwanted pregnancies: A fertility decision-making model. *Journal of Social Issues,* 1974, *30,* 125–166.

Hill, R., Back, K.W., & Stycos, J.M. Family structure and fertility in Puerto Rico. *Social Problems,* 1955, *3,* 73–93.

Hill, R., Stycos, J.M. & Back, K.W. *The family and population control.* Chapel Hill: University of North Carolina Press, 1959.

Hoffman, L.W. & Hoffman, M.L. The value of children to parents. In J.T. Fawcett (Ed.), *Psychological perspectives in population.* New York: Basic Books, 1974.

Malthus, T.R. *An essay on population (The first essay).* London: J. Johnson, 1798.

Malthus, T.R. *An essay on population (The second essay),* (2nd rev. ed.). London: J. Johnson, 1803.

Mellinger, G.L. Individual and couple fertility as related to party, marital stage, and education: A pilot study. Proposal submitted in response to RFP NICHD-BS-75-2.

Mishler, E.G. & Westoff, C.F. A Proposal for research on social psychological factors affecting fertility: Concepts and hypotheses. In *Current research in human fertility.* New York: Milbank Memorial Fund, 1955.

Namboodiri, N.K., Carter, L.F., & Blalock, H.M., Jr. *Applied multivariate analysis and experimental designs.* New York: McGraw-Hill, 1975.

Newcomb, T.M. Autistic hostility and social reality. *Human Relations,* 1947, *1,* 69–86.

Newman, S.H. & Thompson, V.D. (Eds.). *Population psychology: Research and education issues.* U.S. DHEW, Publication (NIH) 76-574, Government Printing Office, 1976.

Peterson, W. *Malthus*. Cambridge: Harvard University Press, 1979.

Robinson, W. The development of modern population theory. *The American Journal of Economics and Sociology*, 1964, *23*, 375–592.

Rogers, E.M. *Communication strategies for family planning*. New York: Free Press, 1973.

Senior, C. Women, democracy and birth control. *Humanist*, 1952, *5*, 221–224.

Solomon, R.L. An extension of control group design. *Psychological Bulletin*, 1946, *46*, 137–150.

Stycos, J.M. *Family and fertility in Puerto Rico*. New York: Columbia University Press, 1955.

Stycos, J.M. & Back, K.W. *The control of human fertility in Jamaica*. Ithaca: Cornell University Press, 1965.

Thompson, W.C. Population. *American Journal of Sociology*, 1929, *34*, 961–962.

Westoff, C.T., Potter, R.G., Jr., & Sagi, P.C. *The third child: A study in the prediction of fertility*. Princeton: Princeton University Press, 1963.

Westoff, C.T., Potter, R.G., Jr., Sagi, P.C., & Mishler, E.G. *Family planning in metropolitan America*. Princeton: Princeton University Press, 1961.

Whelpton, P.K. & Kiser, C.V. *Social and psychological factors affecting fertility*. 5 Vol. New York: Milbank Memorial Fund, 1946–1958.

Chapter 3

Adams, J.S. Toward an understanding of inequity. *Journal of Abnormal and Social Psychology*, 1963, *67*, 422–436.

Adams, J.S. Inequity in social exchange. In L. Berkowitz (Ed.), *Advances in experimental social psychology* (Vol. 2). New York: Academic, 1965.

Adams, J.S. & Freedman, S. Equity theory revisited: Comments and annotated bibliography. In L. Berkowitz & E. Walster (Eds.), *Advances in experimental social psychology* (Vol. 9). New York: Academic, 1976.

Alinsky, S.D. *Rules for radicals: A practical primer for realistic radicals*. New York: Random House, 1971.

Aronson, E., Bridgeman, L., & Geffner, R. The effects of cooperative classroom structure on student behavior and attitudes. In D. Bar-Tal & L. Saxe (Eds.), *Social psychology of education*. New York: Halsted Press, 1978.

Back, K.W. Influence through social communication. *Journal of Abnormal and Social Psychology*, 1951, *46*, 9–23.

Banton, M. *Race relations*. New York: Basic Books, 1967.

Bartos, O.J. Determinants and consequences of toughness. In P. Swingle (Ed.), *The structure of conflict*. New York: Academic, 1970.

Berkowitz, L. Effects of perceived dependency relationships upon conformity to group expectations. *Journal of Abnormal and Social Psychology*, 1957, *55*, 350–354.

Blake, R.R. & Mouton, J.S. Comprehension of own and outgroup positions under intergroup competition. *Journal of Conflict Resolution,* 1961, *5,* 304–310. (a)

Blake, R.R. & Mouton, J.S. Loyalty of representatives to ingroup positions during intergroup competition. *Sociometry,* 1961, *24,* 177–183. (b)

Blake, R.R. & Mouton, J.S. Overevaluation of own group's product in intergroup competition. *Journal of Abnormal and Social Psychology,* 1962, *64,* 237–238. (a)

Blake, R.R. & Mouton, J.S. Comprehension of points of communality in competing solutions. *Sociometry,* 1962, *25,* 56–63. (b)

Blaney, N.T., Stephan, C., Rosenfield, D., Aronson E., & Sikes, J. Interdependence in the classroom: A field study. *Journal of Educational Psychology,* 1977, *69,* 120–128.

Cantril, H. (Ed.). *Tensions that cause wars.* Urbana: University of Illinois Press, 1950.

Chamberlain, N. *Collective bargaining.* New York: McGraw-Hill, 1951.

Chertkoff, I.M. & Esser, J.K. A review of experiments in explicit bargaining. *Journal of Experimental Social Psychology,* 1976, *12,* 464–487.

Cummings, L.L. & Harnett, D.L. Bargaining behavior in a symmetric bargaining triad. *The Review of Economic Studies,* 1969, *36,* 485–501.

Deutsch, M. A theory of cooperation and competition. *Human Relations,* 1949, *2,* 129–152. (a)

Deutsch, M. An experimental study of the effects of cooperation and competition upon group process. *Human Relations,* 1949, *2,* 199–232. (b)

Deutsch, M. Trust and suspicion. *Journal of Conflict Resolution,* 1958, *2,* 265–279.

Deutsch, M. Cooperation and trust: Some theoretical notes. In M. R. Jones (Ed.), *Nebraska symposium on motivation.* Lincoln: University of Nebraska Press, 1962.

Deutsch, M. Field theory in social psychology. In G. Lindzey & E. Aronson (Eds.), *Handbook of social psychology* (Vol. 1, Rev. ed.). Reading, Mass.: Addison-Wesley, 1968.

Deutsch, M. Conflicts: Productive and destructive. *Journal of Social Issues,* 1969, *25,* 7–41.

Deutsch, M. *The resolution of conflict: Constructive and destructive processes.* New Haven: Yale University Press, 1973.

Deutsch, M. Awakening the sense of injustice. In M. Lerner & M. Ross (Eds.), *The quest for justice.* Toronto: Holt, Rinehart & Winston of Canada, 1974.

Deutsch, M. Equity, equality and need: What determines which value will be used as the basis of distributive justice? *The Journal of Social Issues,* 1975, *31,* 137–150.

Deutsch, M. Recurrent themes in the study of social conflict. *Journal of Social Issues*, 1977, *33*, 222–225.

Deutsch, M. Education and distributive justice: Some reflections on grading systems. *American Psychologist*, 1979, *34*, 391–401.

Deutsch, M. & Krauss, R.M. The effect of threat upon interpersonal bargaining. *Journal of Abnormal and Social Psychology*, 1960, *61*, 181–189.

Diesing, P. *Reason in society*. Urbana: University of Illinois Press, 1962.

Druckman, D. *Human factors in international negotiations: Social-psychological aspects of international conflict*. Beverly Hills: Sage Publications, 1973.

Druckman, D. (Ed.). *Negotiations: Social psychological perspectives*. Beverly Hills: Sage Publications, 1977.

Etzioni, A. The Kennedy experiment. *The Western Political Quarterly*, 1967, *20*, 361–380.

Freedman, J.L. Compliance without pressure: The foot-in-the-door technique. *Journal of Personality and Social Psychology*, 1966, 2, 195–202.

French, J.R.P. & Raven, B. The bases of social power. In D. Cartwright (Ed.), *Studies in social power*. Ann Arbor: University of Michigan Press, 1959.

Gerard, H. B. The effects of different dimensions of disagreement on the communication process in small groups. *Human Relations*, 1953, *6*, 249–271.

Gottheil, E. Changes in social perception contingent upon competing or cooperating. *Sociometry*, 1955, *18*, 132–137.

Grossack, M. Some effects of cooperation and competition on small group behavior. *Journal of Abnormal and Social Psychology*, 1954, *49*, 341–348.

Hamner, W.C. & Baird, L.S. The effect of strategy, pressure to reach agreement and relative power on bargaining behavior. In H. Sauermann (Ed.), *Contributions to experimental economics* (Vol. 7). Tübingen: Mohr, 1978.

Harnett, D.L. & Cummings, L.L. Bargaining behavior in an asymmetric triad: The role of information, communication, and risk-taking propensity. Mimeographed manuscript, University of Indiana, 1968.

Harnett, D.L., Cummings, L.L., & Hughes, C.D. The influence of risk-taking propensity on bargaining behavior. *Behavioral Science*, 1968, *13*, 91–101.

Harnett, D.L. & Vincelette, J.P. Strategic influences on bargaining effectiveness. In H. Sauermann (Ed.), *Contributions to experimental economics* (Vol. 7). Tübingen: Mohr, 1978.

Homans, G.C. *Social behavior: Its elementary forms*. New York: Harcourt, Brace, Jovanovich, 1961.

Homans, G.C. *Social behavior: Its elementary forms* (Rev. ed.). New York: Harcourt, Brace, Jovanovich, 1974.

Hull, C.L. The goal-gradient hypothesis applied to some "field-force" problems in the behavior of young children. *Psychological Review*, 1938, *45*, 271–299.

Hyman, S.E. *The tangled bank*. New York: Grosset and Dunlap, University Library Edition, 1966.

Jervis, A.S. *The logic of images in international relations*. Princeton: Princeton University Press, 1970.

Jervis, A.S. *Perception and misperception in international politics*. Princeton: Princeton University Press, 1976.

Johnson, D.W. & Johnson, R. The instructional use of cooperative, competitive and individualistic goal structures. In H.J. Walberg (Ed.), *Educational environments and effects: Evaluation, policy, and productivity*. Berkeley: McCutchan, 1979.

Jones, E.E. *Ingratiation*. New York: Appleton-Century-Crofts, 1964.

Kahn, N. *On escalation: Metaphors and scenarios*. New York: Praeger, 1965.

Kamin, L.J. *The science and politics of I.Q.* Hillsdale, N.J.: Erlbaum Associates, 1974.

Kelley, H.H. & Schenitzki, D.P. Bargaining. In C.G. McClintock (Ed.), *Experimental social psychology*. New York: Holt, Rinehart & Winston, 1972.

Klineberg, O. *The human dimensions in international relations*. New York: Holt, Rinehart & Winston, 1964.

Komorita, S.S. & Moore, D. Theories and processes of coalition formation. *Journal of Personality and Social Psychology*, 1976, *33*, 371–381.

Křivohlavý, J. *Zwischenmenschliche konflicte und experimentelle spiele*. Bern: Hans Huber, 1974.

Lamm, H. & Kayser, E. The allocation of monetary gain and loss following dyadic performance. *European Journal of Social Psychology*, 1978, *8*, 275–278. (a)

Lamm, H. & Kayser, E. An analysis of negotiation concerning the allocation of jointly produced profit or loss. *International Journal of Group Tensions*, 1978, *8*, 64–80. (b)

Lerner, M.J. The justice motive in social behavior: Introduction. *Journal of Social Issues*, 1975, *31*, 1–20.

Leventhal, G.S. *Fairness in social relationships*. Morristown, N.J.: General Learning Press, 1976.

Levy, S. Experimental study of group norms: The effects of group cohesiveness upon social conformity. Unpublished doctoral dissertation, New York University, 1953.

Lewin, K. Environmental forces in child behavior and development. In C. Murchison (Ed.), *A handbook of child psychology*. Worcester, Mass.: Clark University Press, 1931.

Lewin, K. *A dynamic theory of personality*. New York: McGraw-Hill, 1935.

Lewis, H.B. An experimental study of the role of the ego in work: I. The role of the ego in cooperative work. *Journal of Experimental Psychology,* 1944, *34,* 113–126.

Lewis, H.B. & Franklin, M. An experimental study of the role of the ego in work: II. The significance of task-orientation in work. *Journal of Experimental Psychology,* 1944, *34,* 195–215.

Lindskold, S. Trust development, the G.R.I.T. proposal, and the effects of conciliatory acts on conflict and cooperation. *Psychological Bulletin,* 1978, *85,* 772–793.

Lissner, K. Die entspannung von bedürfnissen durch ersatzhandlungen. *Psychologische Forschung,* 1933, *18,* 218–250.

Lucker, G.W., Rosenfield, D., Sikes, J., & Aronson, E. Performance in the interdependent classroom: A field study. *American Educational Research Journal,* 1976, *13,* 115–123.

Machiavelli, N. *The prince and the discourses.* New York: Modern Library, 1513/1950.

Magenau, J.M. & Pruitt, D.G. The social psychology of bargaining: A theoretical synthesis. In G.M. Stephenson & C.J. Brotherton (Eds.), *Industrial relations: A social psychological approach.* London: Wiley, 1978.

Mahler, W. Erzatzhandlungen verschiedenen Realitätsgrades. *Psychologische Forschung,* 1933, *18,* 27–89.

Maller, J.B. Cooperation and competition: An experimental study in motivation. Ph.D. dissertation, Teachers College, Columbia University, 1929. *Teachers College contributions to education* No. 384. New York: Teachers College, Bureau of Publications, 1929.

Margolin, J.B. The effect of perceived cooperation or competition on the transfer of hostility. Ph.D. dissertation, New York University, 1954.

Marrow, A.J. Goal tension and recall: I. *Journal of General Psychology,* 1938, *19,* 3–35. (a)

Marrow, A.J. Goal tension and recall: II. *Journal of General Psychology,* 1938, *19,* 37–64. (b)

May, M.A. & Doob, L.W. Competition and cooperation. *Social Science Research Council Bulletin* (#25), New York, 1937.

McDougall, W. *Introduction to social psychology.* London: Methuen, 1908.

Mikula, G. & Schwinger, T. Intermember relations and reward allocation: Theoretical considerations of affects. In H. Brandstatter, J.H. Davis, & H. Schuler (Eds.), *Dynamics of group decisions.* Beverly Hills: Sage Publications, 1978.

Miller, N.E. Analysis of the form of conflict reactions. *Psychological Bulletin,* 1937, *34,* 720.

Miller, N.E. Experimental studies of conflict. In J. McV. Hunt (Ed.), *Personality and the behavior disorders* (Vol. 1). New York: Ronald, 1944.

Mintz, A. Non-adaptive group behavior. *Journal of Abnormal and Social Psychology*, 1951, *46*, 150–159.

Mizuhara, T. & Tamai, S. Experimental studies of cooperation and competition. *Japanese Journal of Psychology*, 1952, *22*, 124–127.

Morley, I. & Stephenson, G. *The social psychology of bargaining*. London: Allen & Unwin, 1977.

Moscovici, S. *Social influence and social change*. New York: Academic, 1976.

Murphy, G., Murphy, L.B., & Newcomb, T.M. *Experimental social psychology* (Rev. ed.). New York: Harper and Brothers, 1937.

Osgood, C.E. Suggestions for winning the real war with Communism. *Journal of Conflict Resolution*, 1959, *3*, 295–325.

Osgood, C.E. *An alternative to war or surrender*. Urbana: University of Illinois Press, 1962.

Osgood, C.E. *Perspective in foreign policy*. Palo Alto: Pacific Books, 1966.

Ovsiankina, M. Die Wiederaufnahme unterbrochener handlungen. *Psychologische Forschung*, 1928, *11*, 302–379.

Potter, S. *The theory and practice of gamesmanship*. New York: Bantam Books, 1965.

Pruitt, D.G. & Kimmel, M.J. Twenty years of experimental gaming: Critique, synthesis, and suggestions for the future. *Annual Review of Psychology*, 1977, *28*, 363–392.

Raven, B.H. & Eachus, H.T. Cooperation and competition in means—interdependent triads. *Journal of Abnormal and Social Psychology*, 1963, *67*, 307–316.

Rescher, N. *Distributive justice*. New York: Bobbs-Merrill, 1966.

Rubin, J.Z. Experimental research on third-party intervention: Some generalizations and unanswered questions. Manuscript, Tufts University, February, 1979.

Rubin, J.Z. & Brown, B.R. *The social psychology of bargaining and negotiation*. New York: Academic, 1975.

Sampson, E.E. Studies of status congruence. In L. Berkowitz (Ed.), *Advances in experimental social psychology* (Vol. 4). New York: Academic, 1969.

Sampson, E.E. On justice as equality. *The Journal of Social Issues*, 1975, *31*, 45–64.

Sauermann, H. (Ed.). *Contributions to experimental economics* (Vols. 7 and 8). Tübingen: Mohr, 1978.

Schachtel, E.G. *Metamorphosis: On the development of affect, perception, attention, and memory*. New York: Basic Books, 1959.

Schelling, T.C. *The strategy of conflict*. Cambridge: Harvard University Press, 1960.

Schelling, T.C. *Arms and influence*. New Haven: Yale University Press, 1966.

Sherif, M. *In common predicament: Social psychology of intergroup conflict and cooperation.* Boston: Houghton-Mifflin, 1966.

Sherif, M., Harvey, O.J., White, B.J., Hood, W.R., & Sherif, C. *Intergroup conflict and cooperation: The robbers cave experiment.* Norman, Okla.: University Book Exchange, 1961.

Siegel, S. & Fouraker, L.E. *Bargaining and group decision making: Experiments in bilateral monopoly.* New York: McGraw-Hill, 1960.

Slavin, R.E. Classroom reward structure: An analytical and practical review. *Review of Educational Research,* 1977, *47,* 633–650. (a)

Slavin, R.E. Student learning teams and scores adjusted for past achievement: A summary of field experiments. Center for Social Organization of Schools, Report No. 227, Baltimore, April, 1977. (b)

Slavin, R.E. Effects of biracial learning teams on cross-racial friendship. Center for Social Organization of Schools, No. 240, Baltimore, November, 1977. (c)

Slavin, R.E. Student teams and comparison among equals: Effects on academic performance and student attitudes. *Journal of Educational Psychology,* 1978, *70,* 532–538.

Snyder, G.H. & Diesing, P. *Conflict among nations.* Princeton: Princeton University Press, 1977.

Stevens, C.M. *Strategy and collective bargaining negotiation.* New York: McGraw-Hill, 1963.

Stryker, S. Coalition behavior. In C.G. McClintock (Ed.), *Experimental social psychology.* New York: Holt, 1972.

Tedeschi, J.T., Schlenker, B.R., & Bonoma, T.V. *Conflict power and games.* Chicago: Aldine, 1973.

Terhune, K.W. The effects of personality in cooperation and conflict. In P. Swingle (Ed.), *The structure of conflict.* New York: Academic, 1970.

Thomas, E.J. Effects of facilitative role interdependence on group functioning. *Human Relations,* 1957, *10,* 347–366.

Vinacke, W.E. & Arkoff, A. An experimental study of coalitions in the triad. *American Sociological Review,* 1957, *22,* 406–414.

Von Neumann, J. & Morgenstern, O. *Theory of games and economic behavior.* New York: Wiley, 1944.

Walster, E., Walster, G.W., & Berscheid, E. *Equity theory and research.* Boston: Allyn and Bacon, 1978.

Walton, R.E. & McKersie, R.B. *A behavioral theory of labor negotiations: An analysis of a social interaction system.* New York: McGraw-Hill, 1965.

Workie, A. *The effect of cooperation and competition on productivity.* Doctoral dissertation, Teachers College, Columbia University, 1967.

Zeigarnik, B. Das behalten erledigter und unerledigter handlungen. *Psychologische Forschung,* 1927, *9,* 1–85.

Chapter 4

Ainslie, G. Specious reward: A behavioral theory of impulsiveness and impulse control. *Psychological Bulletin*, 1975, *82*, 463–496.

Arkin, R.M. & Duval, S. Focus of attention and causal attributions of actors and observers. *Journal of Experimental Social Psychology*, 1975, *11*, 427–438.

Baldwin, C.P. & Baldwin, A.L. Children's judgments of kindness. *Child Development*, 1970, *41*, 29–47.

Bandura, A. Self-efficacy: Toward a unifying theory of behavioral change. *Psychological Review*, 1977, *84*, 191–215.

Berglas, S. & Jones, E.E. Drug choice as a self-handicapping strategy in response to noncontingent success. *Journal of Personality and Social Psychology*, 1978, *36*, 405–417.

Berzonsky, M.D. Some relationships between children's conceptions of psychological and physical causality. *Journal of Social Psychology*, 1973, *90*, 299–309.

Brehm, J.W. & Cohen, A.R. *Explorations in cognitive dissonance*. New York: Wiley, 1962.

Brickman, P., Ryan, K., & Wortman, C.B. Causal chains: Attribution of responsibility as a function of immediate and prior causes. *Journal of Personality and Social Psychology*, 1975, *32*, 1060–1067.

Brown, J.S. & Farber, I.E. Emotions conceptualized as intervening variables with suggestions toward a theory of frustration. *Psychological Bulletin*, 1951, *48*, 465–495.

Chapman, L.J. & Chapman, J.P. Illusory correlation as an obstacle to the use of valid psychodiagnostic signs. *Journal of Abnormal Psychology*, 1969, *74*, 271–280.

Duncker, K. On problem-solving. *Psychological Monographs*, 1945, *58*, 5, (Whole No. 270).

Dweck, C.S. The role of expectations and attributions in the alleviation of learned helplessness. *Journal of Personality and Social Psychology*, 1975, *31*, 674–685.

Easterbrook, J.A. The effect of emotion on cue utilization and the organization of behavior. *Psychological Review*, 1959, *66*, 183–201.

Elig, T.W. & Frieze, I.H. Measuring causal attributions for success or failure. *Journal of Personality and Social Psychology*, 1979, *37*, 621–634.

Estes, W.K. Reinforcement in human behavior. *American Scientist*, 1972, *60*, 723–729.

Festinger, L. *A theory of cognitive dissonance*. Evanston, Ill.: Row, Peterson, 1957.

Festinger, L. *Conflict, decision, and dissonance.* Stanford: Stanford University Press, 1964.

Fischoff, B. Hindsight ≠ foresight: The effect of outcome knowledge on judgment under uncertainty. *Journal of Experimental Psychology: Human Perception and Performance,* 1975, *1,* 288–299.

Flavell, J.H. Metacognition and cognitive monitoring: A new area of cognitive developmental inquiry. *American Psychologist,* 1979, *34,* 906–911.

Frankel, A. & Snyder, M.L. Poor performance following unsolvable problems: Learned helplessness or egotism? *Journal of Personality and Social Psychology,* 1978, *36,* 1415–1423.

Galper, R.E. Turning observers into actors: Differential causal attributions as a function of empathy. *Journal of Research in Personality,* 1976, *10,* 328–335.

Garcia, J., Ervin, F., & Koelling, R.A. Learning with prolonged delay of reinforcement. *Psychonomic Science,* 1966, *5,* 121–122.

Gould, R. & Sigall, H. Effects of empathy and outcome on attribution: Examination of the divergent-perspectives hypothesis. *Journal of Experimental Social Psychology,* 1977, *13,* 480–491.

Harvey, J.H. & Kelley, H.H. Sense of own judgmental competence as a function of temporal pattern of stability-instability in judgment. *Journal of Personality and Social Psychology,* 1974, *29,* 526–538.

Heider, F. Social perception and phenomenal causality. *Psychological Review,* 1944, *51,* 358–374.

Heider, F. *The psychology of interpersonal relations.* New York: Wiley, 1958.

Hoffman, M.L. Development of moral thought, feelings, and behavior. *American Psychologist,* 1979, *34,* 958–966.

Hollon, S.D. & Beck, A.T. Cognitive therapy of depression. In P.C. Kendall & S.D. Hollon (Eds.), *Cognitive-behavioral interventions: Theory, research, and procedures.* New York: Academic, 1979, pp. 153–203.

Irwin, F.W., Smith, W.A.S., & Mayfield, J.F. Tests of two theories of decision in an "expanded judgment" situation. *Journal of Experimental Psychology,* 1956, *51,* 261–268.

Janis, I.L. & Mann, L. *Decision-making: A psychological analysis of conflict, choice, and commitment.* New York: Free Press, 1977.

Jones, E.E. The rocky road from acts to dispositions. *American Psychologist,* 1979, *34,* 107–117.

Jones, E.E. & Berglas, S. Control of attributions about the self through self-handicapping strategies: the appeal of alcohol and the role of underachievement. *Personality and Social Psychology Bulletin,* 1978, *4,* 200–206.

Jones, E.E. & Davis, K.E. From acts to dispositions: The attribution process in person perception. In L. Berkowitz (Ed.), *Advances in experimental social psychology,* (Vol. 2). New York: Academic, 1965, pp. 219–266.

Jones, E.E. & Gerard, H.B. *Foundations of social psychology.* New York: Wiley, 1967.

Jones, E.E. & Goethals, G.R. Order effects in impression formation: Attribution context and the nature of the entity. In E.E. Jones, D.E. Kanouse, H.H. Kelley, R.E. Nisbett, S. Valins, & B. Weiner (Eds.), *Attribution: Perceiving the causes of behavior.* Morristown, N.J.: General Learning Press, 1972, pp. 27–46.

Jones, E.E. & Nisbett, R.E. The actor and the observer: Divergent perceptions of the causes of behavior. In E.E. Jones, D.E. Kanouse, H.H. Kelley, R.E. Nisbett, S. Valins, & B. Weiner (Eds.), *Attribution: Perceiving the causes of behavior.* Morristown, N.J.: General Learning Press, 1972, pp. 79–94.

Kanfer, F.H. Personal control, social control, and altruism. *American Psychologist,* 1979, *34,* 231–239.

Karniol, R. & Ross, M. The development of causal attributions in social perception. *Journal of Personality and Social Psychology,* 1976, *34,* 455–464.

Kelley, H.H. Salience of membership and resistance to change of group-anchored attitudes. *Human Relations,* 1955, *8,* 275–289.

Kelley, H.H. Causal schemata and the attribution process. In E.E. Jones, D.E. Kanouse, H.H. Kelley, R.E. Nisbett, S. Valins, & B. Weiner (Eds.), *Attribution: Perceiving the causes of behavior.* Morristown, N.J.: General Learning Press, 1972, pp. 151–174.

Kelley, H.H. *Personal relationships: Their structures and processes.* Hillsdale, N.J.: Lawrence Erlbaum Associates, 1979.

Kelley, H.H. & Michela, J.L. Attribution theory and research. In M.R. Rosenzweig & L.W. Porter (Eds.), *Annual review of psychology,* (Vol. 31). Palo Alto: Annual Reviews, Inc., 1980, pp. 457–501.

Kendall, P.C. & Finch, A.J., Jr. Developing nonimpulsive behavior in children: Cognitive-behavioral strategies for self-control. In P.C. Kendall & S.D. Hollon (Eds.), *Cognitive-behavioral interventions: Theory, research, and procedures.* New York: Academic, 1979, pp. 37–79.

Kendall, P.C. & Hollon, S.D. *Cognitive behavioral interventions: Theory, research, and procedures.* New York: Academic, 1979.

Kiesler, C.A. *The psychology of commitment.* New York: Academic, 1971.

Kun, A. Evidence for preschoolers' understanding of causal direction in extended causal sequences. *Child Development,* 1978, *49,* 218–222.

Kun, A., Parsons, J.E., & Ruble, D.N. Development of integration processes using ability and effort information to predict outcome. *Developmental Psychology,* 1974, *10,* 721–732.

Kurdek, L.A. Perspective-taking as the cognitive basis of children's moral development: A review of the literature. *Merrill-Palmer Quarterly*, 1978, *24*, 3–28.

Langer, E.J. The illusion of control. *Journal of Personality and Social Psychology*, 1975, *32*, 311–328.

Langer, E.J. Rethinking the role of thought in social interaction. In J.H. Harvey, W. Ickes, & R.F. Kidd (Eds.), *New directions in attribution research*, (Vol. 2). Hillsdale, N.J.: Lawrence Erlbaum Associates, 1978, pp. 35–58.

Langer, E.J., Janis, I.L., & Wolfer, J.A. Reduction of psychological stress in surgical patients. *Journal of Experimental Social Psychology*, 1975, *11*, 155–165.

Lempers, J.D., Flavell, E.R., & Flavell, J.H. The development in very young children of tacit knowledge concerning visual perception. *Genetic Psychology Monographs*, 1977, *95*, 3–53.

Lenauer, M., Sameth, L., & Shaver, P. Looking back at oneself in time: Another approach to the actor-observer phenomenon. *Perceptual and Motor Skills*, 1976, *43*, 1283–1287.

Leon, R.K. Cognitive-behavior therapy for eating disturbances. In P.C. Kendall & S.D. Hollon (Eds.), *Cognitive-behavioral interventions: Theory, research, and procedures*. New York: Academic, 1979, pp. 356–388.

Lepper, M.R. & Greene, D. (Eds.). *The hidden costs of reward*. Hillsdale, N.J.: Lawrence Erlbaum Associates, 1978.

Lewin, K. *A dynamic theory of personality*. New York: McGraw-Hill, 1935.

Lewin, K. Behavior and development as a function of the total situation. In L. Carmichael (Ed.), *Manual of child psychology*. New York: Wiley, 1946, pp. 791–844.

Livesley, W.J. & Bromley, D.B. *Person perception in childhood and adolescence*. London: Wiley, 1973.

Losco, J. & Epstein, S. Relative steepness of approach and avoidance gradients as a function of magnitude and valence of incentive. *Journal of Abnormal Psychology*, 1977, *86*, 360–368.

McArthur, L.A. The how and what of why: Some determinants and consequences of causal attributions. *Journal of Personality and Social Psychology*, 1972, 22, 171–193.

McClintock, C.G. Game behavior and social motivation in interpersonal settings. In C.G. McClintock (Ed.), *Experimental social psychology*. New York: Holt, Rinehart, & Winston, 1972.

McClintock, C.G., Moskowitz, J.M., & McClintock, E. Variations in preferences for individualistic, competitive, and cooperative outcomes as a function of age, game, class, and task in nursery school children. *Developmental Psychology*, 1977, *48*, 1080–1085.

Meichenbaum, D. & Asarnow, J. Cognitive-behavioral modification and metacognitive development: Implications for the classroom. In P.C. Kendall & S.D. Hollon (Eds.), *Cognitive-behavioral interventions: Theory, research, and procedures.* New York: Academic, 1979, pp. 11–35.

Mendelson, R. & Shultz, R.R. Covariation and temporal contiguity as principles of causal inference in young children. *Journal of Experimental Child Psychology,* 1976, *22,* 408–412.

Michotte, A. *The perception of causality.* New York: Basic Books, 1963.

Miller, G.A. *Language and communication.* New York: McGraw-Hill, 1951.

Mischel, W. Processes in delay of gratification. In L. Berkowitz (Ed.), *Advances in experimental social psychology,* (Vol. 7). New York: Academic, 1974, pp. 249–272.

Mischel, W. On the interface of cognition and personality: Beyond the person-situation debate. *American Psychologist,* 1979, *34,* 740–754.

Moore, B.S., Sherrod, D.R., Liu, T.J., & Underwood, B. The dispositional shift in attribution over time. *Journal of Experimental Social Psychology,* 1979, *15,* 553–569.

Nelson, S.A. & Dweck, C.S. Motivation and competence as determinants of young children's reward allocation. *Developmental Psychology,* 1977, *13,* 192–197.

Nemeth, C., Swedlund, M., & Kanki, B. Patterning of a minority's responses and their influence on the majority. *European Journal of Social Psychology,* 1974, *4,* 53–64.

Novaco R.W. The cognitive regulation of anger and stress. In P.C. Kendall & S.D. Hollon (Eds.), *Cognitive-behavioral interventions: Theory, research, and procedures.* New York: Academic, 1979, pp. 241–285.

Orvis, B.R., Cunningham, J.D., & Kelley, H.H. A closer examination of causal inference: The roles of consensus, distinctiveness, and consistency information. *Journal of Personality and Social Psychology,* 1975, *32,* 605–616.

Orvis, B.R., Kelley, H.H., & Butler, D. Attributional conflict in young couples. In J.H. Harvey, W.J. Ickes, & R.F. Kidd (Eds.), *New directions in attribution research,* (Vol. 1). Hillsdale, N.J.: Lawrence Erlbaum Associates, 1976, pp. 353–386.

Peevers, B.H. & Secord, P.F. Developmental changes in attribution of descriptive concepts to persons. *Journal of Personality and Social Psychology,* 1973, *27,* 120–128.

Piaget, J. *Understanding causality.* New York: Norton, 1974.

Piaget, J. & Inhelder, B. *The origin of the idea of chance in children.* New York: Norton, 1975.

Rapaport, D. (Ed.). *Organization and pathology of thought.* New York: Columbia University Press, 1951.

Regan, D.T., Straus, E., & Fazio, R. Liking and the attribution process. *Journal of Experimental Social Psychology,* 1974, *10,* 385–397.

Regan, D.T. & Totten, J. Empathy and attribution: Turning observers into actors. *Journal of Personality and Social Psychology,* 1975, *32,* 850–856.

Rest, S. Schedules of reinforcement: An attributional analysis. In J.H. Harvey, W.J. Ickes, & R.F. Kidd (Eds.), *New directions in attribution research,* (Vol. 1). Hillsdale, N.J.: Lawrence Erlbaum Associates, 1976, pp. 97–120.

Robertson, T.S. & Rossiter, J.R. Children and commercial persuasion: An attribution theory analysis. *Journal of Consumer Research,* 1974, *1,* 13–20.

Rosenzweig, S. An experimental study of "repression" with special reference to need-persistive and ego-defensive reactions to frustration. *Journal of Experimental Psychology,* 1943, *32,* 64–74.

Ross, L., Greene, D., & House, P. The false consensus effect: An egocentric bias in social perception. *Journal of Experimental Social Psychology,* 1977, *13,* 279–301.

Ruble, D.N., Feldman, N.S., & Boggiano, A.K. Social comparison between young children in achievement situations. *Developmental Psychology,* 1976, *12,* 192–197.

Schachter, S. The interaction of cognitive and physiological determinants of emotional state. In L. Berkowitz (Ed.), *Advances in Experimental Social Psychology,* (Vol. 1). New York: Academic, 1964, pp. 49–80.

Shaw, M.E. & Sulzer, J.L. An empirical test of Heider's levels in attribution of responsibility. *Journal of Abnormal and Social Psychology,* 1964, *69,* 39–46.

Shultz, T.R. & Butkowsky, I. Young children's use of the scheme for multiple sufficient causes in the attribution of real and hypothetical behavior. *Child Development,* 1977, *48,* 464–469.

Shultz, T.R. & Ravinsky, F.B. Similarity as a principle of causal inference. *Child Development,* 1977, *48,* 1552–1558.

Sommer, R. *Personal space: The behavioral basis of design.* Englewood Cliffs, N.J.: Prentice-Hall, 1969.

Storms, M.D. Videotape and the attribution process: Reversing actors' and observers' points of view. *Journal of Personality and Social Psychology,* 1973, *27,* 165–175.

Strickland, L.H., Gruder, C.L., & Kroupa, K.W. Response time as a cue in person perception. *Psychological Reports,* 1964, *15,* 827–837.

Taylor, S.E. & Fiske, S.T. Point of view and perceptions of causality. *Journal of Personality and Social Psychology,* 1975, *32,* 439–445.

Tolman, E.C. The determiners of behavior at a choice point. *Psychological Review,* 1938, *45,* 1–41.

Tolman, E.C. & Brunswik, E. The organism and the causal texture of the environment. *Psychological Review,* 1935, *42,* 43–77.

Veroff, J. Social comparison and the development of achievement motivation.

In C.P. Smith (Ed.), *Achievement related motives in children.* New York: Russell Sage, 1969, pp. 46–101.

Weiner, B. A theory of motivation for some classroom experiences. *Journal of Educational Psychology, 1979, 71,* 3–25.

Weiner, B. & Peter, N. A cognitive-developmental analysis of achievement and moral judgments. *Developmental Psychology, 1973, 9,* 290–309.

Wells, G.L. & Harvey, J.H. Do people use consensus information in making causal attributions? *Journal of Personality and Social Psychology,* 1977, *35,* 279–293.

Chapter 5

Bem, D.J. & Allen, A. On predicting some of the people some of the time: The search for cross-situational consistencies in behavior. *Psychological Review, 1974, 81,* 506–520.

Block, J. *Lives through time.* Berkeley: Bancroft Books, 1971.

Chapman, L.J. Illusory correlation in observational report. *Journal of Verbal Learning and Verbal Behavior, 1967, 6,* 151–155.

Chapman, L.J. & Chapman, J.P. Genesis of popular but erroneous diagnostic observations. *Journal of Abnormal Psychology, 1967, 72,* 183–204.

Chapman, L.J. & Chapman, J.P. Illusory correlation as an obstacle to the use of valid psychodiagnostic signs. *Journal of Abnormal Psychology, 1969, 74,* 271–280.

D'Andrade, R. Memory and the assessment of behavior. In H.M. Blalock (Ed.), *Measurement in the social sciences.* Chicago: Aldine, 1974.

Dornbusch, S.M., Hastorf, A.H., Richardson, S.A., Muzzy, R.E., & Vreeland, P.S. The perceiver and the perceived: Their relative influence on the categories of interpersonal cognition. *Journal of Personality and Social Psychology, 1965, 8,* 434–440.

Epstein, S. The stability of behavior: On predicting most of the people much of the time. *Journal of Personality and Social Psychology, 1979, 37,* 1097–1126.

Golding, S.L. & Rorer, L.G. Illusory correlation and subjective judgment. *Journal of Abnormal Psychology, 1972, 80,* 249–260.

Hamilton, D.L. & Gifford, R.K. Illusory correlation in interpersonal perception: A cognitive basis of stereotypic judgments. *Journal of Experimental Social Psychology, 1976, 12,* 392–407.

Hartshorne, H. & May, M.A. *Studies in the nature of character* (Vol. 1), *Studies in deceit.* New York: Macmillan, 1928.

Heider, F. *The psychology of interpersonal relations.* New York: Wiley, 1958.

Jennings, D., Amabile, T.M., & Ross, L. Informal covariation assessment: Data-based vs. theory-based judgments. In A. Tversky, D. Kahneman, &

P. Slovic (Eds.), *Judgment under uncertainty: Heuristics and biases.* New York: Cambridge University Press, 1980.

Jones, E.E. & Goethals, G. Order effects in impression formation: Attribution context and the nature of the entity. In E.E. Jones et al. (Eds.), *Attribution: Perceiving the causes of behavior.* Morristown, N.J.: General Learning Press, 1972.

Jones, E.E. & Harris, V.A. The attribution of attitudes. *Journal of Experimental Social Psychology,* 1967, *3,* 1–24.

Jones, E.E. & Nisbett, R.E. *The actor and the observer: Divergent perceptions of the causes of behavior.* Morristown, N.J.: General Learning Press, 1971.

Jones, E.E., Rock, L., Shaver, K.G., Goethals, G.R., & Ward, L.M. Pattern of performance and ability attribution: An unexpected primacy effect. *Journal of Personality and Social Psychology,* 1968, *10,* 317–340.

Kahneman, D. & Tversky, A. On the psychology of prediction. *Psychologcial Review,* 1973, *80,* 251–273.

Kelley, H.H. The warm-cold variable in first impressions of persons. *Journal of Personality,* 1950, *18,* 431–439.

Landy, D. & Sigall, H. Beauty is talent: Task evaluation as a function of the performer's physical attractiveness. *Journal of Personality and Social Psychology,* 1974, *29,* 299–304.

Lewin, K. *A dynamic theory of personality.* New York: McGraw-Hill, 1935.

Mischel, W. *Personality and assessment.* New York: Wiley, 1968.

Newcomb, T.M. *Consistency of certain extrovert-introvert behavior patterns in 51 problem boys.* New York: Columbia University, Teachers College, Bureau of Publications, 1929.

Nisbett, R.E., Caputo, C., Legant, P., & Maracek, J. Behavior as seen by the actor and as seen by the observer. *Journal of Personality and Social Psychology,* 1973, *27,* 154–164.

Nisbett, R.E. & Ross, L. *Human inference: Strategies and shortcomings of social judgment.* Englewood Cliffs, N.J.: Prentice-Hall, 1980.

Nisbett, R.E. & Wilson, T.D. The halo effect: Evidence for unconscious alteration of judgments. *Journal of Personality and Social Psychology,* 1977, *35,* 250–256.

Norman, W.T. & Goldberg, L.R. Raters, ratees, and randomness in personality structure. *Journal of Personality and Social Psychology,* 1966, *4,* 681–691.

Peterson, D.R. *The clinical study of social behavior.* New York: Appleton-Century-Crofts, 1968.

Ross, L. The intuitive psychologist and his shortcomings. In L. Berkowitz (Ed.), *Advances in experimental social psychology* (Vol. 10). New York: Academic, 1977.

Ross, L., Amabile, T.M., & Jennings, D. Theories, strategies, and shortcomings in the psychology of intuitive prediction. Unpublished manuscript, Stanford University, 1976.

Ross, L., Lepper, M.R., & Hubbard, M. Perseverance in self perception and social perception: Biased attributional processes in the debriefing paradigm. *Journal of Personality and Social Psychology,* 1975, *32,* 880–892.

Ross, L., Lepper, M.R., Steinmetz, J.L., & Strack, F. Social explanation and social expectation: The effects of real and hypothetical explanations upon subjective likelihood. *Journal of Personality and Social Psychology,* 1977, *35,* 817–829.

Sears, R. Dependency motivation. In M.R. Jones (Ed.), *Nebraska symposium on motivation.* Lincoln: University of Nebraska Press, 1963.

Shweder, R. Likeness and likelihood in everyday thought: Magical thinking in judgments about personality. *Current Anthropology,* 1977, *18,* 637–658.

Taylor, S.E. & Crocker, J. The processing of context information in person perception. Unpublished manuscript, University of California at Los Angeles, 1980.

Taylor, S.E. & Fiske, S. Salience, attention and attribution: Top of the head phenomena. In L. Berkowitz (Ed.), *Advances in Experimental Social Psychology* (Vol. 11). New York: Academic, 1978.

Chapter 6

Abraham, K. Contributions to a discussion on tic. In K. Abraham (Ed.), *Selected papers of Karl Abraham, M.D.,* translated by B.D. Strachey. London: London Hogarth Press, 1927.

Ashton, H. & Watson, D.W. Puffing frequency and nicotine intake in cigarette smokers. *British Medical Journal,* 1970, *3,* 679–681.

Barnett, M.L. Alcoholism in the Cantonese of New York City: An anthropological study. In Oskar Diethelm (Ed.), *Etiology of chronic alcoholism.* Springfield: Charles C Thomas, 1955.

Beckett, A.H., Rowland, M., & Triggs, E.G. Significance of smoking in investigations of urinary excretion rates of amines in man. *Nature,* 1965, *207,* 200–201.

Beckett, A.H. & Triggs, E.G. Enzyme induction in man caused by smoking. *Nature,* 1967, *216,* 587.

Benedek, L. Zwangsmässiges schreien in anfällen als postencephalitische hyperkinese. *Z. Ges. Neurol. Psychiatr.,* 1925, *98,* 17–26.

Coan, R.W. Personality variables associated with smoking. *Journal of Personality and Social Psychology,* 1973, *26,* 86–104.

Drill, V. (Ed.). *Pharmacology in medicine.* New York: McGraw-Hill, 1958.

Ewing, J., Rouse, B., & Pellizzari, E.D. Alcohol sensitivity and ethnic background. *American Journal of Psychiatry,* 1974, *131,* 206–210.

Fenna, D., Mix, L., Schaefer, O., & Gilbert, J.A.L. Ethanol metabolism in various racial groups. *Canadian Medical Association Journal,* 1971, *105,* 472–475.

Ferenczi, S. Psycho-analytical observations on tic. *International Journal of Psychoanalysis,* 1921, *2,* 1–30.

Ferster, C.B. Comments on paper by Hunt and Matarazzo. In W.A. Hunt (Ed.), *Learning mechanisms in smoking.* Chicago: Aldine, 1970.

Goodman, L.S. & Gilman, A. *The pharmacological basis of therapeutics.* New York: Macmillan, 1958.

Greenberg, L.A. Alcohol in the body. *Scientific American,* 1953, *189,* 86–90.

Haag, H.B., & Larson, P.S. Studies on the fate of nicotine in the body. I: The effect of pH on the urinary excretion of nicotine by tobacco smokers. *Journal of Pharmacology and Experimental Therapeutics,* 1942, *76,* 235–239.

Heimstra, N.W., Bancroft, N.R., & DeKock, A.R. Effects of smoking upon sustained performance in a simulated driving task. *Annals of the New York Academy of Sciences,* 1967, *142,* 295–307.

Herman, C.P. External and internal cues as determinants of the smoking behavior of light and heavy smokers. *Journal of Personality and Social Psychology,* 1974, *30,* 664–672.

Hunt, W.A. (Ed.). *Learning mechanisms in smoking.* Chicago: Aldine, 1970.

La Barre, W. Some observations on character structure in the Orient, II. The Chinese, Pt. 2. *Psychiatry,* 1946, *9,* 376.

Larson, P.S., Haag, H.B., & Silvette, H. *Tobacco.* Baltimore: Williams & Wilkins, 1961.

Lin Tsung-yi. A study of the incidence of mental disorder in Chinese and other cultures. *Psychiatry,* 1953, *16,* 313–336.

MacAndrew, C., & Edgerton, R.B. *Drunken comportment: A social explanation.* Chicago: Aldine, 1969.

Marcovitz, E. On the nature of addiction to cigarettes. *Journal of the American Psychoanalytic Association,* 1969, *17,* 1074–1096.

McKennel, A.C. *A comparison of two smoking typologies* (Research Paper 12). London: Tobacco Research Council, 1973.

Nesbitt, P.D. Smoking, physiological arousal, and emotional response. *Journal of Personality and Social Psychology,* 1973, *25,* 137–145.

Perlick, D. The withdrawal syndrome: Nicotine addiction and the effects of stopping smoking in heavy and light smokers. Unpublished doctoral dissertation, Columbia University, 1977.

Schachter, S. *Emotion, obesity, and crime.* New York: Academic, 1971.

Schachter, S. Nesbitt's paradox. In W.L. Dunn (Ed.), *Smoking behavior: Motives and incentives*. Washington, D.C.: V.H. Winston, 1973.

Schachter, S. Nicotine regulation in heavy and light smokers. *Journal of Experimental Psychology: General*, 1977, *106*, 5–12.

Schachter, S., Kozlowski, L.T., & Silverstein, B. Effects of urinary pH on cigarette smoking. *Journal of Experimental Psychology: General*, 1977, *106*, 13–19.

Schachter, S., Silverstein, B., Kozlowski, L.T., Herman, C.P., & Liebling, B. Effects of stress on cigarette smoking and urinary pH. *Journal of Experimental Psychology: General*, 1977, *106*, 24–30.

Schachter, S., Silverstein, B., & Perlick, D. Psychological and pharmacological explanations of smoking under stress. *Journal of Experimental Psychology: General*, 1977, *106*, 31–40.

Shapiro, A.K., Shapiro, E.S., Bruun, R.D., & Sweet, R.D. *Gilles de la Tourette syndrome*. New York: Raven Press, 1978.

Silverstein, B. An addiction explanation of cigarette-induced relaxation. Unpublished doctoral dissertation, Columbia University, 1976.

Smith, G.M. Personality and smoking: A review of the empirical literature. In W.A. Hunt (Ed.), *Learning mechanisms in smoking*. Chicago: Aldine, 1970.

Stewart, O. Questions regarding American Indian criminality. *Human Organization*, 1964, *23*, 61–66.

Surgeon General's Report. The health consequences of smoking. Washington, D.C.: U.S. Department of Health, Education and Welfare, 1972.

Tomkins, S. A modified model of smoking behavior. In E.F. Borgatta & R.R. Evans (Eds.), *Smoking, health and behavior*. Chicago: Aldine, 1968.

Wohlfart, G., Ingvar, D.H., & Hellberg, A.M. Compulsory shouting (Benedek's "Klazomania") associated with oculogyric spasm in chronic epidemic encephalitis. *Acta Psychiat. Scand.*, 1961, *36*, 369–377.

Wolff, P. Ethnic differences in alcohol sensitivity. *Science*, 1972, 449–450.

Wolff, P. Vasomotor sensitivity to alcohol in diverse Mongoloid populations. *American Journal of Human Genetics*, 1973, *25*, 193–199.

Chapter 7

Adams, J.S. Inequity in social exchange. In L. Berkowitz (Ed.), *Advances in Experimental Social Psychology*, (Vol. 2). New York: Academic, 1965.

Allport, G.W. The historical background of modern social psychology. In G. Lindzey & E. Aronson, *The Handbook of Social Psychology*, (Vol. 1). Reading, Mass.: Addison-Wesley, 1968.

Aronson, E. & Carlsmith, J.M. Performance expectancy as a determinant of actual performance. *Journal of Abnormal and Social Psychology*, 1962, *65*, 178–183.

Arrowood, A.J. Social comparison theory: Revived from neglect. *Contemporary Psychology*, 1978, *23*, 490–491.

Arrowood, A.J. & Friend, R. Other factors determining the choice of a comparison other. *Journal of Experimental Social Psychology*, 1969, *5*, 233–239.

Austin, W. Equity theory and social comparison processes. In J.M. Suls & R.L. Miller (Eds.), *Social comparison processes*. Washington: Hemisphere Publishing, 1977.

Back, K. Influence through social communication. *Journal of Abnormal and Social Psychology*, 1951, *46*, 9–23.

Bennett, E.B. Discussion, decision commitment, and consensus in "group decision." *Human Relations*, 1955, *8*, 251–274.

Berger, S.M. Social comparison, modeling and perseverance. In J.M. Suls & R.L. Miller (Eds.), *Social comparison processes*. Washington: Hemisphere Publishing, 1977.

Bernard, L.L. *Instinct: A study in social psychology*. New York: Holt, 1926.

Bernard, L.L. *Social psychology*. In *Encyclopedia of social science*, (Vol. 14). New York: Macmillan, 1934, pp. 151–157.

Dreyer, A. Aspiration behavior as influenced by expectation and group comparison. *Human Relations*, 1954, *7*, 175–190.

Festinger, L. Wish, expectation, and groups standards as factors influencing level of aspiration. *Journal of Abnormal and Social Psychology*, 1942, *37*, 184–200.

Festinger, L. Informal social communication. *Psychological Review*, 1950, *57*, 271–282.

Festinger, L. A theory of social comparison processes. *Human Relations*, 1954, *7*, 117–140.

Festinger, L., Gerard, H.B., Hymovitch, B., Kelley, H.H., & Raven, B.H. The influence process in the presence of extreme deviates. *Human Relations*, 1952, *5*, 327–346.

Festinger, L., Schachter, S., & Back, K. *Social pressures in informal groups: A study of human factors in housing*. New York: Harper, 1950.

Festinger, L. & Thibaut, J. Interpersonal communication in small groups. *Journal of Abnormal and Social Psychology*, 1951, *46*, 92–99.

Festinger, L., Torrey, J., & Willerman, B. Self-evaluation as a function of attraction to the group. *Human Relations*, 1954, *7*, 161–174.

Friend, R.M. & Gilbert, J. Threat and fear of negative evaluation as determinants of locus of social comparisons. *Journal of Personality*, 1973, *41*, 328–340.

Gerard, H.B. The effect of different dimensions of disagreement on the communication process in small groups. *Human Relations*, 1953, *6*, 249–271.

Goethals, G.R. & Darley, J.M. Social comparison theory: An attributional approach. In J.M. Suls & R.L. Miller (Eds.), *Social comparison processes.* Washington: Hemisphere Publishing, 1977.

Hakmiller, K.L. Threat as a determinant of downward comparison. *Journal of Experimental Social Psychology*, 1966, *Suppl. 1*, 49–54.

Heider, F. *The psychology of interpersonal relations.* New York: Wiley, 1958.

Hochbaum, G.M. The relationship between group members' self-confidence and their reaction to group pressures to uniformity. *American Sociological Review*, 1954, *19*, 678–688.

Hoffman, P.J., Festinger, L., & Lawrence, D.H. Tendencies toward group comparability in competitive bargaining. *Human Relations*, 1954, *7*, 141–159.

Hyman, H.H. The psychology of status. *Archives of Psychology*, Columbia University, No. 269, 1942.

Hyman, H.H. *Readings in reference group theory and research.* New York: Free Press, 1968.

Jones, E.E. & Gerard, H.B. *Foundations of Social Psychology.* New York: Wiley, 1967.

Kelley, H.H. The two functions of reference groups. In G.E. Swanson, T.M. Newcomb, & E.E. Hartley (Eds.), *Readings in Social Psychology* (2nd ed.). New York: Holt, 1952.

Kelley, H.H. Attribution theory in social psychology. In D. Levine (Ed.), *Nebraska Symposium on Motivation.* Lincoln: University of Nebraska Press, 1967.

Kelley, H.H. The process of causal attribution. *American Psychologist*, 1973, *28*, 107–128.

Latané, B. (Ed.). *Studies in social comparison.* New York: Academic, 1966.

Lewin, K. *Dynamic theory of personality.* New York: McGraw-Hill, 1935.

Lewin, K. *Principles of topological psychology.* New York: McGraw-Hill, 1936.

Lewin, K. Group decision and social change. In T.M. Newcomb & E.L. Hartley (Eds.), *Readings in social psychology.* New York: Holt, 1947.

Lewin, K., Dembo, T., Festinger, L., & Sears, P.S. Level of aspiration. In J.M. Hunt (Ed.), *Personality and the behavior disorders.* New York: Ronald, 1944.

McDougall, W. *An introduction to social psychology.* London: Methuen, 1908.

Merton, R.K. & Kitt, A. Contributions to the theory of reference group behavior. In R.K. Merton & P.F. Lazarsfeld (Eds.), *Continuities in social research: Studies in the scope and method of "The American Soldier."* New York: Free Press, 1950.

Murphy, G. & Murphy, L.B. *Experimental social psychology.* New York: Harper & Brothers, 1931.

Newcomb, T.M. *Personality and social change*. New York: Dryden, 1943.

Radloff, R. & Bard, L. A social comparison bibliography. In B. Latané (Ed.), *Studies in social comparison*. New York: Academic, 1966.

Schachter, S. Deviation, rejection and communication. *Journal of Abnormal and Social Psychology*, 1951, *46*, 190–207.

Schachter, S. *The psychology of affiliation*. Stanford: Stanford University Press, 1959.

Schachter, S. & Singer, J.E. Cognitive, social and physiological determinants of emotional state. *Psychological Review*, 1962, *69*, 379–399.

Sherif, M. A study of some social factors in perception. *Archives of Psychology*, No. 187, 1935.

Siegel, A.E. & Siegel, S. Reference groups, membership groups, and attitude change. *Journal of Abnormal and Social Psychology*, 1957, *55*, 360–364.

Singer, J.E. Social comparison—progress and issues. *Journal of Experimental Social Psychology*, 1966, *Suppl. 1*, 103–110.

Singer, J.E., Baum, C.S., Baum, A., & Thew, B.D. Mass psychogenic illness: The case for social comparison. Paper presented at the annual meeting of the Organization for Industrial Hygienists, 1979.

Stouffer, S.A., Lumsdaine, A.A., Lumsdaine, M.H., Williams, R.M., Jr., Smith, M.B., Janis, I.L., Star, S. A., & Cottrell, L.S., Jr., *The American soldier*. New York: Wiley, 1949.

Suls, J.M. Social comparison theory and research: An overview. In J.M. Suls & R.L. Miller, *Social comparison processes*. Washington: Hemisphere Publishing, 1977.

Suls, J.M. & Miller, R.L. (Eds.). *Social comparison processes: Theoretical and Empirical Perspectives*. Washington: Hemisphere Publishing, 1977.

Thornton, D. & Arrowood, A.J. Self-evaluation, self-enhancement and the locus of social comparison. *Journal of Experimental Social Psychology*, 1966, *Suppl. 1*, 40–48.

Wrightsman, L.S. Effects of waiting with others on changes in level of felt anxiety. *Journal of Abnormal and Social Psychology*, 1960, *61*, 216–222.

Chapter 8

Abelson, R.P., Aronson, E., McGuire, W.J., Newcomb, T.M., Rosenberg, M.J., & Tannenbaum, P. *Theories of cognitive consistency: A sourcebook*. Chicago: Rand-McNally, 1968.

Adorno, T.W., Frenkel-Brunswick, E., Levinson, D., & Sanford, R.N. *The authoritarian personality*. New York: Harper & Row, 1950.

Allport, G.W. The historical background of modern social psychology. In G. Lindzey (Ed.), *Handbook of social psychology* (Vol. 1). Cambridge, Mass.: Addison-Wesley, 1954, pp. 3–56.

Andrews, F.M. Estimating the construct validity and correlated error components of the rated-effectiveness measures. In F.M. Andrews (Ed.), *Scientific productivity,* Cambridge: Cambridge University Press, 1979, pp. 405–422.

Andrews, F.M. & Crandall, R. The validity of measures of self-reported well-being. *Social Indicators Research,* 1976, *3,* 1–19.

Asch, S.E. *Social psychology.* Englewood Cliffs, N.J.: Prentice-Hall, 1952.

Asch, S.E. Forming impressions of personality. *Journal of Abnormal and Social Psychology,* 1946, *41,* 258–290.

Back, K. The exertion of influence through social communication. *Journal of Abnormal and Social Psychology,* 1951, *46,* 9–23.

Bartlett, F.C. *Remembering: A study in experimental and social psychology.* Cambridge: Cambridge University Press, 1932.

Blake, R.R., Rosenbaum, M., & Duryea, R. Gift-giving as a function of group standards. *Human Relations,* 1955, *8,* 61–73.

Bower, G.H. & Karlin, M.B. Depth of processing pictures of faces and recognition memory. *Journal of Experimental Psychology,* 1974, *103,* 751–757.

Bower, G.H., Monteivo, K.P. & Gilligan, S.G. Emotional mood as a context for learning and recall. *Journal of Verbal Learning and Verbal Behavior,* 1979, *17,* 573–585.

Brown, R. *Social psychology.* New York: Free Press, 1965.

Byrne, D. Interpersonal attraction and attitude similarity. *Journal of Abnormal and Social Psychology,* 1961, *62,* 713–715.

Combs, A.W. & Snygg, D. *Individual behavior: A perceptual approach to behavior.* New York: Harper & Brothers, 1949.

Cooley, C.H. *Human nature and the social order.* New York: Scribner, 1902.

Coombs, C.H. *A theory of data.* New York: Wiley, 1964.

Darley, J.M. & Latané, B. Bystander intervention in emergencies: Diffusion of responsibility. *Journal of Personality and Social Psychology,* 1968, *8,* 377–383.

Dixon, N.F. *Subliminal perception: The nature of a controversy.* London: McGraw-Hill, 1971.

Erdelyi, M.H. A new look at the New Look: Perceptual defense and vigilance. *Psychological Review,* 1974, *81,* 1–25.

Fenigstein, A. & Carver, C.S. Self-focusing effects of heartbeat feedback. *Journal of Personality and Social Psychology,* 1978, *11,* 1241–1250.

Gill, M. (Ed.). *The collected papers of David Rapaport.* New York: Basic Books, 1967.

Heider, F. *The psychology of interpersonal relations.* New York: Wiley, 1958.

Heider, F. & Simmel, M. An experimental study of apparent movement. *American Journal of Psychology,* 1944, *57,* 243–259.

Henley, S.H.A. Cross modal effects of subliminal verbal stimuli. *Scandinavian Journal of Psychology,* 1975, *16,* 30–36.

Hunt, P.J. & Hillery, J.M. Social facilitation in coaction setting: An examination of the effects over learning trials. *Journal of Experimental Social Psychology,* 1973, *9,* 563–571.

Hyde, T.W. & Jenkins, J.J. The differential effects of incidental tasks on the organization of recall of a list of highly associated words. *Journal of Experimental Psychology,* 1969, *82,* 472–481.

Innes, J.M. & Young, R.F. The effect of presence of an audience, evaluation apprehension and objective self-awareness on learning. *Journal of Experimental Social Psychology,* 1975, *11,* 35–42.

Jones, E.E. *Ingratiation.* New York: Appleton-Century-Crofts, 1964.

Jones, E.E. & Berglas, S. Control of attributions about the self through self-handicapping strategies: The appeal of alcohol and the role of underachievement. *Personality and Social Psychology Bulletin,* 1978, *4,* 200–206.

Jöreskog, K.G. & Sörbom, D. *LISREL IV.* Chicago: National Education Resources, Inc., 1978.

Keenan, J.M. & Bailett, S.D. Memory for personally and socially significant events. In R.S. Nickerson (Ed.), *Attention and performance VIII.* Hillsdale, N.J.: Lawrence Erlbaum Associates, 1979.

Kleinsmith, L.J. & Kaplan, S. Paired associate learning as a function of arousal and interpolated interval. *Journal of Experimental Psychology,* 1963, *65,* 190–193.

Kleinsmith, L.J. & Kaplan, S. Interaction of arousal and recall interval in nonsense syllable paircd-associate learning. *Journal of Experimental Psychology,* 1964, *67,* 124–126.

Koller, P.S. & Kaplan, R.M. A two-process theory of learned helplessness. *Journal of Personality and Social Psychology,* 1978, *36,* 1177–1183.

Krech, D. & Crutchfield, R.S. *Theory and problems of social psychology.* New York: McGraw-Hill, 1948.

Kunst-Wilson, W.R. & Zajonc, R.B. Affective discrimination of stimuli that cannot be recognized. *Science,* 1980, *207,* 557–558.

Lewin, K. *Resolving social conflicts.* New York: Harper & Brothers, 1948.

Lott, B. Behavioral concordance with sex role ideology related to play areas, creativity, and parental sex typing of children. *Journal of Personality and Social Psychology,* 1978, *36,* 1087–1100.

Markus, H. & Smith, J. The influence of self-schemas on the perception of others. In N. Cantor & J. Kihlstrom (Eds.), *Personality and cognition.* Hillsdale, N.J.: Lawrence Erlbaum, 1980.

Marrow, A. *The practical theorist.* New York: Basic Books, 1969.

Matlin, M.W. Response competition, recognition, and affect. *Journal of Personality and Social Psychology*, 1971, 295–300.

McDougall, W. *Introduction to social psychology*. London: Methuen, 1908.

Mead, G.H. *Mind, self and society*. Chicago: University of Chicago Press, 1934.

Milgram, S. Behavioral study of obedience. *Journal of Abnormal and Social Psychology*, 1963, *67*, 371–378.

Moreland, R.L. & Zajonc, R.B. Is stimulus recognition a necessary condition for the occurrence of exposure effects? *Journal of Personality and Social Psychology*, 1977, *35*, 191–199.

Moreland, R.L. & Zajonc, R.B. Exposure effects may not depend on stimulus recognition. *Journal of Personality and Social Psychology*, 1979, *37*, 1085–1089.

Murphy, G., Murphy, L.B., & Newcomb, T.M. *Experimental social psychology* (Rev. ed.). New York: Harper, 1937.

Neisser, U. *Cognitive psychology*. Englewood, N.J.: Prentice-Hall, 1967.

Newcomb, T.M., Turner, R.H., & Converse, P.E. *Social psychology: The study of human interaction*. New York: Holt, Rinehart, & Winston, 1965.

Patterson, K.E. & Baddeley, A.D. When face recognition fails. *Journal of Experimental Psychology: Human Learning and Memory*, 1977, *3*, 406–417.

Powell, F.A. Source credibility and behavioral compliance as determinants of attitude change. *Journal of Personality and Social Psychology*, 1965, *2*, 669–676.

Rogers, T.B., Kuiper, N.A. & Kirker, W.S. Self-reference and the encoding of personal information. *Journal of Personality and Social Psychology*, 1977, *35*, 677–688.

Rosenberg, M.J. When dissonance fails: On discriminating evaluation apprehension from attitude measurement. *Journal of Personality and Social Psychology*, 1965, *1*, 28–42.

Sadella, E.K. & Loftness, S. Emotional images as mediators in one-trial paired-associates learning. *Journal of Experimental Psychology*, 1972, *95*, 295–298.

Shand, A. Character and emotions. *Mind*, 1896, *21*, 203–342.

Sherif, M. & Hovland, C.I. *Social judgment: Assimilation and contrast effects in communication and attitude change*. New Haven: Yale University Press, 1961.

Simon, H.A. Discussion: Cognition and social psychology. In J.S. Carroll & J.W. Payne (Eds.), *Cognition and social behavior*. Hillsdale, N.J.: Lawrence Erlbaum Associates, 1976, pp. 253–268.

Skinner, B.F. Why I am not a cognitive psychologist. *Behaviorism*, 1977, *5*, 1–10.

Smith, G.J.W., Spence, D.P., & Klein, D.S. Subliminal effects of verbal stimuli. *Journal of Abnormal and Social Psychology*, 1959, *50*, 167–176.

Snyder, M. Self-monitoring of expressive behavior. *Journal of Personality and Social Psychology*, 1974, *30*, 526–537.

Snyder, M. & Swann, W.B., Jr. Hypothesis-testing processes in social interaction. *Journal of Personality and Social Psychology*, 1978, *36*, 1202–1212.

Stevens, S.S. A metric for social consensus. *Science*, 1966, *151*, 530–541.

Stevens, S.S. *Psychophysics and social scaling*. Morristown, N.J.: Bobbs-Merrill, 1972.

Verplanck, W.S. A glossary of some terms used in the objective science of behavior. *Psychological Review*, 1957, *64*, Supplement, Part 2.

Wicklund, R.A. & Duval, S. Opinion change and performance facilitation as a result of objective self-awareness. *Journal of Experimental Social Psychology*, 1971, *7*, 319–342.

Wilson, W.R. Unobtrusive induction of positive attitudes. Unpublished doctoral dissertation, University of Michigan, 1975.

Wilson, W.R. Feeling more than we can know: Exposure effects without learning. *Journal of Personality and Social Psychology*, 1979, *37*, 811–821.

Wundt, W. *Outlines of psychology*. Leipzig: Wilhelm Englemann, 1907.

Zajonc, R.B. Feeling and thinking: Preferences need no inferences. Paper delivered at the meeting of the American Psychological Association, New York, September, 1979.

Chapter 9

Ansoff, H.I. *Corporate strategy*. New York: McGraw-Hill, 1965.

Balderston, G.C. *Group incentives, some variations in the use of group bonus and gang piece work*. Philadelphia: University of Pennsylvania Press, 1930.

Barnard, C. *The functions of the executive*. Cambridge: Harvard University Press, 1938.

Bennis, W.F. Organizational developments and the fate of bureaucracy. *The Industrial Management Review*, Cambridge: The Massachusetts Institute of Technology, 1966.

Cameron, K. Measuring organizational effectiveness in institutions of higher education. *Administrative Science Quarterly*, 1978, *23*, 604–629.

Cartwright, D. & Zander, A. *Group dynamics, research and theory*. New York: Harper & Row, 1968.

Christopher, W.E. *The achieving enterprise*. New York: American Management Association, 1974.

Cyert, R.M. & March, J. *A behavioral theory of the firm*. Englewood Cliffs, N.J.: Prentice-Hall, 1963.

Deniston, O.L., Rosenstock, I.M., & Getting, V.A. Evaluation of program effectiveness. *Public Health Reports*, 1968, *83*, 323–336.

Deniston, O.L., Rosenstock, I.M., Welch, W., & Getting, V.A. Evaluation of program efficiency. *Public Health Reports,* 1968, *83,* 603–610.

Dent, J.K. Organizational correlates of the goals of business managements. *Personnel Psychology,* 1959, *12,* 365–393.

Deutsch, M. The effects of cooperation and competition upon group process. *Human Relations,* 1949, *2,* 129–152, 199–231.

Dustin, D. Member reaction to team performance. *Journal of Social Psychology,* 1966, *69,* 237–243.

Etzioni, A. Two approaches to organizational analysis. *Administrative Science Quarterly,* 1960, *5,* 277–278.

Forward, J. Group achievement motivation and individual motives to achieve success and to avoid failure. *Journal of Personality,* 1969, *37,* 297–309.

Forward, J. & Zander, A. Choice of unattainable group goals and effects on performance. *Organizational Behavior and Human Performance,* 1971, *6,* 184–199.

Frank, J. Individual differences in certain aspects of the level of aspiration. *American Journal of Psychology,* 1935, *47,* 119–128.

Gantt, H.L. *Work, wages, and profits.* New York: The Engineering Magazine Company, 1910.

George, C.S. *The history of management thought.* Englewood Cliffs, N.J.: Prentice-Hall, 1968.

Georgiou, P. The goal paradigm and notes towards a counter paradigm. *Administrative Science Quarterly,* 1973, *18,* 291–310.

Glaser, R. & Klaus, D. A reinforcement analysis of group performance. *Psychological Monographs: General and Applied,* 1966, *80,* Whole No. 621.

Granger, C.H. The hierarchy of objectives. *Harvard Business Review,* 1964, *42,* 63–74.

Gross, B.M. What are your organization's objectives? *Human Relations,* 1965, *18,* 195–216.

Horwitz, M. The recall of interrupted group tasks: an experimental study of individual motivation in relation to group goals. *Human Relations,* 1954, *7,* 3–38.

Janis, I. *Victims of groupthink.* Boston: Houghton-Mifflin, 1972.

Kanter, R. *Commitment and community, communes and utopias in perspective.* Cambridge: Harvard University Press, 1972.

Korten, D.C. Situational determinants of leadership structure. *Journal of Conflict Resolution,* 1962, *6,* 222–235.

Latham, G.P. & Kinne, S.B. Improving job performance through training in goal setting. *Journal of Applied Psychology,* 1974, *59,* 187–191.

Latham, G.P. & Saari, L.M. The effects of holding goal difficulty constant on assigned and participatively set goals. *Academy of Management Journal,* 1979, *2,* 163–168.

Latham, G.P. & Yukl, G.A. Assigned versus participative goal setting with educated and uneducated woods workers. *Journal of Applied Psychology,* 1975, *60,* 299–302. (a)

Latham, G.P. & Yukl, G.A. A review of research on the application of goal setting in organizations. *Academy of Management Journal,* 1975, *18,* 824–845. (b)

Lawrence, P. & Lorsch, J.W. *Organization and environment.* Homewood, Ill.: Irwin, 1967.

Lewin, K. *A dynamic theory of personality.* New York: McGraw-Hill, 1935.

Lewin, K., Dembo, T., Festinger, L., & Sears, P. Level of aspiration. In J.M. Hunt (Ed.), *Personality and the behavior disorders.* New York: Ronald, 1944.

Lewis, H. An experimental study of the role of the ego in work. *Journal of Experimental Psychology,* 1944, *34,* 113–126.

Locke, E. Toward a theory of task motivation and incentives. *Organizational Behavior and Human Performance,* 1968, *3,* 157–189.

Mager, R.F. *Preparing instructional objectives.* Palo Alto: Fearon Press, 1962.

Mager, R.F. *Goal analysis.* Belmont, Cal.: Fearon Press, 1972.

McBurney, W.J. *Goal setting and planning at the district sales level.* New York: American Management Association, 1963.

Miller, J.G. *Living systems.* New York: McGraw-Hill, 1978.

Mohr, L.B. The concept of organizational goal. *American Political Science Review,* 1973, *62,* 470–481.

Mooney, F.A. & Reilly, A.C. *Onward industry.* New York: Harper, 1931.

Pepitone, E. Responsibility to group and its effects on the performance of members. Unpublished doctoral dissertation, The University of Michigan, 1952.

Perrow, C. The analysis of goals in complex organizations. *American Sociological Review,* 1961, *26,* 854–866.

Raven, B. & Rietsema, J. The effects of varied clarity of group goals and group path upon the individual and his relation to his group. *Human Relations,* 1957, *10,* 29–44.

Ronan, W.W., Latham, G.P., & Kinne, S.B. Effects of goal setting and supervision on worker behavior in an industrial situation. *Journal of Applied Psychology,* 1973, *58,* 302–307.

Ryan, T.A. Goal setting in group counselling. *Educational Technology,* 1973, *13,* 19–25.

Seashore, S. Criteria of organizational effectiveness. *Michigan Business Review,* 1965, *17,* 26–30.

Shaw, M. *Group dynamics: the psychology of small group behavior*. New York: McGraw-Hill, 1976.

Stedry, A. & Kay, E. *The effects of goal difficulty on performance*. Crotonville, N.Y.: Behavioral Research Service, General Electric Company, 1964.

Steers, R.M. & Porter, L.W. The role of task-goal attributes in employee performance. *Psychological Bulletin*, 1974, *81*, 434–452.

Thibaut, J. & Kelley, H. *The social psychology of groups*. New York: Wiley, 1959.

Thomas, E.J. & Zander, A. The relationship of goal structure to motivation under extreme conditions. *Journal of Individual Psychology*, 1959, *15*, 121–127.

Thompson, J. *Organizations in action*. New York: McGraw-Hill, 1967.

Thompson, J. & McEwen, W.J. Organizational goals and environment: goal setting as an interaction process. *American Sociological Review*, 1958, *23*, 23–31.

Wallroth, C. An analysis of means-end structure. *Acta Sociologica*, 1968, *11*, 110–118.

Warner, W.K. & Havens, A.E. Goal displacement and the intangibility of organizational goals. *Administrative Science Quarterly*, 1968, *12*, 539–555.

Wieland, G. The determinants of clarity in organization goals. *Human Relations*, 1969, 22, 161–172.

Yuchtman, E. & Seashore, S. A system resource approach to organizational effectiveness. *American Sociological Review*, 1967, *32*, 891–903.

Zajonc, R. The effects of feedback and the probability of group success on individual and group performance. *Human Relations*, 1962, *15*, 149–161.

Zajonc, R. & Taylor, R. The effects of two methods of varying group task difficulty on individual and group performance. *Human Relations*, 1963, *16*, 359–368.

Zander, A. Group aspirations. In D. Cartwright & A. Zander (Eds.), *Group dynamics research and theory*. New York: Harper & Row, 1968.

Zander, A. *Manager, group and company*. Stockholm, Sweden: Swedish Institute for Administrative Research, 1969.

Zander, A. *Motives and goals in groups*. New York: Academic, 1971.

Zander, A. The purposes of national associations. *Journal of Voluntary Action Research*, 1972, *1*, 20–29.

Zander, A. *Groups at work*. San Francisco: Jossey-Bass, 1977.

Zander, A. The psychology of group processes. *Annual Review of Psychology*, 1979, *30*, 417–451.

Zander, A. & Armstrong, W. Working for group pride in a slipper factory. *Journal of Applied Social Psychology*, 1972, 2, 193–207.

Zander, A., Fuller, R., & Armstrong, W. Attributed group pride or shame in group or self. *Journal of Personality and Social Psychology*, 1972, *23*, 346–352.

Zander, A., Forward, J., & Albert, A. Adaptation of board members to repeated success or failure by their organization. *Organizational Behavior and Human Performance*, 1969, *4*, 56–76.

Zander, A. & Medow, H. Individual and group levels of aspiration. *Human Relations*, 1963, *16*, 89–105.

Zander, A., Medow, H. & Efron, R. Observers' expectations as determinants of group aspirations. *Human Relations*, 1965, *18*, 273–287.

Zander, A. & Newcomb, T., Jr. Group levels of aspiration in United Fund campaigns. *Journal of Personality and Social Psychology*, 1967, *6*, 157–162.

Zander, A. & Ulberg, C. The group level of aspiration and external social pressures. *Organizational Behavior and Human Performance*, 1971, *6*, 362–378.

Zander, A. & Wulff, D. Members' test anxiety and competence: determinants of a group's aspirations. *Journal of Personality*, 1966, *34*, 55–70.

Chapter 10

Adorno, T.W., Frenkel-Brunswik, E., Levinson, D.J., & Sanford, R.N. *The authoritarian personality*. New York: Harper & Row, 1950.

Allport, G.W. *Personality: A psychological interpretation*. New York: Holt, 1937.

Asch, S.E. Review of "A theory of cognitive dissonance." *Contemporary Psychology*, 1958, *3*, 194–195.

Back, K. Influence through social communication. *Journal of Abnormal and Social Psychology*, 1951, *8*, 251–274.

Bavelas, A. *Morale and the training of leaders*. In G. Watson (Ed.), *Civilian morale*, Boston, Houghton-Mifflin, 1942.

Bem, D.J. & Funder, D.C. Predicting more of the people more of the time. *Psychological Review*, 1978, *85*, 485–501.

Campbell, A., Eberhart, S., & Woodward, P. *Public reactions to the atomic bomb and world affairs. Part II: Findings of the intensive surveys*. Ithaca: Cornell University Press, 1947, pp. 80–310.

Cantril, H. *Invasion from Mars*. Princeton: Princeton University Press, 1940.

Festinger, L. *A Theory of Cognitive Dissonance*. Stanford, Calif.: Stanford University Press, 1957.

Festinger, L. & Katz, D. *Research methods in the behavioral sciences*. New York: Dryden, 1953.

Hartshorne, H. & May, M. *Studies in deceit*. New York: Macmillan, 1928.

Hertzman, M. & Festinger, L. Shifts in explicit goals in a level of aspiration experiment. *Journal of Experimental Psychology*, 1940, *27*, 439–452.

Hovland, C.I., Janis, I.L., & Kelley, H.H. *Communication and persuasion*. New Haven: Yale University Press, 1953.

Hovland, C.I., Lumsdaine, A.A., & Sheffield, F.D. *Experiments on mass communication*. Princeton: Princeton University Press, 1949.

Hull, C.L. *Principles of behavior*. New York: Appleton-Century-Crofts, 1943.

Lazarsfeld, P.F., Berelson, B., & Gaudet, H. *The people's choice*. New York: Duell, Sloan and Pearce, 1944.

Lewin, K. *Dynamic theory of personality*. New York: McGraw-Hill, 1935, pp. 1–42.

Lewin, K. Formalization and progress in psychology. *University of Iowa Studies in Child Welfare*, 1940, *16*, No. 3, 9–42.

Lewin, K. Forces behind food habits and methods of change. *Bulletin of the National Research Council*, 1943, *108*, 35–65.

Lewin, K. *Field theory in social science*, New York: Harper, 1951.

Lewin, K., Lippitt, R., & White, R. Patterns of aggressive behavior in experimentally created "social climates." *Journal of Social Psychology*, 1939, *10*, 271–299.

Lippitt R. An experimental study of authoritarian and democratic group atmospheres. *University of Iowa Studies in Child Welfare*, 1940, *16*, 45–195.

Lippitt R. *Training in community relations*. New York: Harper, 1949.

Lippitt, R. & White, R. The "social climate" of children's groups. In R. Barker, J. Kounin, & H. Wright (Eds.), *Child behavior and development*. New York: McGraw-Hill, 1943.

McClelland, D.C., Atkinson, J.W., Clark, R.A., & Lowell, E.L. *The achievement motive*. New York: Appleton-Century-Crofts, 1953.

Newcomb, T.M. *Consistency of certain extrovert-introvert behavior patterns in 51 problem boys*. New York: Columbia University, Teachers College, Bureau of Publications, 1929.

Newcomb, T.M. *Personality and social change*. New York: Dryden, 1943.

Rosenthal, R. *Experimenter effects in behavioral research*. New York: Appleton-Century-Crofts, 1966.

Schachter, S. Deviation, rejection and communication. *Journal of Abnormal and Social Psychology*, 1951, *46*, 190–207.

Schachter, S. *The psychology of affiliation*. Stanford: Stanford University Press, 1959.

Sherif, M. A study of some social factors in perception. *Archives of Psychology*, 1935, No. 187.

Spence, K.W. The postulates and methods of behaviorism. *Psychological Review*, 1948, *55*, 67–78.

Thorndike, E.L. The law of effect. *American Journal of Psychology*, 1927, *39*, 212–222.

Index